Rituals of Failure

RITUALS OF FAILURE

WHAT SCHOOLS REALLY TEACH

Sandro Contenta

between the lines

Published by
Between The Lines
394 Euclid Ave., #203
Toronto, Ontario
M6G 2S9

Cover and interior design by Counterpunch
Typesetting by Counterpunch
Backcover photograph by Nino Bruni
Printed in Canada

Between The Lines gratefully acknowledges the financial support of the
Canada Council, the Department of Communications, the Ontario Arts
Council, and the Ontario Ministry of Culture, Tourism, and Recreation
through the Ontario Publishing Centre.

Kool G Rapp and DJ Polo, "Road to the Riches" published by Warner Bros.

Canadian Cataloguing in Publication Data

Contenta, Sandro
   Rituals of failure : what schools really teach

Includes bibliographical references and index.
ISBN 0-921284-71-3 (bound)   ISBN 0-921284-70-5 (pbk.)

1. Education – Canada.   I. Title

LA412.C65 1993   370'.971   C93-094712-6

"Every new child is nature's chance to correct culture's error."
— *Ted Hughes*

Contents

Acknowledgements

I owe an enormous debt to many people who helped me complete this work. First, I wish to thank the children and teenagers who trusted me with their thoughts and feelings during my visits to schools in Nova Scotia, Quebec, Ontario, and British Columbia. Discussing life with them was pure joy. For solutions to the many problems with schools, educators need only ask the people they serve. I also wish to thank the principals and teachers who welcomed me into their schools and classrooms.

I am grateful to the *Toronto Star* for its continued interest in education and for giving me the time to write this book. I especially wish to thank former city editor Lou Clancy for allowing me the freedom to pursue many of the issues that eventually formed the themes of this work.

I am indebted to Geoffrey York, Fergus Coyle, and Ed Innocenzi who, in different ways, provided critical advice and insights. An immense thank-you to John Ferri for patiently editing the first draft of the manuscript, and for long evenings of stimulating conversation. Soothing support also came from Leslie Fruman, Roberto Bruni, and Natividade Calvario. It is my good fortune to have all these people as dear friends.

I am also grateful to Don Rutledge for his wise guidance, and to Marg Anne Morrison and Robert Clarke for their meticulous editing of the final manuscript. Thanks to Kathleen Kenna for her Vancouver hospitality, and to the Ontario Arts Council and the Canada Council for their financial support.

Finally, a special thanks to my family for its unquestioned love, and to my mother, Giuseppina, for teaching by example about love and revolt. This book is dedicated to her.

Introduction

When John Polanyi wants to tell a story of scientific discovery, he uses a slide picture of a naked toddler. Her arms are outstretched, there's a look of rapture on her face, and she's scampering with complete abandon towards an unknown beyond the limits of the photograph. It may seem a lighthearted way for the Nobel Prize-winning chemist to introduce such a serious subject. But Polanyi sees infants as budding scientists filled with "that impulse to adventure, a desire to venture into the world and embrace it." There is wonder in their eyes.

The child is a pure romantic, intoxicated and consumed by a love of life, an ardent need to know, at once frustrated and gratified. The caress of a parent delights her body and language delights her mind. With every discovery the universe brightens as in a divine flight of lucidity. But her joy is not naive. She has bumped her head on enough furniture to know intuitively that pain and suffering also come freely. The world is as scary as it is beautiful, and paradox is not an easy concept for toddlers to grasp. Someday, with love and despair in her heart, she may pause and consider that the choice between revolt and suicide lies uncomfortably close. But in these early years she is singleminded. Her search for understanding reveals more uncertainty, yet she presses on in a kind of inspired revolt: Life teaches her fervour!

What happens to all those budding scientists and their inspired impulse to adventure? With the best of intentions, the school system retards it badly. "It's there and we wipe it out," says one of Toronto's top science teachers.

For their part, most students see school as a complete waste of time, as a kind of endurance test not unlike a jail sentence. When Chris Ward was Ontario's education minister, he complained in March 1988 that students had come to see a high school diploma as a useless piece of paper and this gave them little incentive to graduate. He then suggested there was something about schools that caused students to act like zombies. "Too many of those who remain in school have simply turned off and sealed their minds to what is being taught," he said. Schools have a lot to do with this mass mental tuning out.

A 1987 federal government report, *Canada's Youth "Ready for Today,"* surveyed more than 2,000 students aged 15 to 24 and asked them if they liked going to school. Only 23 per cent of high school students said they did. Next question: "Are your courses interesting?" Again, only 23 per cent said they were. Next: "Is your school work meaningful and important?" Just under one-third, 32 per cent, said yes. Finally: "Is your learning going to help you later in life?" Less than half, 41 per cent, said yes. The report concluded: "For most young people, going to school is the equivalent of going to work for adults. If the environment is negative rather than positive – life is an ordeal." If schools were shopping malls they would be out of business.

Bernard Shapiro, Ontario's exceptional deputy minister of education in the late 1980s, says teachers are developing students who are scientifically illiterate, meaning they can't think for themselves. They are producing students ignorant of the skills scientists use to make sense of the world: asking questions, making observations, doing research, and conducting tests to draw logical conclusions, a process driven by what John Polanyi calls "inspired groping." Not for a moment, however, does Shapiro suggest that the scientific method is the road to the "truth." Literate people, he says, should understand the scientific method but also recognize that it provides only certain kinds of answers, having both strengths and limitations. In the end, it's only one way of looking at the world, of constructing a mental narrative that helps us make sense of it. But students, and far too many teachers, seem incapable of conceiving this. Thinking critically is not their forte. But who can blame the students? Generally, they're too busy being spoon-fed by teachers, and all they have to do is burp now and then.

In Room 16, on the second floor of Vancouver's Grace* Elementary School, sat Karen Riley's* class of grades 3 and 4 students. Having two grades in one class has been one of the improvements in some inner city schools since the late 1980s; the theory being that a teacher is able to follow a child's development for longer than just one year. Directly across the hall were large paintings by Riley's pupils celebrating those things society has decided amount to good manners. A couple of weeks earlier, the staff had decided the school's children needed a good dose of etiquette. Not that they had been more unruly of late; everyone just thought it would be a good idea. They adopted a 1942 British book on manners (someone just happened to have one, said a teacher) as their guide, and for two weeks the kids were expected to open doors for teachers, say please, excuse me, and thank you whenever proper etiquette dictated. A funny thing happened, though.

"The kids were worse than they've ever been," said Riley, still shaking her head. "The entire school . . . they were wild, they were rude, they were running around. They were just awful." She agreed it may have been a rebellious show of strength, a united front, a collective thumbing of the nose, but she wasn't completely convinced. "Sometimes I think it's the air pressure or a change in the temperature."

As Riley waved me into her classroom, the children sat in five straight rows, their heads lowered, eyes fixed on the tops of their desks. Riley sat at her desk on the opposite side of the room, facing the door. She told me to settle down at the back and only a head or two looked up as I made my way down the middle aisle. I sat down and a curious sensation touched me that had little to do with the miniature chair I had balanced myself on. I felt I had disrupted a sacred ritual. In a monotonous, hypnotizing drone, a woman's voice on a tape recorder at the side of the classroom conducted a math drill. The children had a script of the plotline and filled in the blanks at each pause.

---

* Not real names. Throughout the book, other names of schools, teachers, and students are real unless otherwise indicated.

"6 times 4 equals . . . 7 times 8 equals . . . 2 times 2 equals . . . ."

A pause and then: "Isn't this fun?" the disembodied voice asked. The children groaned, "Yeeessss."

"6 times 3 equals . . . ."

Plastered all over the classroom walls were directives; variations of the socialist realism billboards that line the streets of some totalitarian countries. At the front of the class under the heading "OUR GOALS" was written: "Excellent work habits/ Self-control/ Quiet work manners/ Organization/ Positive attitudes/ Think before you act/ Smiling faces/ Honesty/ Responsibility/ Self-respect/ Independently working hard with maturity and with a good attitude/ Well groomed."

"1 times 8 equals . . . ."

Also at the front, another poster: "Only one person speaks at a time/ We do assigned work/ We whisper/ We make politeness count."

One child gave up, put down his pencil, and strained his neck to look out the window. Behind two rows of shelves that separated the open windows from his desk, the sun was shining. The shelves were lined with cardboard boxes labelled "Language Drill," "Phonics Drill," "Reading Drill." If language is a living thing, it was suffocating in coffins twice the size of shoe boxes.

"9 times 8 equals . . . ."

Children filled in the blanks mechanically to the lifeless chant. The public address system then crackled above the drill; first the sound of chimes and then a voice: "Excuse the interruption. Karen, will you pick up the interphone please?" Riley walked out and the class stirred. Children talked quietly to each other, one got up to stretch. Unfortunately for the kids, the new context had absolutely no effect on the tape recorder and The Voice said, "Well, you've almost made it. You're on the last part of this paper. Just think how good you're going to feel when it's all over. Keep doing your best. 4 times 9 equals . . . ."

Near the teacher's desk, another poster: "Make the letters touch the lines/ Make the letters round and fat/ Make the letters close together/ Put a finger space between the words and don't forget to miss one space."

Riley returned and made her way slowly up and down the rows. The Voice: "Be brave, you're almost there." It ended a moment later and a couple of kids let out a muffled shout of joy, "Yaahh."

The Voice: "Well, congratulations. You did it. Doesn't it feel good?"

For a husky boy at the front the end couldn't have come too soon. He stood up and shook his right hand wildly, trying desperately to regain the flow of blood. Riley examined the drill sheet of a child with freckles. He had one wrong answer. She said, "Oh, that's too bad." Then she told him to do the whole drill over. She looked at me and smiled. "I just feel so badly for him but that's the name of the game."

At the front of the class, another poster: "Our word for this week is/ FRIENDLINESS."

At the end of the math drill, Riley told the children to pat themselves on the back for a job well done. Hands immediately wrapped themselves around necks, tapping. Those who got all the answers right were, in Riley's words, "Free like the birds on the trees." Throughout history, however, freedom has been a fickle matter. Riley soon commanded that everybody stop in their tracks. The noise level had surpassed some sort of standard and she made short work of it with a single word: "Freeze!" And that's exactly what happened.

The children held their positions as if Riley had hit the pause button: one shaking slightly to keep his right foot in the air, another in the act of throwing a card down, some with their faces in books. And so they remained, statues with twitching signs of life.

"Would everybody freeze, please? If this doesn't stop I'm going to have to say no free time, and that would be very unfair to the children who've worked hard and got it and to the children who are almost there. That's the second time I've warned you. If I have to quieten you again, that's it. There are people who are trying to work and they need quiet." She let a few moments go by, enough to let the message sink in, and then released the pause button that returned the children to life.

What happens to our budding scientists and impulsive adventurers? Most of them are zapped frozen in time and space like the image of the little girl in Polanyi's slide. They are controlled by an awesome show of power, a practice of school teachers for decades. Twenty years ago at my elementary school in the east end of Montreal, the bell ending recess and lunch was also endowed with the power to stop us cold, in suspended animation, something our parents could only dream about.

"At times I wonder what the motivation is in the child," said Riley. "I'm always astonished at how if I say, 'stand up,' they all stand up. Nobody says, 'No, I'm not going to.'" Well, at least not out loud. Besides, conformity has little to do with motivation and much more to do with the exercise of power. Riley has it; the children don't.

Everyone realizes there are problems with our schools, but few people understand the real reasons. It is open season on schools, and provinces across Canada have gone through massive, often bitter debates on the quality of their education systems. The hunt isn't confined to Canada alone. During the past decade, in an anxious search for a social panacea, schools in Great Britain and the United States have also been poked, stirred, and shaken into a state of confusion. Much of the concern focuses on the year 2000, the latest symbol of Western angst, as we move not only into a new century, but a new millennium. In a way, the Western world is like John Polanyi's toddler, freefalling into the many unknowns of the twenty-first century. But unlike the child, there's little rapture on our faces. We are clearly aware of the problems we will take with us into the next century if we haven't dealt with them by then. We also know that the challenges that threaten our existence – environmental collapse and the still real threat of nuclear devastation – are of our own making. Perplexing concepts such as "information explosion" and "global economy" are quite naturally greeted with mistrust, but our reactions elicit a frightened sense of nostalgia unknown to children. Progress beckons but its call bewitches as in a great myth.

It's no coincidence, then, that this anxiety has been the focus of reports on education from British Columbia to Newfoundland over the past decade. Canadian governments and businesses are determined to compete more vigorously in the global market. But they must contend with a population that is becoming increasingly aware that every new turn of the industrial engine further chokes the environment. Today we face this deepening paradox and we have turned to schools for an answer. But first, perhaps out of panic or for old time's sake, we are kicking the hell out of them.

Across the country, business leaders are the ringleaders. Schools, they claim, produce a bunch of illiterates who can't even make the correct change as sales clerks. They point to an extensive national survey by Southam in 1987 that labelled 4.5 million Canadians illiterate, one-third of whom were high school graduates. Drop-out rates hover at about 35 per cent nationally and the aimless revolt of teenage subcultures has the uneasy feel of something sacred unraveling.

Business people call for tighter controls, such as province-wide standardized tests. Students who don't make the grade should be granted, in the words of the Ontario Chamber of Commerce, "the right to fail." Overall, business leaders push for a "back-to-basics" approach that essentially amounts to more of the kind of teaching conducted by Karen Riley. The direction of school reform today suggests that political leaders are ready to oblige. In the face of challenges that threaten our very existence, we seem to demonstrate that unique ability to look forward and fall backward at the same time. It's as though we're stuck somewhere between a recognition that survival demands creative solutions and a desire to preserve our culture by continuing to act in ways that got us into trouble in the first place. Schools today are mired in this contradiction.

"We say that as a society we want independent learners, critical thinkers. I'm not so sure society really wants that," says Angus McNeil, the principal of Coal Harbour High School near Dartmouth, Nova Scotia. "If you put these guys out there who can think for themselves, they're not going to be told what to do anymore.

"It's a mixed message to the kid," McNeil continues. "What do we value? Obedience, respect for authority; we tend not to want that challenged. We discipline kids for challenging it. 'We want you to be a critical thinker but you open your mouth, buddy, and you're dead meat.' I mean, look, if we started today and said, 'Every kid in this province is going to come out with critical thinking skills,' my God, they'd tear the place apart! They'd start saying, 'We're not going to kill any more of that ozone stuff and we're not going to create any more greenhouse effect. We're going to make the world safe to live!'

"There's almost a lack of trust and honesty in the whole system. The creative, intelligent teacher feels stifled. He has to present himself in a dignified manner. What we want everybody to do is talk in monosyllables and monotones. Education is a process, it's not a dozen eggs. But what we've got today isn't a joy or a lifelong pursuit. It's drudgery. It's 'meet the test and be evaluated.' It's a system of hurdles and I'm not sure I can overcome that or change it."

The seemingly immovable force McNeil feels unable to resist has been identified by educational researchers as the "hidden curriculum" of schools. Through the structure and practice of schooling, it constitutes a kind of arithmetic of socialization that tries to burrow deep inside the children and mold their very spirits. It is primarily an invisible operation that often suffocates the natural impulse to adventure that John Polanyi speaks of. Its lessons are passivity and submission, and it is responsible for an education system that fails both students and society. The hidden curriculum is the subject of this book.

1

EGERTON RYERSON AND
THE HIDDEN CURRICULUM

Resistance to schooling is so widespread among students it is tempting to see it as something instinctual. This seemed to be the case the day I began grade 1, my first day of school. The school was a squat building in Montreal's east end and the schoolyard was filled with children and, mostly, their mothers. At the door of the school, a boy wailed at the top of his lungs. It was a breathless, anguished scream that seemed to announce his imminent expiry, cut short by shrieks that resounded a block away. He tore at his mother's dress, and entreaties by teachers only made matters worse. Whether the boy sparked a chain reaction or whether it had previously eluded my frozen senses, I'm not sure. But suddenly I heard cries erupting all over the yard as if some grievous choir was painfully working its way to a crescendo of soprano madness. I threw my mother a gaze that pleaded, "Look, I've always trusted you, but do you think maybe, just maybe, these people know something we don't?" She paused and then walked me into the school with the determination of someone who accepts only the destiny that remains after hand-to-hand combat.

Intense aversion to schooling has a long history. It hit massive proportions when Egerton Ryerson, probably the best known of Canada's fathers of education, set up a school system for all of Ontario in the mid-nineteenth century. Ryerson saw free and compulsory schooling as a great act of democracy, but many parents didn't agree. They resented that their children were legally forced to attend and noted with reason that many teachers were incompetent, drunk, or child molesters. School burning was not uncommon and some teachers were literally chased out of town by angry mobs of parents and students. When teachers punished children by keeping them after school, the parents vehemently protested and often broke into the school to free them. School administrators branded these rebels as bad parents for undermining the school's authority and refusing to replicate its stiff, often brutal, discipline at home. Corporal punishment was officially sanctioned and meted out with the zeal and self-imposed burden of those who believe they know best. Sociologist Bruce Curtis, in his book *Building the Educational State: Canada West, 1836–1871,* notes that many of the most violent struggles in school involved attempts by students to leave school rather than be beaten by teachers, and attempts by teachers to force students to accept the beatings.

At Saltfleet Township in 1859, for instance, a young teacher was locked in the school house for an hour by his students after unsuccessfully trying to punish some of them. After they released him, archival records state, the students "threw mud and mire into his face and over his clothes" while parents encouraged them. At Brantford in 1863, a teacher named W. Young was assaulted by one of his students to the point that his successor claimed, "Mr. Young's head, face and body was, if I understand rightly, pounded literally to jelly." Young himself attributed the assault and other resistance to "my efforts to introduce good order & discipline."

The resistance from parents and pupils made clear to teachers that there were limits to the amount of corporal punishment they could get away with. Curtis notes that in 1836 one Ontario teacher wrote: "A few days ago I slightly chastised a little girl in my school for an act of wilful disobedience and in the evening her father came to me in a fearful rage, was with difficulty induced to refrain from violently assaulting me, and after much abusive language said if his child 'did not behave herself in school, turn her out' but if I ever touched her again he would stamp the guts out of me."

Curtis argues that the resistance of students and parents was largely directed by their aversion to the massive transformation in the role of schools. Under Ryerson, schools went from focusing on the teaching of basic literacy skills to molding social identities. Ryerson established what is now known as the hidden curriculum – a system that, through the structure and pedagogy of school, tries to shape the behaviour of students. The aim was to develop people who willingly accepted the status quo, and this was to be done by establishing school rituals that implicitly taught passivity and submission. This system tried to reach deep into the selves of students and eliminate their resistance. But people don't lie down and play dead when someone tries to mess with their insides.

There are few agreements in education. Everyone and their relatives seem to have a different idea of what schools should be doing. When there is agreement, it's usually around what the goals of education should be – developing literate thinkers instead of sheep, productive and nice people instead of axe murderers. Ask them how to achieve these goals and you're back to dealing with disagreement. On one point though, conservative, liberal, and radical sociologists all agree: schools play a primary role in "reproducing" the social and economic relationships of our society. Of course they disagree on exactly how it's done and whether it's good or bad. But nonetheless the metaphor of reproduction dominates educational research.

The reproductive role of schools dates back to Egerton Ryerson. His time was the twilight of the Family Compact – the oligarchy of aristocrats, merchants, bankers, and clergymen who ran colonial affairs – and the common folk were getting restless. In fact, it was a period of major social and political upheaval that culminated in the rebellion of 1837, which threatened the powers that be. In the book *Egerton Ryerson and His Times*, the editors Neil McDonald and Alf Chaiton argue that Ryerson believed the political system was losing its legitimacy. The civil disorder, Ryerson thought, was the result of mass ignorance and the republican influence of American teachers and textbooks in the largely private schools of Upper Canada.

Amidst this social turmoil, the notion of childhood was taking shape among English Canadians. Historian Philippe Aries was among the first, in 1962, to argue that the notion of childhood as a separate time of life didn't exist prior to the early sixteenth century. Until then, children took part in adult life not long after infancy, upon mastering spoken language.

By and large, there were few adult "secrets" kept from children; they slept in the same rooms, they went to war, and in the Middle Ages gambling was a favourite pastime of the young.

The origins of childhood parallel the development of the printing press and the spread of literacy. Schools sprung up in those areas of Europe where literacy was most valued, such as the British Isles. And where there were schools, the notion of childhood developed rapidly. Schools can be traced back to the Middle Ages, but it was not until the spread of books in the sixteenth century that knowing how to read and write fluently became important.

Media critic and educator Neil Postman, in *The Disappearance of Childhood*, maintains that literacy changed the social status of the young. "Because the school was designed for the preparation of a literate adult, the young came to be perceived not as miniature adults but as something quite different altogether – unformed adults." The school's task was to form them, to take them through the steps towards literacy and adulthood, starting with memorizing the alphabet. Grade levels became the most graphic markers of the steps to literacy and adulthood. As children progressed through the grades, their understanding of the adult world grew in proportion to their mastery of reading and writing. Literacy became the key to unlocking adult secrets.

Once childhood was invented, adults tried to uncover the "nature" of children, and the eighteenth-century philosopher John Locke played a significant role in this process. Locke was responsible for the well known analogy that at birth a child's mind is a blank tablet, or *tabula rasa*. Parents, educators, and other adults were therefore responsible for imprinting the appropriate social script on the child's mental slate. Postman notes that in the book *Some Thoughts Concerning Education*, Locke argued that developing a child's powers of reason was a crucial step towards adulthood. Part of developing this faculty, Locke suggested, involves a kind of education that manipulates the child's emotions. "Esteem and disgrace are, of all others," he wrote, "the most powerful incentives to the mind, when once it is brought to relish them. If you can get into children a love of credit, and an apprehension of shame and disgrace, you have . . . put into 'em the true principle."

Locke's metaphor of the *tabula rasa*, Postman says, sees children as unwritten books whose pages need filling. To become an adult a child has to acquire the sort of intellect expected of a good reader: the capacity to think logically and sequentially, the capacity to manipulate high orders of abstraction, and the capacity to defer gratification. In the world of book learning, the exuberance of children had to be contained and modified. Self-control and discipline were valued, the kind that sits children in straight rows and demands absolute quiet and concentration. In short, the kind of discipline that prevails in schools today. Postman writes: "The capacity to control and overcome one's nature became one of the defining characteristics of adulthood and therefore one of the essential purposes of education; for some, *the* essential purpose of education." This was not an uncommon view among school reformers in Canada West during the mid-nineteenth century and later.

In Europe, the notion of childhood was first embraced by the more affluent and literate middle classes who could afford the children's fashions and books that began to be produced at the end of the sixteenth century. It did not filter down to the lower classes until the mid-1800s with the advent of universal education. As historian Neil Sutherland suggests in his book *Children*, English Canadian society showed little awareness of children as individuals until the 1880s. Indeed, it was during this period that school authorities stopped referring to students as "scholars" and began calling them "school children." By the 1890s, children were increasingly seen as morally deficient and a threat to the well-being of society. It's no coincidence that this view gained prominence at a time when literacy was flourishing in Canada. By the 1890s, more than 400 newspapers were being published and books of fiction were widely read. School officials feared these books like the plague. In 1849, the *Journal of Education for Upper Canada* described fictional books as containing "the power of spreading a pestilential miasma." A year later, the journal continued its relentless attack on fiction, saying it could "lay the foundation of a life of vice and crime." These books were thought to completely captivate the reader, breaking down the person's individual discipline and rationality and thereby threatening the social order. For school reformers, it became imperative that children read books that disseminated what they saw as "useful knowledge," such as lessons in natural science or the scriptures.

The political and economic elite of Canada West believed the status quo was at stake when Ryerson began designing Ontario's new school system. Ryerson believed a publicly funded, universal school system would create stability by training the population in their duties towards the political order. Neil McDonald, author and professor of education at the University of Manitoba, argues that Ryerson set up the first Canadian system of mass social control which was later used as a model for other provinces. Ryerson's ideas served as the prototype for such men as S.P. Robins in Protestant Quebec, David J. Goggin on the Prairies, and John Jessop in British Columbia.

In his 1846 report outlining a plan for a school system in Ontario, Ryerson summarized his concept of education this way: "By education I mean not the mere acquisition of certain arts or of certain branches of knowledge, but that instruction and discipline which qualify and dispose the subjects of it for their appropriate duties and employments of life as Christians, as persons of business and also as members of the civic community."

Neil McDonald argues that Ryerson believed social class was divinely ordained. Unfortunately, those destined to spend their lives with sore necks from looking up had forgotten why they should be there. Ryerson wanted the working class to understand it was in everyone's best interest to allow what he believed to be the more enlightened, the ruling elite, to rule. "Ryerson was not concerned in altering the 'divinely ordained' social order," McDonald writes, "but in the interests of 'social progress' was concerned that the 'lower orders' adopt the more acceptable and trustworthy values of the middle class. In effect, it was an attempt to convince the working classes that their interests were also those of the middle and upper classes, and that as a collectivity, there was a 'common' or 'public good' towards which all must work." And so the "common good" as democratic pacifier was institutionalized in schools. "From the outset," McDonald contends, "it was intended that schools support a political system about which there was to be no serious examination or questioning."

It can be argued that Ryerson, an ordained Methodist minister, was simply trying to develop a more loyal and informed public to complement the social and economic changes of the time. Like other school reformers at the time, Ryerson believed in a form of liberal education that taught "disciplined intelligence" and knowledge to be used to carry out the will of God. By improving moral behaviour, Ryerson believed people would keep themselves in line without the state having to use physical force. But while Ryerson's intentions were far from sinister, the long-term results of the system he laid down continue to have a numbing effect on the minds of students today. Ryerson's formula was a simple one. By getting the poor to accept the values of their "betters," they end up defining their own self-worth in ways that are in the best interests not of their own class but of the one that dominates them. In this idea lies the genesis of the reproductive role of Canadian schools.

It is when things become familiar that we possess them unconsciously. At the cornerstone of Ryerson's reforms was what Bruce Curtis calls "the construction of routines and rituals of obedience." The idea was to turn the school into a mode of disciplinary power. "The sight of the school, the consciousness that one was drawing near to the school, would induce certain kinds of behaviour, of self-regulation," Curtis writes. "Pedagogical authority would become effective and legitimate by being implanted in the selves of students."

Until the late 1830s, Ontario schools were under the control of the community and local trustees and together they determined the curriculum taught and the teachers hired. With the School Act of 1846, Ryerson began centralizing control of Ontario's school systems. The act and subsequent legislation gave Ryerson, as Chief Superintendent of Schools, broad powers of curriculum control based on the ability to withhold annual grants to schools. For the first time, the central authority was able to influence what happened in schools by establishing criteria for hiring teachers, approving texts, and laying down regulations that superintendents were supposed to follow. In centralizing control, Ryerson was very much adopting the industrial model of organization – a not surprising result given that mass education followed urban industrialization.

There was of course pressure from employers who were demanding a disciplined labour force that moved to the tick of the mechanical clock and worked to the pace of machines and prescribed schedules. This was no easy task for rural children raised on agrarian rhythms. They got up at dawn, went to sleep when the sun set, and generally measured time by the cycle of seasons. When October came around and potatoes had to be harvested, attendance at schools plummeted. And when haymaking commenced in July, schools could be assured that the stronger boys would be working the fields. School administrators were keen to make schools as regular as clockwork. If children were to internalize what Ryerson believed were appropriate behaviours, their ways of acting had to become routine and second nature.

Nothing enforces routines like hierarchy, with its rigid, lockstep lines of command designed to keep people in their allotted places. Schools came to reflect the hierarchical nature of workplaces and were built, organized, and run like factories. Urban schools built at the turn of the century were three or four stories high and had long corridors with classrooms on either side. They were so similar in structure to factories that some, like Toronto's Brant Street Public School, were actually made to be converted to factories if enrolment declined. My high school in Montreal went from being a factory to a school and back to a factory in little more than a decade.

Along with industry's architecture came its management techniques, which continue to prevail today. School systems across the country have central offices, or boards of education, filled with senior management, which provide money, supplies, and equipment. It's not unlike the industrial model of a main plant with warehouse or distribution centres spread across the country. Inside schools the similarities continue. Individual schools have principals, department heads, and classroom teachers supervising students. Factories have superintendents, department heads, and supervisors running the plant and overseeing workers.

Dale Shuttleworth, assistant superintendent at the York Board of Education in Metropolitan Toronto, notes that principals-in-training must be adept at time-tabling, a skill often seen as more important than their abilities as curriculum leaders. In the end, the control and efficient movement of students from one class to another play a larger role than the needs of individual students. In his essay, "Public Education: An Industrial Model in the Post-Industrial Age," Shuttleworth writes: "This efficiency of production ethic has strong origins in the assembly line model, as envisioned by Henry Ford."

Through a kind of osmosis, this hierarchical structure has come to seem natural to both students and workers. As such, it significantly determines how people function by framing the acceptable and the unacceptable. For instance, the spoon-feeding of information becomes the preferred style of teaching when authority travels in a line perpendicular to students.

In short, Ryerson laid the groundwork for a school system that has since changed little in structure and function. The grading system of the Victorian common school permitted better supervision of pupils and encouraged uniformity and competition. "Knowledge was broken into pieces, reduced to its elements and compartmentalized; pupils themselves were viewed as raw material to be processed," says George S. Tomkins in his book *A Common Countenance: Stability and Change in the Canadian Curriculum.* "School rituals such as recitation in unison, the practice of 'penmanship' . . . and the precise division of the day into periods likewise stressed the order, obedience and uniformity characteristic of the factory system."

This call to obedience was enshrined in the School Act of 1846 where, for the first time, the duties of a teacher were officially outlined. Teachers were required to "maintain proper order and discipline" and were instructed to pay the "strictest attention to the morals and general conduct of their pupils." By their own example, teachers were expected to impress upon students "the great rule of regularity and order – a time and a place for everything, and everything in its proper time and place." They were to teach the principles of "Truth and Honesty; the duty of respect to superiors, and obedience to all persons placed in authority over them." They were also to encourage "cleanliness, neatness and decency" in their students and personally inspect them every morning to ensure that their hands and faces were washed, their hair combed, and their clothes clean and mended.

The goal was to shape the moral behaviour of students. Uniform textbooks, a byproduct of an increasingly centralized school system, played a significant role in ensuring this end. Tomkins notes that in British Columbia, for instance, textbooks took a literal interpretation of the Bible and expressed a belief in orthodox Christian doctrines. For example, the textbook *Outlines of General History* taught that the world was created in 4004 B.C. and treated Adam's fall, Noah's flood, and the Tower of Babel as true historical events. Tomkins also notes that grammar texts, readers, geography books, and chemistry books included scriptural references. After 1870, public school authorities throughout the province proclaimed a new public curriculum of civic virtues including thrift, orderliness, family responsibility, time-work discipline, and respect for property and godliness. These "virtues" were also transmitted by a more sophisticated effort to try and spoon-feed children what school authorities saw as appropriate knowledge.

Prior to the reforms of the 1840s, spelling, for instance, was seen as a preparation for reading through the learning of letters and the combination of them into syllables and words. Children were taught letters through the forming of consonant-vowel pairs to be sounded, such as ba, be, bi, bo, bu. Words of one, two, or more syllables were then pronounced and spelled. Words in spellers were classified by length, and before beginning to read, children were expected to master the spelling of long words. "Rote learning resulted in children being able to spell complicated words while still being unable to spell monosyllabic ones," Tomkins states. Egerton Ryerson legitimately denounced this "letters to words" method as "irrational drudgery" and helped replace it with what was known as the Prussian "whole word" method. Pupils learned words as whole units instead of as groupings of letters. For example, the teacher would write "barber" on the blackboard, often associate it with a picture, then erase the word and ask students to spell it from memory. This "look and say" method was followed by questions to make sure the student acquired the officially sanctioned meaning of a word. Indeed, Curtis argues that the transmission of "correct meaning" became the focus of the new reading method. "'To think for oneself' in bourgeois school reform was not an abstract capacity to be exercised as one thought fit. On the contrary, bourgeois school reform sought to produce students who would think particular things and who would think in particular ways: but *freely*, in a self-disciplined manner," Curtis writes in his essay "The Speller Expelled." Sadly, it's the kind of teaching that still rules today.

Related to teaching literacy in Ryerson's time was the teaching of penmanship based on what was believed to be scientific principles embodied in manuals and teachers' textbooks. According to Tomkins, one textbook urged pupils, using goose quill pens, to write in unison "so that they not only made the same letter but the same part of the letter at the same time." The text prescribed nine steps to starting a writing lesson, including "Place the right hand upon the inkstand," and ten in closing it, such as "Close the inkstands." Such methodology, says

Tomkins, "had a military precision." This method is not far removed from the writing instructions teacher Karen Riley had posted on the wall of her Vancouver classroom. Then and now, penmanship exemplified the uniformity among students that schools tried to achieve.

Reading and writing skills were to be taught within the context of "humanistic" pedagogy. Humanistic theory was a sharp break from how classes were conducted in the first two decades of the nineteenth century, when "monitorial schools" were the norm in England and the New England states. Students were taught by rote in groups as large as 600 under the control of a single teacher. The teacher would pass bits of information to child monitors who in turn would pass it on to the group of children under their supervision. Ryerson rejected this approach, as Curtis indicates, "for its failure to adequately penetrate to the core of the consciousness of the human subject." Ryerson preferred the kind of "humanistic" education espoused at the time by Horace Mann, the secretary of the Massachusetts Board of Education. The theory tried to maintain order by developing students who were emotionally dependent on the approval of teachers. Ryerson quoted Mann to show how the theory worked:

> When a difficult question has been put to a young child, which tasks all his energies, the Teacher approaches him with a mingled look of concern and encouragement; he stands before him, the light and shade of hope and fear alternately crossing his countenance; and if the little wrestler with difficulty triumphs, the Teacher felicitates him upon his success; perhaps seizes, and shakes him by the hand in token congratulation; and, when the difficulty has been really formidable, and the effort triumphant, I have seen the Teacher catch up the child in his arms, and embrace him, as though he were not able to contain his joy . . . and all this has been done so naturally and so unaffectedly as to excite no other feeling in the residue of the children than a desire, by the same means, to win the same caresses . . . .

In a sense, children were to be loved into submission. Teachers would, in effect, be able to control students with a glance, a gesture, or a tone of voice. Humanistic education helped develop children who disciplined and regulated themselves in search of approval. But in case this conditional love wasn't enough to keep students in line, it was backed up by the power of the rod. The School Acts and regulations preserved and strengthened the power of teachers to use corporal punishment.

Curtis notes that prior to the reforms of the 1840s, corporal punishment was regulated directly by the community. "If teachers used violence defined locally as excessive, students were capable of responding directly and in kind." This changed under the School Acts, and parents or students could be fined or jailed for "disturbing" a school. Disturbing was broadly defined to include everything from making noise to challenging the authority of the teacher. The evidence of the teacher was usually enough to make the case. Furthermore, when teachers used violence against students that parents found excessive, such disputes were to be resolved through school arbitrations and not the courts. In short, humanism in education was preached only after schools had legally monopolized the use of violence.

Overall, Ryerson's reforms reflected the world view of a ruling, and mostly educated, elite and their practice of noblesse oblige, an attitude which in education has evolved, at best, into misguided paternalism. The problem with those at the bottom is that they don't think and act enough like those at the top. "The whole dream of democracy," wrote nineteenth-century novelist Gustave Flaubert, "is to raise the proletariat to the level of stupidity attained by the bourgeoisie." Ryerson's reforms, Curtis argues, amounted to a process of "self-making." The aim was to achieve a kind of moral metamorphosis: to change the way people looked at themselves and the world around them; to get children to internalize authority or power relations in a way that made them seem natural. Basically, to elevate the status quo to the level of truth. By the turn of the century, the hidden curriculum of submission and passivity was firmly in place through the structure, routine, and practice of schooling.

Not surprisingly, Ryerson's ideas evolved into an appallingly elitist system. The high school entrance examinations, implemented by Ontario in 1870, went a long way to ensuring this. They became the chief sorting device for the school system and reinforced the hierarchical nature of schools by accentuating the division between common (elementary) and secondary schools. For most of the first half of the twentieth century, most children left school after grade 8, having been inculcated with a benign respect for God, King, and Country. For decades, high schools remained an elitist enclave. Of the grade 2 students in Ontario in 1952–53, only 22 per cent went on to complete high school. The figures were similar for other provinces. At the time, this exclusiveness wasn't cause for too much concern. The Canadian economy, still largely resource-based, didn't need many skilled or professional workers. But the late 1950s brought radical change. The baby boom (Canada led the Western world), high youth unemployment, and the technological needs of a changing society forced the school system to open up. These economic and social changes paved the way for the first serious attempt at transforming the school system that Ryerson had built. This attempt came in the form of a movement called "progressive education."

In their essay "Back to Basics," Jack Quarter and Fred Mathews, professors of applied psychology at the Ontario Institute for Studies in Education (OISE), argue that the educational changes were partly designed to put schools in tune with the new economy. Large bureaucracies were being set up in the public and private sectors, government services were expanding, and American multinationals were setting up shop in Canada. New management positions were being created that had to be filled. Workers capable of operating more complex machines were also in demand. In the face of all this the labour force needed upgrading, and schools were expected to train students for the new roles.

In response to these pressures in the early 1960s, Conservative prime minister John Diefenbaker offered to cover 75 per cent of the costs for new commercial or vocational high schools across the country. Ontario bought into the system extensively. When industrial engines roar in Canada, nowhere do they roar louder than in Ontario. In the first year of the Diefenbaker plan, 124 vocational schools were approved, representing 90 per cent of all such projects in Canada. By the end of the six-year federal project, nearly 60 per cent of the 635 vocational wings in schools or full vocational schools were built in Ontario. A still more highly stratified school system was developed to correspond to the highly stratified economy. Education administrators responded by segregating students on the basis of deemed ability – what became known as the practice of "streaming." In Ontario, under the Robarts Plan, students were categorized into seven different streams of study. Three separate groups were set up: arts and science, science and technology, and trades, business, and commerce. Within each group, students were slotted into two subgroups: an advanced, five-year program heading to university, and a four-year program spilling out into the "world of work." The seventh stream was a two-year program which essentially trained students for dead-end jobs. Those in the program were labelled "terminal students." Thus students were categorized into convenient administrative boxes, vertically and horizontally.

It was at this time that the practice of streaming proliferated to the point where it became perhaps the most graphic example of the hidden curriculum. Locking students into one stream of study or another involves a judging, sorting, and slotting process that earns schools the mechanical metaphors often used to describe them. Those streamed high are eligible for university and considered "winners" while those streamed low are barred from university and labelled "losers."

But while these categorizations were fundamentally restrictive, they were interpreted by many educators at the time as providing an opportunity for mainly working-class teenagers who otherwise would drop out to continue studying. Teachers who experienced those years say a sense of egalitarianism permeated the system and was further enhanced by the social and political transformations of the 1960s. The social movement of the time, which grew out of the civil rights struggle in the United States and spilled northward, was in essence a demand for a more democratic society and a tearing down of systemic barriers that prevented disadvantaged groups from gaining a fair share of the economic and social pie. This democratic push led to many innovations, including, for example, the financing of programs to help inner-city children in the early 1970s and the adoption of anti-racism policies in schools.

Within this new liberal reality it became apparent that strict discipline, widespread failures, and standardized tests discarded too many students. This not only contradicted the humanitarian thrust of the period but failed to make economic sense as well. Schools had to become more flexible in order to graduate more people to fill the new jobs of a booming and changing economy.

By the late 1960s, the Hall-Dennis report, *Living and Learning,* in Ontario, the Commission on Education by the B.C. teachers' union, and the Worth Commission in Alberta began espousing progressive or "child-centred" learning. This became the driving rhetoric of schools across the country. While it was inspired by the social and economic realities of the time, the roots of progressive education can be traced back to Jean-Jacques Rousseau, who believed that each and every child's "soul" was inherently good and must be protected from the leveling effect of civilization. Rousseau's ideas influenced such important educators as Johann Pestalozzi, Friedrich Froebel, and A.S. Neill. The progressive method recognizes that children are not homogeneous. They develop at different rates and in different ways. The task of teachers is to ensure that each one acquires a passion for learning while reaching his or her potential. Children should not be treated like widgets or human receptacles into which adults pour half-truths. Central to the philosophy is the belief that everyone should be treated with dignity.

In the United States, this progressive wind led to the growth of the free school movement in the late 1960s. The movement tried to disregard the compulsory aspect of education by not enforcing state laws of attendance. Free schools substituted hierarchical authority with democracy. Authority over curriculum, classroom attendance, conduct, and evaluation were placed in the hands of teachers, parents, students, and administrators. Students were allowed to choose their own activities which, as sociologist Christopher Hurn says, "would enable them to understand, to question, and to grow emotionally as well as intellectually." Children were to be motivated by a desire to master their environment and not by grades or fear of failure. Children were not compared to others and evaluated simply to give them an idea of their progress. Teachers were to shed their veneer of expertise and reveal themselves as human beings, guiding students in their work.

What were called open schools also set up shop at the time but were less innovative, keeping traditional methods of evaluation and a traditional curriculum. The biggest change with open schools was to redefine the structure of the classroom, getting students to work in groups and giving them the freedom to talk and move around. By allowing students to be more active in the structuring of their work, open schools hoped to do away with the tight controls needed to keep students sitting quietly and passively as teachers droned on in their traditional method of teaching the whole class simultaneously.

Both free and open schools met with limited success. Hurn writes that free schools, because of their commitment to achieving democratic consensus, had trouble getting everyone to agree to basic rules and procedures. In the classroom, problems of authority, discipline, and motivation became increasingly difficult to resolve to everyone's satisfaction. And, without the traditional sanctions of punishment and grades, it often required exceptionally talented and charismatic teachers to inspire effort and loyalty in students.

Open schools seem to have had more success. Joyce Epstein and James McPartland conducted the largest American study of open schools on more than 14,000 students in Howard County, Maryland. They found no consistent relationship between open classrooms and test scores across all grades in language skills, reading comprehension, or mathematics. In other words, the study found that open classrooms have no discernible effect on students' learning. Students performed no better or worse than those in traditional classrooms. The researchers did find, however, that open classrooms increased the self-reliance of students. "In open classrooms," Hurn says, "children are less likely to report being uncomfortable in disagreeing with their friends, in putting forward new controversial ideas, and in thinking about the possibility of leaving their home and families." Hurn adds that the success of open schools can be gauged on a much simpler level. Unlike free schools, open schools have withstood the test of time and many continue to prosper. The Toronto Board of Education, for instance, has several "alternative" schools that have operated successfully for two decades.

In Canada, progressive pedagogy first gained prominence in the 1930s. In 1931, Saskatchewan led the way by embracing elements of the philosophy and Alberta made it the focus of its curriculum in the late 1930s. Ontario did the same in 1937 but, as with Saskatchewan and Alberta, settled for a system where rhetoric and practice didn't meet. Progressive philosophy never trickled down to the classroom, largely because Ontario teachers continued to conduct classes in the way they themselves had been taught.

Student teachers were trained in what were called "normal schools," first set up in Ontario in 1843. The early normal schools were run much like military camps, where even conversations between male and female students were prohibited. Indeed, in 1878, the ability to put students through military drills became a requirement for a first class Ontario teaching certificate for men. While the more overtly militaristic methods of normal schools were dropped over the years, the implicit ones remained when progressive theory entered schools in the 1930s. Student teachers continued to be trained in a lockstep process similar to the one endured by elementary school children. They were examined on the details of the elementary school curriculum and learned through a close study of textbooks. They were trained to swallow, and when they graduated and conducted their own classes they expected their students to open wide. In short, drilling breeds drilling.

The school system is notorious for refusing to learn from experience. Thirty years later, with the Hall-Dennis report, Ontario politicians and school authorities made the same mistake of failing to equip teachers to handle the reforms. The landmark report was written by educator Lloyd Dennis and Supreme Court Judge Emmett Hall. Its progressive philosophy was summarized in the report's preamble entitled, "The truth shall make you free." The report influenced schools for more than a decade and produced the most flexible school system in Canadian history.

In elementary schools, the notion of "social promotion" took root. Children who didn't learn as quickly as their peers were no longer kept behind and stigmatized as failures. Instead, they were passed with an understanding that, as far as anybody knew, they could blossom into top students the next year. It's one thing, however, to stigmatize students with failure and quite another to simply pass them without ensuring that they have at least learned some things. Bernard Shapiro, formerly the head of OISE, notes that this was one of the mistakes made in the province's open schools. Shapiro believes open schools remain a valuable model for school reform. He says they offer the kind of structure that allows learning to become more important than teaching. The greater freedom created by the open classroom, however, should go hand-in-hand with a greater sense of responsibility. In the past, Shapiro argues, too many teachers in open schools didn't ensure that students were learning and standards came tumbling down.

In high schools the credit system was introduced in the early 1970s. Students were free to choose whatever courses they liked and schools were free to offer whatever they could dream up. Until the mid-1970s, there were no mandatory or core subjects, but there were problems. As the children of the baby-boom years left high school, the schools were hit with a severe drop in enrolment. This caused some anxiety – provincial funding was tied to the number of students schools served – and it triggered a scramble for bodies. Less demanding courses were designed to attract students and this further eroded standards. Schools had already interpreted *Living and Learning* to mean that all standards were destructive, and teachers were grading students according to whatever criteria they chose. In the late 1970s, universities complained loudly that marks had become meaningless. A 70 per cent average in one school could be the same as a 50 per cent in another school and a 90 in a third school. By 1980, the popular perception among parents, employers, and many teachers was that students were coasting their way through school.

Greg Murtah, a history teacher at the time, says the progressive approach never really had a chance. Ontario's ministry of education never officially endorsed the new philosophy. Still, the rhetoric of progressive education was so influential that the system couldn't help but respond. Teachers tried to embrace the new philosophy but received little training to help them do so. Progressive education was a fundamentally different approach than they had been using for many years. Instead of treating the 30 or so students they faced as though they were a homogeneous group, teachers were expected to individualize their instruction according to the strengths and weaknesses of each student. At the same time, they had to continue teaching the official curriculum. In history, for example, getting students to memorize the seven causes of the American revolution and regurgitating them on examinations wasn't good enough. Students were expected to participate in their learning, perhaps by taking on the role of a black slave at the time. The student was to arrive at his or her own understanding of the period through the use of information found outside the approved textbook. Progressive education required teachers who exercised less control and had a solid understanding of the subject matter. They could no longer hide behind the presumed authority of textbooks.

"It wasn't the messiah that was the problem, it was all those damn disciples that got in the way," Murtah says, referring to teachers.

"I blame what people did with Hall-Dennis," adds Ron Watts, then principal and vice-chancellor of Queen's University in Kingston, Ontario. "The whole education process was brought into disrepute because the parents turned against it. They wanted to see their children progress through the system but when they realized that the standards had been watered down, they lost respect for it.

"Ultimately, I think we've been beating around the wrong bush all along," Watts says. "It's not the curriculum that's the answer, it's the teacher. A lousy curriculum taught by a brilliant teacher will bring the student alive. A superb curriculum taught by a lousy teacher will kill him."

Watts' analysis is accurate. The school system desperately needs better teachers, but even the most able have difficulty sustaining their commitment. Like their students, they too are victims of a system where hierarchy reigns and rocking the boat is not tolerated. A sizeable chunk of teachers are a kind of walking wounded who sound like they've had their enthusiasm slowly cut out with a blunt scalpel. They seem forever shadowed by a mind-numbing awareness of how immensely complex the problems with schools are and, feeling powerless in the face of the hidden curriculum, resignation is their lot. So they judge, sort, and slot students into one educational future or another and greet with cynicism new initiatives like progressive education or, more recently, "holistic language." Experience has taught them it's only a matter of time before these new initiatives are brought under control by the hidden curriculum. Such was the fate of progressive education. Its attempt to humanize schooling resulted in a system that sorts and slots with a limited amount of compassion – a system that strokes and kicks at the same time.

Educational rhetoric has changed since Ryerson's time, but the practice of schooling has essentially remained the same. Control continues to be exercised through a system in which tasks are assigned and completed, much as they are in a factory. While the hidden curriculum is ubiquitous, researchers argue that its pillars are the school's rigid hierarchical structure, a dominant teaching method that spoon-feeds children, and the sorting and slotting of students into categories of "winners" and "losers." Underlying it all is an obsession with sequence and control.

Remember Karen Riley's classroom at Grace Elementary School in

Vancouver? The workings of the hidden curriculum are graphically seen in the kind of drilling she was conducting with a tape recorder. Despite decades of anxious debate on education, drilling is a teaching method that persists in many classrooms across the country, and its continued use demonstrates how little schools have changed since Ryerson's days. In his authoritative history *The Development of Education in Canada,* C. E. Phillips notes that pupils in the mid-1800s were asked to memorize portions of textbooks and recite them back to the teacher word for word. Drilling by rote, Phillips states, "required above all docility and obedience in the pupil, and in the teacher an ability to make punishment an imminent reality . . . . No occasion was given, if it could be avoided, for requiring the pupil to think."

Drilling is an ancient schooling ritual. It is essentially unquestioned, sacred, and followed blindly. David Gierak, a drama teacher in Alliston, Ontario, puts it this way: "School is like some science fiction novel of a post-nuclear world where people walk around dazed, carrying on the traditions of the ancients, not knowing what they mean or why they're doing them; doing them only because the ancients performed them before the bombs dropped."

Gierak believes the rituals throw so many students into apathy that if he saves one or two of them, if he helps them learn to think, he considers it a great success. After all, by the time Gierak faces his students in high school, most have learned the rituals well. They start performing them the day they enter school and the idea is to act as though there were no other way to act. When the tape recorder in Riley's class asked the children, "Isn't this fun?" they not only responded to a machine, of all things, but, mimicking its drone, they lied and said yes. As Riley put it, it's the name of the game and the kids know it. To win, they must think and act the way schools want them to think and act. It's a process that tries to reach deep into the child.

In his cogent analysis of American society, *Culture Against Man,* anthropologist Jules Henry writes that "School metamorphoses the child, giving it a Self the school can manage, and then proceeds to minister to the Self it has made." Riley's ability to "freeze" her children at will demonstrates the extent to which the metamorphosis is essentially a mechanical one, resembling the tape recorder she used for the drill. This transformation of a child's insides, this mass homogenizing, occurs not so much through the learning of subject content as through the communication of what Jules Henry describes as "noise."

Human beings have the capacity to learn several things at once, and when Riley's children sit in the classroom they're being bombarded by messages from all sides. The drone of the tape recorder, the straight rows, the competitiveness of students, the posters invoking attitudes, the tone of the teacher's voice, and the ringing of the bells are messages the children pick up in the form of background noise. This "white noise" permeates the system and results in the subtle but relentless ways that schools perform what many argue is their central function – to socialize children in the dominant myths of our culture. The noise often comes to students in the form of unquestioned rituals and is part of the hidden curriculum. By focusing mainly on the structure and practice of schools, I will try to explore how these rituals reflect the myth of progress – the tale of Western culture's steady climb to consumer heaven.

"Every culture lives within its dream," writes Lewis Mumford. The dream is composed of collective social myths that frame the acceptable and the unacceptable. The belief in the scientific method as the only approach to knowledge, the view of the universe as a machine which can be broken down into constituent parts, the view of life as a competitive struggle for existence, and the belief in unlimited material progress through economic and technological growth: these are all examples of dominant ideas that make up our culture's myth of progress. It's a myth – a story – with a sequential narrative that quantifies, grades, and labels the universe in an illusory search for absolute truths. The Pavlovian shuffling of students in and out of classes at the ring of bells, the sorting and slotting process of streaming, the sequential curriculum that transforms knowledge into an assembly line, the hierarchical structure that discourages questioning, and the sanctity of competition – are all school rituals dedicated to the deity of progress.

We've reached a point where our myths no longer serve us, yet we continue to serve our myths. And with schools reflecting the society they serve, the hidden curriculum is working to quicken our demise. Teetering on the thin line between nuclear destruction and environmental collapse has made us somewhat anxious. As our trust in political leadership diminishes, our demand that schools do more grows.

Developing "critical thinkers" has become a rallying cry for school reform, but few reformers have tried to uproot the hidden curriculum. It is left to continue its socializing work, and for many students the assault is relentless. They resist the essentially dehumanizing nature of schooling, but their revolt is aimless, performed as a matter of principle, a way of regaining dignity, and forever at the mercy of a supreme lesson of the hidden curriculum – resignation.

2

THE THREE Rs:
RESISTANCE, REBELLION,
AND RESIGNATION

At the end of the week, on sunny spring days, schools are like pots of simmering water with teachers sitting on the lids. By late in the afternoon the risk of boiling over is great. We can perhaps blame this delicate state of affairs on the impertinence of sunshine. For students bored out of their minds, the pull of the outside is irresistible. I've been in schools, Coal Harbour in Nova Scotia, for example, where the steam escapes with a rush and whole classes are cancelled because students simply don't show up. And it's not as though they skip class and disappear. They usually just hang out around the school, shooting the breeze, virtually unaware of their own defiance. There are few instances when revolt is so spontaneous and natural. "I rebel, therefore we exist," wrote Albert Camus.

Skipping is the physical manifestation of a more widespread form of resistance that takes place in the classroom. There, many talented truants religiously practice a mental tuning out, no matter what the weather. Physical and mental skipping is a signal from students that they alone have final control over their bodies and minds. This suits the hidden curriculum just fine. Its function is to sort and slot people into "stations and callings" that are often not of their choosing. Its insidious power is often to get people to do it to themselves, of which more will be said later. Those who skip lose marks for not showing up, precipitating their being stamped "losers." Those with truant minds are learning to cope with the monotonous jobs many of them will be forced to take in the future. They're learning how to stay down and dancing.

Students outside of the university-bound courses resist the system far more overtly than those on what society considers to be the winning path. Ron Kendall is familiar with both groups of students. He used to be principal of West Park Secondary School, a Toronto school exclusively for basic-level students in vocational courses, but is now vice-principal of North Toronto Collegiate Institute, a school exclusively for those in the advanced, university-bound program.

"At West Park they don't understand why there have to be any rules," Kendall says. "If they're there, they're meant to be destroyed. The kids here [North Toronto] don't openly resist the rules. They try to bend, they try to connive; what we have are kids who are not getting 80 per cent like their classmates and this causes some frustration. They try to test you but not in those epic ways. I haven't come across a legendary rule breaker yet. I can think of two kids here who are really rebellious but, in a sense, they're the Holden Caulfield types. Yeah, they'll probably become lawyers."

High school students react to schools in ways that fall into four general groups, not unlike those described by British educator David Hargreaves. The first is what might be called the *conformists* – those students who completely buy into the system and embrace its values without being aware of its essentially arbitrary nature. They are mainly found in the path leading to university and have their eyes locked on high-status jobs.

The second group is made up of students who do well in school and are also largely in the university-bound streams. Most of them are not much excited by schooling, describe it as a kind of game, and learn to mechanically play by the rules that will produce the best results. They see school as the accumulation of credentials that pave a path to the top. With the odd grudge now and then, they live by the rules. We'll call them the *technocrats*.

The third group is composed mainly of students who are not in the university-bound program. Like the technocrats, they generally see schooling as a game and are resigned to its inevitability. Generally defined by society as losers, they've given up on the system and make the achievement of personal happiness their goal. They shuffle through the routine of school, bored out of their minds, and in the end they resist with a shrug and a daydream. They are what Hargreaves calls the *indifferent*. Overwhelmed by lethargy, they drift through the school day as though iron weights hung from their bodies. The technocrats and the indifferent make up the majority of students, meaning that most students are aware yet resigned.

The fourth group has been rejected most thoroughly by the "game." They generally do poorly in academic subjects and are labelled as having bad attitudes or behavioural problems. They turn schools into combat zones: the school does everything it can to keep them under control and they in turn see it as their moral duty to defy all rules. Like most students who resist, they practice an aimless form of rebellion which in the end simply allows schools to dismiss them more readily. They are the *rebels*.

As with all categories, there are many individuals who straddle two groups or who embrace elements of several. Some students have the presence of mind and strength of character to rise above the overwhelming cynicism of a rigidly stratified system. There are, for instance, some very bright rebels, capable of working at an advanced level when they want to. But the student who writes anti-racism articles for the student newspaper, plays in a rock band, and is capable of maintaining university-stream marks is the clear exception. More often than not, good students of this kind are being smothered.

Awareness and resistance go hand-in-hand. Despite the stereotypes many adults have of teenagers, a simple talk with them makes clear that most are anything but clued out. Personal experience is the best teacher. When you spend years walking around in a miniature version of society, seeing its workings up close, there's no hiding the ugliness. The issue is not whether teenagers are aware but rather what they do with their awareness.

Much of the resistance is aimless, but it demonstrates that students don't roll over and play dead when faced with the hidden curriculum. Human nature is such that we resist attack, if for no other reason than self-preservation. Students resist the rigid controls of schools and the ceaseless judgements that label them winners or losers. They all feel their very dignity is at stake. For many, their resistance turns to outright rebellion; for most, it leads to resignation.

In schools, mass resistance takes many forms. Most students are relentlessly trying to slow down the schooling process. It's not exactly a storming of the ramparts. It's an hour-by-hour, day-by-day struggle to subvert; the kind of work slowdown that would make the most militant union proud.

What students say is a common stunt was pulled on teacher Paul Orshak one day at the start of his "People in Society" course at Toronto's Brother Edmund Rice Catholic Secondary School, in the city's west end. Three students walked in, greeted a few friends, and then in one way or another made clear they had forgotten their textbooks. They happily followed Orshak's order to go get them. When they returned, they shuffled around for a while, and by the time they were ready for the class, a full ten minutes had passed. Not by coincidence, it was a sunny Friday afternoon.

It was a grade 11, basic-level class, the bottom of Ontario's three-tiered program of study in high schools. Only students in the "advanced" level of study are eligible for university. Those in the "general" stream can go on to community college while those in the "basic" program head for work after high school. There is a pattern which indicates that people from low-income families, and generally the "socially disadvantaged," end up at the bottom. The statistics are downright embarrassing for a society that utters words like equality as though it believes them. Students in these lower streams say they're generally looked upon as losers – a relentless judgement that erodes dignity.

On the blackboard, Paul Orshak was outlining the different stages of human development as seen by Erik Erikson and Sigmund Freud. Phil sat at the front with a smile on his face. He was one of the teenagers who had arrived without a textbook. Immediately after retrieving it, he began pawing Antonella, sitting next to him. She fought him off with a left hook to the shoulder that didn't phase Phil one bit. "It's summer and I'm grooving," he said. "Man, you get a girl, you lie on the grass, I'm grooving."

"God, that's all you talk about," said Antonella. "Can't you shut up, I haven't had lunch yet."

"Do you want something to eat?" Phil asked, raising his eyebrows and cracking a big smile while leaning over.

"Ah, go home," Antonella shot back.

"Go get a nose job."

"Go get a body job," said Antonella, unperturbed.

Phil let out one more, "Ah, go home," and then suddenly added, "Sir, who pays these people, people like Freud?"

Orshak told the students they would watch a movie on neurosis in their next class. He launched into an explanation of the film but one student cut him off, complained he was giving away the plot.

"I was just whetting your appetite," Orshak said.

"Wet, oh, I like that word," Phil groaned from the front of the class.

"Phil, you know what I like about you?" Orshak said. "If I stand here for an hour I might think of something."

"Ah sir, we know you really like Phil," a student said.

From the back of the class, Tony got up and strutted slowly to the garbage can in front. His swagger had a calculated muscle-man spring to it, leaving the impression that he should be taller. His long hair was severely slicked back over his ears and hung over his forehead in a big wave. He's a member of the subculture teenagers call "ginos." He returned to his seat and put up his hand.

"Sir, I need to go to the washroom," Tony said.

"Every day we meet at this hour and you say, 'Sir, I've got to go to the washroom,' and it takes you seven minutes to come back. I think you're going and taking something," Orshak said.

"Sir, I do nothing!" Tony said, indignant.

"If I see a puddle, you'll go," Orshak said.

The fact that sex dominates the thoughts of 17-year-olds should be no surprise. They openly express their sexuality even though the structure and practice of schooling act like a wedge between body and mind. The hidden curriculum is obsessed with squares and straight lines. The assembly line is an appropriate metaphor for a system that sorts and slots people into boxes of deemed ability. Along the way it sits students in straight rows, controls their movement, asks them to perform linear and sequential tasks, spoon-feeds them content, and emphasizes cognitive and abstract skills – practices which alienate many students from their own natural feelings. Added to this is the enforcement of a sometimes ridiculous morality. When I visited a high school in Alliston, Ontario, teenagers related with incredulity the time their vice-principal tried to stop hugging and kissing in the hallway. He decreed that students must keep a specified distance from each other and then walked around with a ruler, pouncing to measure the space between bodies. Only slightly more serious is Ontario's AIDS education curriculum that emphasizes chastity until marriage as the safest prevention. No doubt this is the case, but teenage hormones don't make for a captive audience.

Once, as I was waiting for the start of a movie, I overheard two young women talking behind me who looked about 16 years old: "She went up to Michael and kissed him and, like, I knew it was his birthday and all that but I couldn't stand it. I just wanted to grab her by the hair and throw her down. It was really weird; it was like my whole body was jealous."

"I know what you mean," said her friend. "I feel like that too sometimes."

These are the questions that interest teenagers; the love-and-death musings of humanity that adults learn to sweep under the rug. It's one reason teenagers are so fascinated by music. Romantic pop songs, unlike schools, seem to speak directly to their concerns.

Schools may want to deny the pleasures of the flesh, but in their own way teenagers won't let them. They know full well that flaunting their sexuality ruffles the adults who run schools, and they do it with joy. A favourite practice of young women at Edmund Rice is to hike up their mandatory plaid skirts into miniskirts. Of course part of this sexuality is an acting out of sexist roles fostered by the mass media. But it's also an expression of the larger desire of teenagers to understand and respond to the emotions swelling inside them. So students bring their own agendas into the classroom, whether teachers like it or not. If they want to have any kind of control at all, teachers have to compromise and strike a deal. In this sense schooling is a clash between machine and human resistance, youthful and exuberant. In the end, the sorting and slotting machine gets its way – this is a simple question of power – but not before resistance has forced accommodation, creating an unwritten agreement between students and teachers. The system bears down on students, and they push back. A deal is struck, consent is won, revolt is contained, but the peace is an uneasy one.

In Paul Orshak's class, Phil's wisecracks are very much within the bounds of the informal contract. Orshak is clearly one of Edmund Rice's better teachers. Administrators see him as someone who can engage students, and students see him as someone who sincerely wants them to succeed. "With Mr. Orshak, learning is fun," says one student, expressing a rare sentiment in schools.

Orshak is tall, has wispy brown hair, and generally presents a slovenly but comfortable appearance, replete with suspenders. Most of all, he is a master of repartée. His lessons are full of banter and witty exchanges with students.

"They know when a person's kidding or when a person's trying to hurt. These kids have known a lot of criticism that hurts," says Orshak, referring to students placed in the basic-level program of study.

"When I first came here four years ago it was a total shock," Orshak adds. "You go to university and you learn all this stuff that you can pass on and then you end up with a group of basic-level kids and you never use it. You never use what you learn."

Like so many others, Orshak emerged from his training as a teacher well versed in the lecture mode of education, the one that treats students like blank slates. After a year he realized that this demand for attention would not wash with students on the losing side of the credentials race.

"There's a wall that goes up between you and your students," he says. So he took a clue from them and incorporated into his teaching the banter they used among themselves.

One day after class, while I am asking Orshak about his teaching style, a former student drops by to say hello. He is a sturdy fellow completing his first year of community college, and he had grown up in the working-class neighbourhood that surrounds Edmund Rice. He says Orshak's classes were "like the streets."

"You know, like when you're hanging out, you're always trying to get each other. You know, if someone insults you, you have to pick up on it really quick and get him back. It's always back and forth, back and forth. That's what it's like with Mr. Orshak."

"But I don't think you could do this kind of teaching at Lawrence Park," Orshak says, referring to a high school in an affluent part of Toronto which offers only the advanced, academic program of study, leading to university.

So Edmund Rice students succeeded in bringing their street culture into the classroom and pushed Orshak to modify his teaching method in order to accommodate it. It was either change his style or face a wall of blank stares. The result is the unwritten agreement. Without these agreements, student revolt would be much greater.

These informal agreements have been described by American researchers Arthur Powell, Elinor Farrar, and David Cohen in their book *The Shopping Mall High School: Winners and Losers in the Educational Marketplace.* In some classrooms, teachers accept one-word answers or students who simply regurgitate; in others, students are expected to expand or build on ideas they encounter in literature or textbooks. In some, homework is part of the agreement; in others, homework is sacrificed in exchange for just showing up. In one Edmund Rice class, the reward was a game of password during the last ten minutes of the period if the class went smoothly. The most common understanding is that everyone would much rather be somewhere else, so the goal is to do the minimum required to get through the class and then scram.

In some schools, usually those in affluent neighbourhoods, parents are also part of the agreement. As Paul Orshak says, his style of teaching would not be acceptable at Lawrence Park Collegiate Institute, where everyone understands that the country's future professional elite is being trained. Even in these elite schools, however, some teachers will reward students simply for performing as expected, like trained seals.

On a hot spring day Tony Angiolillo and I were sitting on swings in a parkette in front of Brother Edmund Rice High School. It was lunchtime and across the street a crowd of teenagers at the corner was busy doing their brand of street theatre. Tony falls in the indifferent category, and he admitted he consciously chose to work below his ability.

"If I try, I could do really well, but I don't," he said. "I screw around too much, I like to have a good time rather than get the business done. I don't like competing in school. I don't think competing in school is needed. You know, you always get people saying, 'Oh, look at me, I got 50 on 50 and I didn't even study.' People walk around saying they're the best and how far they're going to go. It really disgusts me."

A few minutes later, a couple of students from the street corner crowd wandered over to where Tony and I were chatting. Tony knew them but he became hesitant and evasive with my questions, so after a few minutes we headed for the cafeteria. The lunch period was over and the cafeteria was empty except for the caretaker. Tony chatted with him in Portuguese, and their banter made it clear he had done so many times before.

"The thing about schools," Tony said, "is that there's no community. Nobody wants to be with anybody, really."

Graduating, Tony said, is "the last thing on my mind. Being happy is important to me, not worrying about little things. A lot of people I know just let little things get to them."

Spending time with his girlfriend was more important than anything else, especially school. "Everywhere you go, people are always telling you, 'You have no time for nothing else.' If you work they say, 'Don't tell me you need time for a social life!' and if you're at school they say, 'Don't talk to us about no social life or work problems.'"

"I've always been scared about getting old. When I turned 17 I almost started to cry," he said seriously. "I enjoy being young because a teenager is enjoying yourself and I think this is the only time to have a good time. You know, when I become older, let's say I become a construction worker, then that's all I'm going to be – a construction worker. When I'm older, you know, I'm going to have to work every day. I'm going to have to be there always or I'm going to lose the job and I won't be able to support my family. Like, I watched my father and mother work every day, just to get food on the table. But you know, when you've gone through life like that and you've seen them do it, I guess you're not as scared, really, because you've been through it and you know that's what you have to do. If you had a life where everything is nice and your parents are always behind you in what you do, you would probably be more scared because you've never faced anything on your own."

We talked about pollution and poverty, about happiness, and many more things. Tony was at once earnest and engaging. "You know, I really think about these things a lot," he said, as though not sure he should admit to it.

"Do you think you could do anything about any of this?" I asked.

"If I was president or prime minister of either America or Canada, there wouldn't be a poor country in this world. I would guarantee it. Really, I would make sure there wasn't a Third World country around.

But you know, I don't think there's much you can do yourself unless you're in a high position."

For youths like Tony, awareness is smothered by a sense of power-lessness. They fight back by refusing to take part in the game, and they work below their potential. Resignation is triumphant.

The self-defeating resistance inherent in Tony Angiolillo's attitude was documented on a larger scale by British researcher Paul Willis. In his 1977 book, *Learning to Labor: How Working Class Kids Get Working Class Jobs*, Willis signalled a break from the wholly mechanistic Marxist theories of social reproduction. Until Willis, Marxist theorists saw school as a kind of black box where students are loaded on a conveyor belt, remain passive throughout the indoctrination process, and eventu-ally roll off as perfectly formed widgets. Perhaps many businessmen and politicians would like it to work that way, and the essential aspects of schooling – its emphasis on control, its spoon-feeding of information, and its assembly-line sorting and slotting process, or streaming – try to deliver just that. But in his landmark study, Willis concluded that non-dominant groups in society don't take their domination lying down.

Using the anthropologist's tool of ethnography, Willis observed the lives of a group of working-class students he called "the lads." The lads completely rejected the underlying values of school, particularly its emphasis on social mobility through credentials. Through part-time jobs and the work experiences of their parents, the lads had a sense that social mobility was a farce and messages from the school to the contrary were greeted with cynicism. The lads completely dismissed the school's rules and saw "intellectual" work and "pen pushing" as effeminate. Their preference for manual labour, however, was not due to a passive accep-tance of their place in the class structure. They instead saw manual labour as liberating. They believed it was more challenging and they val-ued the macho comradeship of their fathers' shop-floor culture, which they were mimicking in school. Their home culture, therefore, played a significant role in determining their ambitions. (Feminist researcher Angela McRobbie has criticized Willis for ignoring the role that family patriarchy plays in reproducing a dominant sexist ideology. She noted that while the lads were learning to flex their macho muscles and thereby continuing the rule of patriarchy, working-class girls were apprenticing in submission.)

The lads' rejection of the values schools disseminate fell short of being a political statement; it did not represent a show of solidarity with the working class. Their resistance was largely aimless. It was a response to the contradictions they saw between the lofty rhetoric of equality and social mobility and the reality of their day-to-day lives, contradictions easily apparent in the values and practices of schools. In the end, by rejecting the system, by being counter-culture, the lads precipitated their streaming into low-level courses of study, to help an unequal economy reproduce itself. As Willis put it: "There is an element of self-damnation in the taking on of subordinate roles in Western capitalism." Willis' lads can be found in almost any school.

George Harvey Collegiate Institute is in a mainly working-class neighbourhood in the city of York in Metropolitan Toronto. The surrounding streets have a mixed population, mostly Italian but with a large black community. George Harvey offers only a small program of academic, advanced-level courses. Most of its courses are in the technical fields, such as computers, business, drafting, and mechanics. For many years the school has had one of the better basketball teams in the Metro Toronto area. In 1989 the team did poorly, but this didn't stop the fans from turning every game into a neighbourhood street party.

The spectators' bleachers rest on a concrete deck high above the basketball court, its upper-most row of seats a stretch away from the metal rafters on which the fans bang loudly every time a George Harvey player scores a basket. During the game I was at, some spectators were transfixed by the action on the court, others just hung out. The preferred attitude was supercool, and the muffled sounds of reggae from someone's "boom-box" seemed to bind everyone in a kind of fluid harmony. Standing beside me was a black teenager wearing a black leather cap. He wore a large medallion around his neck that hung down to his stomach. He locked his gaze on a girl walking towards him from the opposite end of the stands. As she approached he smiled and their clenched fists touched in greeting. "Vibrations," she said. "Constant vibrations," he replied.

In this setting, it was easy to spot Maurice Thomas. Sitting alone on a bench in the middle of the stands, he was the only white student in a crowd of about one hundred spectators. "I've been wondering about that myself," he said when I asked him about his distinctive presence. "I just transferred to this school from Pembroke a couple of days ago and I can't figure this out."

Thomas played basketball at his previous high school and had come to the game with the thought of joining the George Harvey team. "It doesn't look like this is for me," he said, looking around. Without knowing it, Thomas had walked into the heart of a powerful subculture that revolves around the school's all-black basketball team. For most white students, attending basketball games would amount to trespassing on someone else's turf. The players themselves admit there are some white students in the school with the talent to make the team. "I think they're just intimidated, they know they wouldn't fit in," said Roy Mohamed, the team's manager and disc jockey for the parties thrown by the players after the games.

Like the members of all subcultures, the students at George Harvey have their codes of behaviour. These determine whether someone is in or out. The groups form around a fixed point: school sports teams, clubs, musical genres, and their attendant fashions – "b-boys" and hip hop, for instance, or "skids" and heavy metal. Some of the divisions are also along racial lines. There are few white b-boys, and among Italian youths the "ginos" are a distinct subculture. Some groups may act in harmony with school rules while others, like Paul Willis' lads or the George Harvey players, will do everything they can to reject them.

As a general rule, the kids who reject the rules at any school are made up of those who are not in what the school hierarchy and society consider a winning stream of study. Their counter-culture provides a defence against the judging, sorting, and slotting process that places them in the lower levels of study, bars them from going to university, and takes a kick at their spirit. It doesn't stop the process, but in their rebellion they find dignity and a sense of community, one in which *they* set the rules. Their days are filled with gestures of defiance, ranging from skipping class to doing drugs. These groups are very close-knit. Sometimes, when one individual in the group decides to drop out of school, the rest follow him.

But whether they're defiant or comfortable within the school's mainstream, teenage subcultures always represent an attempt to wrestle some control from a system that determines where students should be, when they should be there, and what they should do while they're there. The George Harvey basketball team, for instance, has extended its turf from the court to the school's main hallway. A row of glass doors separates "their" hallway from the lobby in the school's main entrance. At lunchtime the players or other group members will stand by the entranceway like doormen at an exclusive club.

"This is our hallway; all the excitement happens here. It's where the action is, you know, the jokes, the fun, the laughter, stuff like that," said Roy Mohamed. He was dressed in the standard b-boy look: off-white windbreaker with rainbow stripes and matching pants, baseball cap, gold chains, and rings on every finger.

At lunchtime the hall was filled with students and the players acted like delighted hosts, making sure everyone was having a good time. The guys on the team said other students respected their turf and often avoided it by taking detours when going to classes. Likewise, they didn't hang out on other floors. "On the third floor, that's the boring floor; you got the brainers there," said Roy, referring to the university-bound students.

"Yeah, they say, 'Well, I'm moving up now, I'm moving to the third floor,'" laughed Bobby Llewellyn, one of the ball players.

"Yeah, remember Sean," Roy said. "Sean was like us and then, 'Ah, I'm moving up!' They're the guys who say they're the best but basically, they're just one of us."

"So they actually hang out up there and don't come down?" I asked.

"Yeah, you don't see them no more," Roy said. "If they have to go to class they go up and around."

We were standing in a loose circle in the middle of their hallway and it was lunchtime. A passing girl caught Roy's attention: "Hey baby." The atmosphere was pure joy. There was more than just strength in numbers, there was personal freedom as well. It felt like the scene at the ballgame. The teenagers seemed to soar on a kind of mellifluous vitality. Guys moved in and out of our group, bouncing like electrons. When a stern-looking teacher walked by, she seemed terribly out of place. With a twitch full of disapproval, she glared at the lively scrum, but the students acted as if she didn't exist.

At the heart of the subculture were members of the team: Bobby Llewellyn, Bobby Reynolds, Ron Hamilton, Dave Williams, Wayne

Simpson, Gary Jackson, and, finally, Roy Mohamed. Most of them had Caribbean backgrounds, and this added a further element of cultural alienation to their resistance. They admitted to only one firm condition of membership in their group.

"You got to be able to hack our criticism," Roy said. "Some people can't. If you can't take it, you'll be crying every day. Like what are you going to do when we start talking about your girlfriend?"

"Talk about yours?" I ventured.

"You got it," he said.

In the locker room after one game, Bobby Llewellyn, the team's star player, practiced some of his "criticism." A teammate walked out of the shower and as he dried himself Llewellyn shouted: "Hey look at you, man. How you gonna turn on some woman? With your nose?" Llewellyn then overheard a former player tell me he's thinking of going to university. "You go to university?" Llewellyn said in a mocking shriek. "Man, Freddy's freakin'. Imagine seeing Freddy at U of T. Man, you're freakin' Freddy, you're freakin'."

In the corner of the locker room, a student played team hairdresser and gave the ball players the box-shaped haircut popularized by disco queen Grace Jones. Llewellyn described it as "wearing your hair like a hat." But Llewellyn was not adverse to style. One day he proudly pointed out to me that he was wearing his track suit inside out because, "It's original, man."

Most players on the team were taking general-level courses, in the middle of Ontario's three streams of study. The general level has been sharply criticized in studies commissioned by the ministry of education for being a watered-down version of advanced-level studies without any of the incentives. Those in the advanced stream are driven by the need for high marks in order to get into university. The general level is theoretically for students heading to community college, but as one Toronto principal said, "That's the school system's biggest lie." In fact, most of the students who go to community college are from the advanced level. These are students who either failed to get the marks to go onto university or chose not to. College administrators, given the choice between low-scoring applicants from the advanced-level and general-level students, tend to pick from the former group. So for the general-level student, what's the point of attending school if all they'll get is a diploma, which employers claim is of dubious value? Why put up with all the controls of school if there's no payoff at the end of the line? This lack of purpose in their education fueled a kind of guerrilla war between the George Harvey players and school authorities.

Nothing angered them more than reminders from teachers of the school's basic rule: If they failed half their subjects, they would be taken off the team. This may have represented a genuine interest in their welfare on the part of school authorities, but for the players it was an outright threat of losing the only thing about school that gave them self-esteem, on and off the court.

"Playing ball means that all the girls talk to you," said Roy. "You can walk through the hallway and say, 'Hey, I made this shot and I did this dunk.'

"Yeah, you're really noticed being with the team," he continued. "It's like, you know, you got the nerds and you got the cooler guys and we're the cooler guys. Like when we went to New Brunswick for a game, this school was dead."

The sense of vitality the players felt on the basketball court and in "their" hallway was entirely absent when they sat in class. The standard complaint about boredom was heightened by the fact that George Harvey had adopted a system of longer classes. The year is divided into two terms. In the first term, students study the same four courses every day, each running for about 75 minutes instead of 45. Then they take a different set of courses the next term. A majority of Ontario schools have adopted this system on the grounds that subjects can be taught better with longer periods. But with everything else about schools staying the same, the players saw it as an extended sentence.

"What's so boring about school?" I asked them.

"The school itself. You have the same classes, every single day," said Llewellyn, his voice trailing off like a recording slowing down. "You come to school five days a week, same four classes each day and every day. So it gets after a while, after the first month, school's just *boring*."

"There's a teacher in this school who just talks all period long," said Dave Williams. "He gives you no work, right. And I told him, I said, 'Sir, it's better if you were a college teacher or a university teacher.' You know, he thinks he's a philosopher."

"How can you change this school to make it more bearable?" I asked.

"Blow it up and give it a new name," Llewellyn said.

When the guys described their schooling experience, they saw themselves as factory workers under the watchful eye of foremen. They even referred to the teachers as bosses.

"Teachers in this school think they're it," Roy said. "They think they're the boss by just trying to bug you every time when you come to school. They keep bugging you and bugging you, provoking you, stuff like that. And the principal and the bosses, you know, they think they own the school. So you have to abide by the way they want everything run."

The school had strict rules on dances, for instance, and these rules irritated the players to no end. School authorities, they said, would allow them to hold dances immediately after school but not in the evenings. The later time slot was reserved for dances organized by the student council that, the players said, most black students refused to attend.

"Every school I've been to," said Ron Hamilton, "the student body does not want to admit that it's the black people that carry the swing around the school, you know what I'm saying? When it comes to a dance, it's only black people who are dancing, and they refuse to admit that. So if they have a dance and they have some DJ who plays the right music for the majority of people that are there, okay. But, you know, they always get some gino guy that's going to play all kinds of gino music and then nobody's going to buy no tickets and nobody's going to show up, right."

"So why don't you elect someone to the student council that's going to listen to you?" I asked. "You guys can put together a lot of votes."

"Look, we just come to school and the bell rings, we come and we go, you know," Ron Hamilton said.

"The whole system, you know, it's already put down on a platter, that's how it is since day one. It's going to be too hard to change," said Nugent, a black student who hung around with the players.

"If we have a black guy being the president, he's going to abide by what the bosses believe," Llewellyn said. "And anyway, we don't give a shit. You see, we don't go out of our way. The dances, we like them at night. They say, 'No,' so we say, 'Fuck you,' and leave it at that. There's no point in fighting it. If you win, you'll still lose."

"Yeah, even when you're right, you're wrong. It's a lose-lose situation," Nugent said.

For students who have never read Franz Kafka, they have an eerie understanding of his existential philosophy. They describe the school system as an infinite labyrinth governed by laws that have nothing to do with human nature and therefore make no sense at all. On one level it is ironic that in their desire to escape the dominant system, they create a new system with rules that seem as rigid and exclusive as the one they disdain. Is it surprising, for instance, that there's an element of misogyny in the values that bind them? In order to find dignity they duplicate the very structures that the dominant culture uses to maintain its status. There is further irony in the fact that this process of duplication virtually guarantees the permanence of their marginal status.

This process continues when subcultures step outside the school walls and become youth gangs. These groups look very much like walking rock videos, and in this sense they are somewhat prepackaged by the mass media. But the messages embodied in these subcultures go deeper than just their styles. In his study of the punk movement, *Subcultures: The Meaning of Style,* British researcher Dick Hebdige writes: "The punks appropriated the rhetoric of crisis which had filled the airwaves and editorials throughout the period and translated it into tangible (and visible) terms. In the gloomy, apocalyptic ambience of the late 1970s . . . it was fitting that the punks should present themselves as 'degenerates'; as signs of the highly publicized decay which perfectly represented the atrophied condition of Great Britain."

The forces that bear down on Tony Angiolillo and the George Harvey basketball team extend far beyond the school walls. These forces form the pillar of a collective social tale, and teenage subcultures are its mirror image.

The auditorium at Malvern Collegiate was packed. It was a community meeting for Toronto's east end, and it was billed as a "Gang Forum – Education, Solutions, Tips for Parents." It was a warm spring night in 1989 and the Metro Toronto region had been seized by a kind of gang hysteria. For months the mass media had been filled with stories of youth gangs roaming the streets like violent caricatures of mad shoppers.

They would "swarm" solitary victims, beat them up, and strip them of leather jackets or other chic items of clothing. It was not a safe time to be nicely dressed. The threat seemed to be everywhere. A couple of terrifying stories – one of a mother who watched her daughter get beaten up and another of a teenager stabbed to death in a dance club – were repeated in the media so often they seemed to magically reproduce. Every day, the media revealed the name of a new gang until it became impossible to keep count. One night the "Untouchables" would allegedly be responsible for a beating at one end of the city and the next night be the cause of trouble at the other end. Either turf meant nothing to these gangs or they had a broad network of cells that would be the envy of the most sophisticated revolutionary group. It caused genuine fear in the 300 or so parents at Malvern Collegiate that spring night, and they looked to the panel of "experts" to confirm their fears.

A dozen people were on the panel; four of them cops and the rest made up of local politicians, a school official, a youth worker, and Rob Tucker, head of a group called the Council on Mind Abuse. Tucker told the audience that the youth gangs were like satanic cults whose aim is to destroy society's moral code of "love, compassion, and trust." He then gave the example of a 13-year-old whom a youth gang had encouraged to rebel against his parents. For his initiation ritual, they lured him to a basement where they mutilated animals and used the blood to leave thumb prints on the wall. "I'm really scared about this," he concluded. This sent the teenager sitting in front of me into hysterics, the kind of laugh that bursts through clenched lips in a spray, causing the whole body to heave. More subdued but equally mocking snickers came from the 50 or so teenagers in the last three rows of seats.

Gordon Rasbach took a more tentative approach in his presentation. He was a police officer with a squad set up by the Metro Toronto force to deal with the youth gangs. He had interviewed dozens of teenagers involved in the violence and was described by police as an expert in the field. He estimated that 80 per cent of gang members were from middle-class and affluent families. The groups have no membership, hierarchy, or turf. "We're using the term gang for lack of a better word," he said. "We call it gangs because that's what the media call it."

This point of view did not go over well with George Thompson, the staff superintendent of 55 Division, the police department responsible for much of Toronto's east end. He walked to the microphone with the self-confident gait of a man accustomed to making his presence felt.

"Make no mistake about it, there are gangs out there," he boomed in a low, surly voice.

"Right on!" shouted a voice from the crowd as applause broke out.

They may not be well organized, Thompson continued, but the dictionary definition of a gang is a group that exhibits "anti-social behaviour," and there are many of those around.

Gordon Rasbach returned to the microphone and said that parents should be concerned if their children begin wearing clothes they can't afford, particularly those with labels like Roots, Club Monaco, and Hugo Boss. "They like to look their best," he said.

By now, teenagers were streaming out in disgust, shaking their heads at what they saw as yet another example of collective adult stupidity.

"Listen to those people," said Chris, a 16-year-old from Danforth Technical School. "I got told I'm socially deprived, socially depressed, and my parents don't care. You know, you go through history and everybody's always taking a problem and passing the blame onto somebody else."

Turning a social phenomenon into a police matter inevitably fuels the alienation that drives most teenagers to join what are more accurately called subcultures. As Constable Rasbach suggested, the label of "gangs" attached to these roaming cliques of teenagers is a media creation, one that very much disturbs teenagers.

"It's to sell newspapers," Chris said. "If they get something with a gang, someone hurt, or someone dying, that's what they do, they blow it up and it sells newspapers. Like, I mean, there was an article in the newspaper a year ago about a skateboard gang called the Untouchables. Now, they went from a skateboard gang to Metro's most notorious police-hitting, kid-kicking gang!"

A teenager named Bob said he used to hang out with a group of guys, a gang with no name. "I've seen it all. I've been through it all," he said, sounding like an ancient mariner. "I've seen 10 people jump on one person and beat him up and I've seen 30 people fight 30 people. I've seen it all and I've done it all."

"Okay, so why did you do it?" I asked.

"Because everybody's on a power trip. You see movies and you look at the guy and you say, 'Oh, I can be like him.' So you try and live the adventure. Life is boring, right, so you try to make something happen."

"So you're bored and you're after adventure and power?"

"Yeah, we're just trying to create adventure but sometimes you get so caught up in the sense of adventure that you cross the line between reality and a movie and then you get into real trouble, trouble you didn't expect to get in. Then once you're into it, people are saying, 'Look at what you've done!' and by the time you realize what you've done, you don't want to back out so you try and play it off as if it wasn't a big deal," Bob said.

"It's to make a name for yourself so you can be the flavour of the month," added Chris. "Say me and him go out and he beats up 12 people and I beat up 14 people. Whoever comes out the toughest or the baddest, he's the one who usually has the followers around him."

"Until someone pulls a bigger scam," Bob said. "Like if you come up with a challenge and you conquer the challenge, like, 'Look at him, he's in the spotlight for a night.' Like he gets all that power and authority for a while. On the street, you get power from it. Just think, you could be by yourself or you could have 30 or 40 people following you around, asking you what *you* want to do and where *you* want to go. Which would you rather be?"

Power is not an abstract concept for these teens. They simply exercise it within their own context, mimicking the grab and pull of the adult world they see around them. Toronto filmmaker and writer Kevin McMahon argues that swarming is the teenage equivalent of predatory corporate takeovers in a culture that teaches by the example of its actions and not by its lofty and often hollow rhetoric. But in the end, their "magical" re-creation of our brutal culture is performed not in the mindless fashion of automatons but with the frightening attitude that what's good for the master is good for the slave. While swarming may make good training for future corporate roles, teenagers are also thumbing their nose at the hypocrisy of adult rules. In one swarming attack, a group of teenagers beat up an adult, took only one dollar from his wallet, and then threw it down a sewer as he watched. One student at Brother Edmund Rice School explained swarming this way: "Power, they want power. They want to have a name, they want to be known; it's like being a lawyer." Another student added, "The only difference between some kids beating up some guy and the way businessmen do things is that the businessman is going to get away with it 'cause he can get some big shot lawyer to defend him. But what can we get? You know, money talks."

In his seminal study, "Subcultural Conflict and Working-class Community," British sociologist Philip Cohen details the birth of the mods and skinheads in England's inner city in the early 1960s. Cohen argues that they represented a magical attempt to recover a sense of community. The mods and skinheads emerged, he notes, at a time when working-class communities in London's inner city were experiencing severe physical and psychological changes. Whole neighbourhoods were labeled slum areas in the late 1950s and bulldozed to make room for subsidized, high-rise apartments, an architectural form not conducive to community street life. Middle-class families moved in to buy the remaining large homes, immigrants arrived in greater numbers, working-class youths saw their mothers enter the workforce, traditional craft jobs declined, and conspicuous consumption roared louder than ever.

Schools were ill-equipped to cushion the blow. Teachers imposed middle-class values and expectations on working-class students, many of whom felt, with justification, that they were being prepared for unskilled, dead-end jobs. No longer able to take refuge in the stability of their working-class communities, they formed groups that tried to re-create a feeling of belonging through exclusive codes of behaviour. The pill-popping mods donned tight dress pants and thin lapels in a self-conscious exploration of the reckless consumerist values embodied by the upwardly mobile class. The skinheads, however, acted differently. Cohen describes their style, violence, and reactionary values as a "caricature of the model worker, the self-image of the working class distorted through middle class perceptions; a meta-statement about the whole process of social mobility."

There are some obvious parallels between the transformation of inner-city London and the changes in Canadian inner cities, such as the razing of neighbourhoods to make room for the Don Mount Court and Regent Park housing projects in Toronto. The period since the late 1950s has also seen a steady decline in the role of churches and schools as centres of both middle-class and working-class communities. The notion of a "neighbourhood school" continues to be eroded as students and parents go on shopping sprees for the right French immersion, gifted, or sports program.

The large numbers of new Canadians entering our schools are most vulnerable to this sense of having the ground removed from under their feet. The fear and culture shock that immigrants experience are great, and schools do little to help. The resulting alienation is a significant factor in their banding together to regain a sense of belonging and self-esteem. But they too have been assigned the label "gangs" and in some cases are being handled by police. In 16 Vancouver schools in 1989, police regularly patrolled the hallways on the lookout for gang members with names like the Viet Chings, Barrio Latinas, East Van Saints, Patok Boys, Red Eagles, Clark Parkers, and Los Diablos. Like their Toronto counterparts, these are loosely knit groups with no membership or turf, and anyone is free to adopt their names.

Erik Wong, a Vancouver high school teacher, was asked in 1989 by the municipal government to improve the public's understanding of youth subcultures. For years he had watched schools alienate immigrant students and spent a lot of time speaking to the students outside the classrooms. In Vancouver, the typical teenager who turns to a subculture for support comes from a low-income immigrant family. In school these students are usually enrolled in English-as-a-second-language classes and doing poorly. In fact, Wong said, "they see school as being meaningless. They walk around in a group and as a group they get a sense of self-esteem, a sense of self-concept, and a sense of power, because as individuals in this society they don't have that . . . . Their sense of being able to rebel against us, their sense of being able to stand apart from us and in fact see us cower with fear of what they represent is their sense of getting revenge."

Teenagers belonging to large cliques do sometimes get involved in petty crimes, but most of the time they just hang out in shopping malls. This too is reasonable – indeed almost natural – in a consumer-crazed society where shopping malls have become the modern version of community centres. The small ones call themselves "neighbourhood malls." The larger ones advertise themselves as places where the family can spend a day sitting by water fountains, watching a movie, or playing at indoor amusement parks. But membership in this community has a price. I once asked a friend who used to run one of the largest shopping malls in Metro Toronto what its main purpose was. "You see that floor," he said pointing down. "It's wiped clean, right. That's what we want to do to the minds of shoppers – wipe them clean so all they think about is shopping." And if that doesn't work, if the visitors don't buy, mall owners can throw them out. This is exactly what happened to many Toronto teenagers in the spring of 1988.

The Eaton Centre is the most well known of Toronto's shopping malls, located on prime real estate in the heart of downtown. One of its advertising campaigns is a poster showing a woman in upscale dress, sculpted features, and surrounded by shelves of books and the words: "For me, shopping is not so much a collection of goods as it is an exercise in the development of personal taste." It's one of those "soft" ads that links consumerism to the building of our inner emotions.

Every Tuesday night, hundreds of teenagers exercise their own personal taste by donning the latest teenage fashions and going to a half-price movie at the mall. At the height of the media's gang hysteria, store owners decided that the teenagers heading to the mall's movies weren't good for business. So on a rainy Tuesday night, the newly formed police gang-squad swooped into action and stopped the youths from hanging out in the mall while waiting for the movies to begin.

I watched one teenager, who was perhaps 16 years old, walk into the mall's movie entrance on Dundas Street. A few moments later, a police officer ordered him to get out. The youth looked bewildered as a security guard bombarded him with questions – name, address, date of birth – while refusing to explain how the information would be used. The guard then handed the teenager a ticket that barred him "indefinitely" from the centre.

"What do you mean, indefinitely?" the youth asked.

"It means forever."

"What did I do?"

"Your problem kid is that you don't listen!" a nearby cop shouted, grabbing a hold of the youth. Suddenly, the teenager found himself suspended in mid-air and being hurled through the doors. During his flight out, he smashed into an elderly woman in a fur coat. "Oh my back!" she screamed as police rushed to her side like children anxious to repair what a second earlier they had taken pleasure in smashing. I stopped the teenager as he stormed towards Yonge Street, past two police officers on horseback. "I didn't do nothing, man. Nothing!" he said, his face twitching from helpless anger.

The teenager can be excused for feeling confused and angry. He was enticed by cultural messages that encouraged him to find a sense of community within the cathedrals of consumerism. When he tried to do so, he was arbitrarily prevented from taking part.

The latent function of subculture, Philip Cohen writes, is "to express and resolve, albeit 'magically', the contradictions which remain hidden or unresolved in the parent culture." Today, the central contradictions are formidable: how do we reconcile the future Utopia promised by the myth of economic progress when we know it's polluting us to death? How do we satisfy our longing for a sense of community in a survival-of-the-fittest society that rewards unbridled individualism? Teenagers are highly sensitive to these contradictions, as they hover in a kind of twilight zone where their presence is appreciated only when they passively embrace adult rites, which most of them recognize as hypocritical and heartless. It creates a cynicism that has spread deep into the lives of middle-class youths. Indeed, we are now witnessing a new development that did not exist when Cohen's research was published in 1972. He believed subcultures could only be produced by the working class. "I do not think the middle class produces subcultures," he wrote, "for subcultures are produced by a dominated culture, not by a dominant culture." While the working class continues to produce subcultures, the middle class has now joined the act. As Toronto police officer Gordon Rasbach noted, the large majority of teenagers who swarm are from middle-class families.

The middle class has not been immune to the erosion of community. The earliest and strongest sense of belonging is developed in the family. More than ever before, however, middle-class youths are dealing with the psychological trauma of family breakups. In 1987, the number of divorces in Canada increased 11 per cent from the previous year to 86,985. An American study released in 1989 found that the effects of divorce on children are lasting. In the longest study of its kind, psychologist Judith Wallerstein of the University of California tracked 60 middle-class families for 10, and in some cases, 15 years after divorce. At the start of the study, all of the children were doing well in school. After a divorce, children often assumed the role of helping the parent through depressions and generally trying to hold the parent together psychologically. Wallerstein called this the "overburdened child" syndrome. By the fifth year after divorce, 37 per cent of the children were depressed, could not concentrate in school, had trouble making friends, and suffered from a wide range of behavioural problems. By the end of the study, Wallerstein wrote, 41 per cent of the children were "entering adulthood as worried, underachieving, self-deprecating and sometimes angry young men and women . . . . An alarming number of teenagers felt abandoned, physically and emotionally."

The frenzy over international competition is another pressure assaulting the family unit. It has struck middle-class parents with the fear that they may no longer be able to pass on their status to their children. This need for success spurs some parents to try to create superkids before their children even walk into kindergarten. The middle-class child is scheduled to death with after-school lessons in dance or piano and later a part-time job thrown into the mix. All of this occurs within a school environment where the pressure to compete is increasing, entrance to universities is becoming more difficult, and many teenagers suspect that all their hard work might just turn them into overqualified labourers doing menial jobs. And finally, there's the ubiquitous sense of boredom and cynicism that envelops teens. For some, subcultures have become the outlet for rebellion.

On January 4, 1960, Albert Camus died instantly when the car in which he was a passenger slammed into a tree at high speed. He was 46 years old. In his pocket was a train ticket indicating he had changed his mind at the last minute and had decided to make the journey by car instead. It was a brutally absurd death for the man Jean-Paul Sartre described as the "Descartes of the Absurd." We are left with his work, a central theme of which is the act of revolt.

"Awareness, no matter how confused it might be, develops from every act of rebellion," Camus wrote in his essay, *The Rebel*. Rebellion cannot exist without a sense that injustice reigns. Slaves who rebel are saying "enough is enough" and serving notice that a line has been crossed that dehumanizes them to a point they can no longer tolerate. Rebellion, wrote Camus, "is profoundly positive in that it reveals that part of man which must always be defended." Rebellion, then, is an act of solidarity. It defines a primary value by affirming the human dignity common to all. For Camus, this act of physical rebellion has evolved into metaphysical rebellion – the revolt of "man" against an absurd existence in which suffering ends only in death. Human beings reject this destiny and our revolt, paradoxically, expresses a desire for order – a demand to be as united with the universe as the stars. This passion for unity is a harrowing one, and in its pursuit we have lost sight of the very limits that define our existence – those limits struck between our demand for an absolute meaning to life and the obstinate silence of the heavens. Faced with this relentless relativity we take a maddening leap, scream "all or nothing," and murder becomes a matter of indifference. The freedom limited by a respect for a common dignity is replaced by the unlimited right of the powerful to dominate. Rebellion loses sight of the cry for human justice that gave it birth, and all great revolutions, fought in the name of power and the illusion of Utopias, end in corruption and nihilism.

The Western world has not fundamentally changed since Camus observed it in the 1950s. We need only look at the matter-of-fact way our environment is raped in the name of economic progress to recognize that nihilism guides our destinies today more fiercely than ever. This is the world teenagers are trying to make sense of, and their response is to be both repulsed and resigned. Pollution and nuclear war are high on the list of concerns for teenagers, but they feel powerless in the face of the persistent threats. Tony Angiolillo at Brother Edmund Rice would change the world if he could, but how can he imagine himself as an agent of change when, at school, he can't even control when he goes to the washroom? "It'll never change" is the refrain of teenagers and, indeed, the refrain of our times.

Schools today continue the historical transformation of rebellion from an act that affirms human dignity to one that imprisons. Paul Willis argued that groups in capitalist societies develop their own ways of doing things in relation to their economic and social positions. Often, these cultural expressions help maintain the status quo. The ugliness teenagers experience outside school is duplicated within its walls. They recognize that much of what is being taught has little relevance to their day-to-day lives. They see the rigid classroom structures of desks in straight rows and the authority of teachers as more appropriate to a factory than a school. They're vaguely aware that a fundamental function of school is to sort, judge, and slot students into boxes that bestow dignity on some while trying to withhold it from others. This forms part of the school's hidden curriculum, but to teenagers there's not much that's hidden. When you're being judged every minute of the day, you begin to understand the pattern. However, as noted earlier, their resistance is performed as a matter of principle, a way of regaining dignity, but virtually always in the context of resignation. Seeing no escape, some opt out of the school game while others resign themselves to mechanically pushing its buttons. Either way, injustice is allowed to continue.

But students do not happily or mindlessly play dead to the hidden curriculum, and in this there is hope. The informal contracts between students and teachers demonstrate that authority is forced to compromise to win the consensus of the less powerful and thereby maintain its own legitimacy.

Italian social theorist Antonio Gramsci argued that in Western societies, social groups must form alliances in order to wield authority over less powerful groups. This authority, however, is not imposed by coercion. The power of dominant groups is seen as legitimate and natural. Once consent is won, what Gramsci calls "ideological hegemony" is achieved. He describes it as a "moving equilibrium," a system that is somewhat pluralistic and must constantly be reproduced anew. It involves continuous struggle and a shifting of alliances that sometimes shatters the prevailing consensus. The social movements of the 1960s are perhaps the most spectacular modern example. Resistance to the dominant ideology is not automatically co-opted; if sustained, it can make a difference. But when a particular ideological hegemony has a solid grip on the reins, less powerful groups often end up making decisions that go against their own best interests, believing that they share the values and potentially the rewards of those who are better off.

The dominant ideology is continually being reconstituted, and within this process resistance can make a difference if it maintains a clarity of purpose. At the heart of youth rebellion is a defence of human dignity against rituals that proclaim the dominion of power. The master demands, "All or nothing," and the slave responds, "Enough is enough." There is no battle more worthy. But for this affirmation of humanity to bear fruit, the opponent that is now largely invisible must be brought into focus. The unquestioned rituals at the heart of the hidden curriculum of schools and society must be seen for what they are – myths rather than truths, social narratives written by people rather than gods. It is an exercise in the highest form of literacy; the "reading" and rewriting of social myths. But here again – despite some worthy attempts that we will look at later – schools fail us by not building on the vague awareness that most teenagers have that something is not quite right. Students get the message that abiding by the rules, no matter how fraudulent they may be, is the only way to succeed. One way or another, schools are producing students who grudgingly perpetuate the status quo with a hidden curriculum that promotes resignation. They are producing a generation of illiterate fatalists.

3

HOME SWEET HOME

"People like to dump on schools but no one looks at the real problem."
Harold Doucet was talking. Actually, it was more like a rant. Doucet is
the principal of St. Patrick's School, which sits on Maitland Street in
the heart of Halifax's poorest neighbourhood, in the city's north end. It
was late Monday morning, an hour or so after a radio station had carried a story on the streaming of inner-city children into programs that
make it impossible for them to go on to university, and more likely for
them to drop out. This pattern can be found in schools across the country, mostly among economically or socially disadvantaged students. It's
a well documented practice, but Harold Doucet has had it with hearing
schools get all the blame.

"For someone to turn around and blame the problem, the lack of
achievement, on schools is totally wrong. They're using us as scapegoats.
Now, I got big shoulders so you can blame me if you want but I'm just
saying that the fact is, I'm not your problem." This was one of the first
things Harold Doucet said to me.

St. Patrick's has classes ranging from junior kindergarten to grade 9.
In the short time Doucet has been principal, he has organized a parent-
teacher association to get parents more involved in the education of their
children, fostered links between the school and community groups, and
solidly supported an innovative reading and writing program known as
"holistic language." But perhaps most important is the warmth he elicits

from children in the primary grades. They constantly stop him in the hallway to say hello, to show him their drawings, or, occasionally, to playfully pat his rotund belly.

But the first morning we met, the radio report and my initial questions threw him into that defensive Pavlovian response that comes so readily to teachers used to getting bashed; he assumed the traditional posture and blamed the victims.

"The kids don't come to school because they don't get up in the morning." he said. "They run around in the streets all night and their parents have no idea where they are."

Doucet then told a story about a child in grade 2 whose mother was a prostitute. "We know she observes her mother having sex in her apartment," Doucet said. "If she (the child) stays in that home much longer, it'll be too late. We might influence a few lives but that's it, the real influence is at home."

Doucet's point was that the home environment has a far greater impact on how well children do in school – and what stream they are eventually placed in – than the school itself. Whether this is indeed true is a longstanding debate in education. But it's safe to say that a child's home environment can make success at school easier or harder. Helen Hill's story shows how the home can make it an uphill climb for some children.

Grace Elementary School is located in Vancouver's poorest neighbourhood. It sits in the downtown core, surrounded and isolated by highways and railroad tracks. The school has two buildings, both of which are almost empty. Grace's enrolment has dwindled from 850 children in 1970 to 225 in 1989.

Robert Penner* has been the school's principal for four years. "We're talking about a subculture of poverty here," he said. "For example, in this area, crime is underreported. If the things that happened here happened to you or I, we'd have a SWAT team out. No crap. 'Get your ass out here or by God I'm going to start shooting!' We would be outraged. There's no outrage here."

---

* Not his real name

In the relentless grind of poverty, outrage is an indulgence that expires with hope. A more common response among children in the neighbourhood is what psychologists call Attention Deficit Disorder, or ADD. Wayne Shaddick, Grace's childcare worker, said the disorder is caused by the stresses of poverty, inside and outside the home. Everything from fights between parents to the regular rumbling of trains through the neighbourhood entombs children in an incessant bombardment of white noise. Once in the imposed silence of a classroom, they find it difficult to concentrate and are easily distracted. Some of them become hyperactive. People suffering from ADD are often injected with the drug Ritalin, a stimulant that, paradoxically, has the effect of slowing them down. Opponents of the drug contend that it merely masks the symptoms without curing the disease. Shaddick said it's not uncommon to find Grace children on Ritalin.

During my second day at Grace, Shaddick introduced me to Brian Hill, a grade 2 student whom Shaddick described as having an above-average IQ and a tendency to retreat into fantasy. Brian often came to school with wild tales that never really happened. "I want to promote some fantasy but I want him to note, 'Now I'm pretending and now I'm not,' or he's going to get too lost," Shaddick said. "A little boy can walk through the world for years at that age without anybody checking, 'Is something wrong here?'"

The next day, Shaddick and I happened to meet Brian's mother, Helen Hill. Her story gives some idea of the trauma children like hers bring to school, and illustrates the kind of home environment Doucet said puts children at a disadvantage when they walk into class for the very first day.

Like many of Grace's students, Brian lived with his mother in a nearby housing project that stood dark and grey less than 100 metres behind the school. Railroad tracks separated the two sites and a fenced-in overpass took you from one to the other. Past a small playground sitting in the shadows of the highrises was a community centre. Inside, its main floor was one big oblong room with offices at either end. A long reception counter with two more offices behind it added to the centre's officious air. The day Shaddick and I were there, a handful of haggard-looking men stared blankly at the noon-day news on a large video screen. Helen Hill sat at a small table against the wall near the entrance. She had just finished cooking for the centre's clients, a job she did part-time. She had another part-time job as a cleaner in one of the apartment buildings in the project.

Hill was 43 years old. She was short, with a pale, puffy face and a small chin. There was a slight quaver in her voice. She had a manner full of softness, and she spoke repeatedly of determination and hope. "I think it's finally over," she said. "I'm not afraid anymore. I'm going for it. I think it's finally over."

Helen was born into a poor family with a father who she said despised her. "He said if he could have committed the perfect murder and gotten away with it, he would have killed me." An undiagnosed case of dyslexia turned Helen's schooling into an implacably miserable experience. "It was torture, absolute torture. I was beaten up by the teacher and I didn't understand. I'd say, 'I can't read this, it's jumping all over' and they'd say, 'I'll show you how it jumps all over' and they'd start beating me up and everything." The beatings, with rulers, straps, and fists, continued for four years. She remained illiterate until she was 13, when her music teacher would put on a Chopin recording to play in the background and patiently teach her to write during the lessons. "There's never a day when I don't think of her in some way," she said.

She dropped out of high school and, after losing several jobs, ended up on welfare. She fell in love and married in December 1980. "I went with my husband for two years and talk about prince charming! He was wonderful." But once they were married, things changed. "He would be nice to a dog but he'd come home and, oh, I hate to use this word, but he'd call me a fuckin' cunt. And he'd say the only way he could tell me and a snail apart is, oh, I had legs." Her husband specialized in psychological terror, practicing a kind of emotional warfare in which Helen was the victim of his attempts to exercise some control over his life. At least once he beat her up severely.

In six years of marriage she figured he worked a total of about five days. He simply refused to find a job. Yet unpaid bills or meager meals drove him crazy with anger. To avoid his wrath, she asked the mail carrier to leave the utility bills in a pair of boots outside the door so her husband wouldn't see them. "I thought he was going to kill me."

Her welfare cheque was $700 a month and twice a year she would buy foods like beans, barley, and noodles in bulk. She cooked everything from scratch and practiced the illusion of plenty. When the food in the refrigerator ran low she would place the remaining items at the front of the shelves. "If he reached in to get something at the back, he would hit something and knock it over and he wouldn't think there wasn't any food." She would also save a meat dinner for once a month, something she still does. "At the end of the month there's no money at all and you're scrounging around to get by. And when you're waiting for the cheque it seems like an eternity. But when you have that (meat) dinner, it helps. I think it's a psychological thing too, but you have to bring all your senses to it."

By 1986, Helen Hill had two children, Brian and Michael, and a haunting fear of hunger. "I would have terrible nightmares of Michael as a baby with sunken eyes, you know, and he would say, 'Mommy, I need some milk.'

"I'd go to bed and, I don't know if your heart's ever ached from beating so fast and so hard, but I'd go to bed and mine would just ache. Then one day I finally snapped."

The family was at the table eating beef stew and Michael wanted help breaking up some pieces of meat. Helen's husband flew into a rage, shouting she had spoiled the child. She took Michael to his room and then watched her husband storm out of the apartment. Early the next morning she picked up a hammer, walked back to her room, and gave her sleeping husband three crushing blows to the head. With blood gushing from his head he ran out the door screaming. Helen said she remembered nothing of the attack. She was convicted of assault, but not sent to jail.

Her son Brian did not witness the beating but heard the screams. Brian looked tiny for a boy his age. When he smiled, which was often, he seemed all cheeks and eyes. His excited talk was filled with expressive *pows* and *aarrs* and *brummbrumms*, depending on whether he was describing a fight, a dog, a car, or anything else that emitted a sound.

Helen said Brian was talking at seven months and had since barely paused for breath. By the age of two he was mesmerized by television, especially commercials. "He gets one glimpse of them and they stay with him for life." A television character named He Man was an early model for Brian. "We're trying to get him out of fantasy but I'm not sure if we can," Helen said, "or maybe he would rather stay in fantasy."

Brian and I were sitting on steps facing the school's main hallway. Excitedly, he jumped from story to story, in one breath describing a narrow escape from skinheads who wanted his firecrackers, then his ambitions to be a lawyer, an actor, or a cop, and how he liked riding in his dad's Mercedes. His dad's Mercedes? I asked him about his parents.

"They kept having arguments and then *boy*," he said, his eyes lighting up. "On the last day, my dad had to be rushed to the hospital. The side you take the nails out, my mother *pow*! With a hammer; the side you take the nails out with."

"What did you do?" I asked.

"When I woke up I just see my mom and dad *vroommm*," he said, thrusting out his arms. "And I said, 'Mom and Dad, they don't allow roller derby in here.' Alright, since we still had the ladder, my dad climbed the roof and then I pulled it up so my mom couldn't get there. I left my dad on the roof with an icepack on his head. My mom got another ladder, I made her fall; she didn't get hurt but I made her fall on my dog. My dog is like really big. So my dog was protecting my dad up on the roof, my mom came up and then he was laying there and then my dog was behind the big, um, box I had there and jumped out of it, *aarr*. And then my mom tripped, *woohoo*, and then fell."

"So you saved your dad?"

"Yeah."

Brian said he liked drawing pictures for Wayne Shaddick. By definition, a childcare worker should be thoughtful and caring, and Shaddick certainly was. Perhaps he cared too much. He struggled openly with the daily disappointment of knowing he would never be given the resources adequate to his task. His tiny office on the school's second floor was crowded with two desks and a filing cabinet and decorated with a handful of posters, one of which read: "It will be a great day when our schools have all the money they need and the military has to hold a bake sale to buy a bomber."

Brian's drawings were of little stickmen who seemed isolated in space: no sky, no ground, no house, no narrative, no context. "This boy has a sense that he is such a small and insignificant figure, that nothing truly eventful happens in his life, which is far from the truth," Shaddick said.

"With Brian you have to question, 'Is this the world he's going to retreat to? Has anybody addressed the violence?' Has anybody sat down and said, 'What are the effects on this young boy? Are we going to repeat the cycle? What's the mental health status of the family?' Those are the bigger questions that I'm not qualified to deal with. My gut tells me that Brian should be getting intense psychiatric treatment. But that's just my gut. I mean, I have a BA with a major in English literature, give me a break!"

A bang on the door and a loud "Mr. Shaddick!" introduced Medi, an Iranian boy who looked to be about 11 years old and was a recent refugee. He was holding a basketball and had a big toothy smile and deep-set eyes. He wore a red sweatshirt and jeans with the zipper down. I asked him how he liked school and he just smiled.

Medi's drawings were filled with violent images from his homeland and his stay in a Turkish refugee camp. His parents were dead and he lived with an older brother. He thought it was ridiculous in the winter to wait in the cold until the right bus arrived. So he would hop the first one that came along and ride for hours all over town, changing buses until he got one that happened to go by his house.

Medi also had a thing for telephones. With them he played a kind of cosmic roulette. When he saw one, he would pick it up and start dialing; no number in particular, just a vague sense that a friendly person, maybe even his parents, would answer. Usually, school staff were already on the line and all he got was a blast of indignation. One day he saw a little red box on the school wall – the fire alarm – pulled it, and got a wonderful reaction.

Medi left Shaddick's office, but a half-hour later came another *bang, bang, bang,* "Mr. Shaddick!"

"He's pretty dependent on me," Shaddick said, opening the door.

Shaddick wanted to emphasize an important point: the school had many children like Brian and Medi who needed a lot more qualified help than he could provide. Yet if asked, school administrators in Vancouver point to childcare workers like Shaddick as evidence that troubled children are being cared for.

"Look, I'm spending a lot of my time rescuing the system, just enough to keep the heat off politicians and to keep the lid on things," Shaddick said calmly. "We provide this middle ground so everybody's happy. We keep these kids from making loud noises. We keep them out of the newspapers, we keep them from getting killed. Again, we're rescuing the system. But are we really helping the kids? No! Are we changing anything? No!"

The stories of Brian and Medi bear witness to the challenges schools face with children who come from disadvantaged backgrounds. When Brian walks into school, he brings personal baggage that proves to be more distracting to his learning than what children from more stable family backgrounds bring in. Poverty creates the further disadvantage of making it difficult for Brian's mother to afford the storybooks more affluent parents buy their children to give them a head start in reading. And can Medi be expected to compete with Canadian students when he has yet to understand the significance of a fire alarm? Indeed, the culture shock faced by new Canadians is no less debilitating than poverty when it comes to success in school. This is certainly the case with Judy.

During my many talks with teenagers, I occasionally met one who moved me completely. Judy, an 18-year-old native of China attending Britannia Secondary School in Vancouver, is one of them. Her story is about a desperate desire to embrace Canadian culture, only to end up emotionally torn.

I met Judy in the spring of 1988 when I walked into the main office of Britannia, a school in the same neighbourhood as Grace. I went to see Vice-Principal Clive Hughes and Judy was sitting at a desk answering telephone calls during a break in her classes.

Clive Hughes is a tall man with glasses, greying hair, and a fatherly manner. He told me a story about the lives of Chinese parents in the neighbourhood. They're from an earlier wave of immigration and, according to Hughes, unlike the wealthy Hong Kong families now moving to the B.C. coast, they live in poverty, usually work 12-hour days, and get gouged by slum landlords. To supplement the poor heating during the winter, many families do as they did in the old country and strike up charcoal burners. The coal emits an enormous amount of heat, as well as carbon monoxide.

"Every winter, kids from this school get asphyxiated. It's horrible!" Hughes said.

"Asphyxiated? "

"Yeah, like dead. Some of them are saved because parents hear them coughing and gasping and get to them on time, but some aren't," Hughes said.

With almost 70 per cent of its students from non-English-speaking families, the school has multilingual workers who help bridge the language gap between home and school. Hughes said the school has one of the lowest drop-out rates in the city, but added that some problems are beyond the school's control. He suggested I talk to Judy and found us a small office where we could be alone.

Judy was wearing a jean jacket, a white T-shirt with blue stripes, blue running shoes, and jeans cut off at the knees. She was a thin and striking young woman. Her black, slightly waved hair was tied back except for a thick strand flowing down the left side of her face. Long lashes shielded deep black eyes that rarely shied away despite the intensity of her story. Somehow, she seemed full of trust, exuding a natural effervescence. She spoke rapidly and leapt from one thought to another, as if an inner stream of chaotic stories were fighting to get out.

She was born in the southern Chinese province of Canton. There, her father was a teacher and she was a top student. When she was 11, her family moved to Vancouver.

"It's so much quieter here," she said. "Like your neighbour – you live in a house for a long time and you might not even know their last name, right? But where I came from it's really crowded and like really opened. It's a lot safer because, you know, it's practically like a whole family or something, because you live in a small town and then people get together and help each other out, right?"

She wanted to fit in from the start. "Like, I wanted to be one of them. I want to fit in because I think Canada is white people, the majority, right?"

She spent her first year and a half in English-as-a-second-language (ESL) classes. She was then mainstreamed into grade 7 and became seized by a profound fear of not being accepted. She surrounded herself with white friends and tried hard to get rid of her accent, to the point where she now lamented her inability to speak fluent Chinese. But throughout, she was determined to remain true to herself and to avoid drugs and drinking.

"I really pushed myself 'cause I really, really wanted to fit in." These are words Judy repeated throughout our conversation as if terrorized by the thought of hovering forever in the empty space between parallel lines. But the more she tried to embrace her new culture, the more she became separated from her own.

"It's like I have to choose between one or the other," she said.

Judy's father worked in a herbal store in Vancouver's Chinatown, and her mother was a dishwasher. "They can't speak English so their bosses kind of use it against them, right, because they know they can't get any further than Chinatown, right? And they work hard and long hours, and they get really, really low pay."

They put all their hopes on Judy, but she said they were incapable of understanding her sense of cultural vertigo. By grade 9, Judy was dating white boys, and her parents rejected this completely. They forbade her to go out evenings and insisted she put off dating until she graduated and had an apartment of her own.

"I couldn't communicate with them and I still can't, but I'm trying. Once we got here I guess the gap is, you know, slowly getting wider and wider 'cause I'm adapting more to the Western culture and they're still back there. 'Cause the way I think is a lot different now. 'Cause I live here and I want to make the best of it and they don't see that."

With teenagers, an essential part of fitting in means wearing the appropriate fashions. To Judy's parents, this was scandalous.

"They don't like the way I fix myself up. My dad complains almost every day, you know. I remember my dad, he got so mad one day. I was wearing these pants – not tight, right, they're slacks, right? – and I remember he got so mad that day. He took my pair of pants and chopped them in half, you know, with a Chinese butcher knife. He chopped them in half and he threw them in my face and he just didn't say anything.

"He would complain too about my hair, that it was too long, you know, 'And if you don't get it cut I'll cut it when you're sleeping.' That would really scare me."

Judy stressed, however, that she wasn't blaming her parents for her troubles. "I could never hate my parents for what they did to me 'cause they're my parents. I respect them. I feel bad because they came here for me and my brother, to have a better future, and they sacrificed so much. That's why I never tell them my problems, because they've been through so much. They're not bad, they can't help thinking that way. I don't want people getting the wrong idea of my parents. I could never blame them."

This lack of bitterness is remarkable for someone who spent many long and lonely nights crying in her room. For comfort, she turned to a string of relationships with boys. It didn't help.

"See, guys can put me right down because they make me feel like I'm so worthless. 'Cause when they reject me, I can't handle it, because I've been rejected so many times. Like I said, I meet the jerks, you know those types, right?"

"How would a jerk reject you?" I asked tentatively.

"It's like, you know, those one-night stands – you know what I mean, right? And like, I'm not that type. And I can't handle rejections. Like I always want someone there. Like ever since I was little I was never close to my parents, right? At that time I didn't realize it but when I got here I see all these TV shows – all my friends, they're so close to their parents – and I started thinking that way. Like I know I can never expect it from my parents, right? I can't even let them touch me, I feel so isolated, you know. I don't know why I can't feel close to them. But they can never give me the same thing so I expect that from a guy. I think a boyfriend could give me all those things like caring, you know, almost like a father figure, I don't know."

In her search for human understanding, Judy was seduced by television's consumer love stories.

"I always seem to bump into those jerks," she said again. "I take it really serious because I want someone to turn to, someone I can hold, you know, hold onto when you're down or something, right? I don't know, I guess I depend on that a lot and I end up getting myself into more trouble. Like, I want a boyfriend, like one of those love stories, you know, live happily ever after, and all that. I believe in those things. Like, a lot of the way I think is from television too, like soap operas. I always think that relationships should be like that, right? It's so simple, so easy. They're so happy in there, you know, and nothing to worry about and they all have nice, high positions." She let out a knowing laugh, as though her experiences had now relegated "living happily ever after" to a childish dream.

By now, I know Judy is prepared to answer anything I ask, and this deep trust from a delicate person fills me with a sense of uneasy responsibility. Also, I fear I'm aware of where her story is leading.

To relieve the pressure, she briefly ran away from home, skipped classes, and dropped out of grade 11. "There were times I felt I had no one to turn to, you know. I felt so isolated, like deep inside. I used to think the walls were coming in."

The month before we talked, Judy had just left another painful relationship. She got drunk, walked into the school's washroom, and slashed her wrists. She woke up in a psychiatric ward, and the surroundings were familiar. It wasn't the first time Judy had tried to kill herself.

"Yeah, like none of my relationships lasted more than two months and this time I just came out of a bad one, right? It was five months long but I found out he was cheating on me all this time – you know, one of *those,* right? – and I couldn't handle it. Maybe I tried too hard, you know, to make it as a commitment and maybe guys are afraid of that. But now I don't think so much of that. That used to be a priority, you know, finding Mr. Right, but not any more."

For being drunk during her suicide attempt, Judy violated a school rule that prohibits drinking on school grounds, and so she was transferred to another school. Six months later she was allowed to return, and Judy was grateful for the care Vice-Principal Hughes had shown towards her.

"Mr. Hughes, he really looked after me and I don't want to let him down, right? He makes me feel like he really cares about me. And I even asked him, 'Like, why do you care about me?' and he said 'cause I'm worthwhile, right, that I'm someone, so I can't let him down."

"I really have a low self-esteem, I really do. I don't know why. The trouble is, I try to please too many people and they reject me. It's like I'm always doing something wrong to make them feel like that; 'cause my parents reject me, right? my boyfriends do, right? and sometimes my friends do, right? It seems like it's my fault 'cause I blame it on myself, I seem to do that. But you know, I just want to belong."

We got up to leave and I felt a need to give her words that would act like a social shield. I told her she wasn't alone in feeling like she did. I told her that friends of mine have been driven to extremes as desperate as hers. I told her we have a society that devours its most sensitive and caring members. I told her it is compassion like hers that will save the planet. I told her she was courageous and bright. I told her many other things, but nothing sounded right.

The modern era of research in achievement by disadvantaged groups was kicked off by James Coleman's 1966 study, *Equality of Educational Opportunity*. It was funded by the U.S. government and designed to statistically confirm the commonly held view that the quality of schooling determined how well students performed. The idea was obvious enough: Disadvantaged children do poorly because they attend bad schools while middle-class students do well because they go to good schools. Coleman went into the research expecting to find this correlation and shocked everyone, including himself, when his results showed nothing of the kind.

"Schools bring little influence to bear on a child's achievement that is independent of his background and general social context," wrote Coleman. "This very lack of an independent effect means that the inequalities imposed on children by their home, neighborhood and peer environment are carried along to become the inequalities with which they confront adult life at the end of school."

The Coleman study ignited a massive controversy mainly because its conclusions refuted the common-sense belief that good schools will teach students better than bad ones. Many educators flatly said Coleman was wrong, although several reviews of his data generally confirmed his conclusions. The weight of time has done much to give the Coleman findings preeminence in the minds of today's teachers. For well-intentioned teachers it provides an explanation for consistently poor results despite their best efforts.

For Brian, Medi, and many others from disadvantaged groups, the traumatic environments of their homes undoubtedly affect how they do in school. Their educational outcomes are further influenced by a home culture where the development of a self-image is shaped by the realities of the workplace. Blue-collar workers have routinized and highly supervised jobs, while those in professional or managerial roles have much greater control over their work. The results of some studies indicate that low-income parents tend to demand conformity and obedience from their children while middle-class parents are more likely to encourage their children to think for themselves. Moreover, middle-class parents tend to have higher aspirations for their children, expecting them to be motivated and attend university. The messages that surround children, in and out of the home, are sure to influence their behaviour.

We are born trying to make sense of our environment. From the very beginning, we seem to recognize that we can only know ourselves by understanding what and who is around us. As we embrace our environment, it embraces us. We look at the world around us, interpret its messages, incorporate it with all that we know and all that we are, and send out our own message for the world to interpret in turn. But this dialectic cares nothing for balance. If the environment we try to interpret is full of malice and deceit, its weight may slowly darken our sense of ourselves. This has been the history of blacks in Nova Scotia, a community that has tried to make sense of more than 200 years of discrimination.

Some 13,000 of the province's 800,000 people are black. Many live in about 30 segregated communities, most of them on the outskirts of cities. In this Canadian form of apartheid, residents must leave their community for services such as education and medical care. Blacks are virtually shut out of positions of authority and as of 1989 Nova Scotia's school system had yet to appoint a black principal. This marginalization is so extensive that blacks have difficulty seeing themselves and each other in positions of authority. One black doctor of West African origin said this mental block forced her to close a medical clinic she had opened in one of the segregated towns in 1968.

"The people just wouldn't come," she said. "They just couldn't believe that any black person could be a doctor. They figured there had to be something wrong. So they just kept going to the hospital in town, where they had to wait in a hallway for hours before they got treated. It was really incredible."

Gerald Clarke, executive director of Nova Scotia's Black Educators' Association, said he's felt the burden of this self-defeating attitude. Clarke said his very success in becoming a vice-principal has tainted him in the eyes of the black community. A black who accepts a job with social status in a racist system raises suspicion.

"They wonder, 'How did he get to be successful? He either cheated or he's in cahoots with the white man.' You see, the people who could become leaders in the black community are always held in suspicion by the community," Clarke said. Black professionals from West Indian or African backgrounds who move to the area are often resented even more. "Differences aren't accepted in the black community. It's not enough to be black; you have to be black and poor. They figure, 'If we all can't make it out, we may as well all stay in.'"

This nihilistic form of rebellion also afflicts black students. Schools place many black students in a dead-end partly by expecting little of them. As a teacher, Clarke was determined to have high expectations of black pupils, but he discovered that some parents did not share the feeling.

"I had a black parent phone me and threaten me with a shotgun because I was [academically] pushing his daughter too much. I knew she was capable of more, but getting pushed was a new experience for them. If I teach black kids to a standard that the system expects for everyone, it has been said of me that 'Mr. Clarke thinks he's white,' and it really hurts."

Mike Whitehead, the counsellor at Coal Harbour High School outside of Halifax, is empathetic. Many black students, he believes, consciously decide they want no part of a racist society. "It's like an elephant in a circus who grows up tied to a stake," said Whitehead. "When he's small, he can't pull the stake out. When he's bigger, he can do it, but he doesn't." In this way, the system perpetuates itself without dirtying its hands. And in this sense, James Coleman is right: A child's environment, inside and outside the home, will influence performance at school.

Few studies could match the scope and detail of Coleman's statistical sample until 1979, when Michael Rutter's study *Fifteen Thousand Hours* found that schools *can* make a difference. More recent and perhaps more extensive statistical research on the matter has been done by British educator Peter Mortimore, who also worked on the Rutter project. Mortimore and his researchers tracked 2,000 students in 50 schools over a period of four years. The 1988 study, *School Matters: The Elementary Years*, found that working-class students in what Mortimore called "effective schools" did better than middle-class students in bad schools on tests of reading, writing, and math. In measuring the progress children made in reading, Mortimore found schools to be many times more important than background factors. Rutter and Mortimore are leaders in what has come to be known as the "effective schools" movement.

They maintain that changes in teaching methods and teacher attitudes, among other things, can significantly improve the performance of students.

In the end, the difference between Coleman and the effective schools movement is one of emphasis. Coleman believes in the transcendent effect of the home environment, while Rutter and Mortimore don't. What no one disputes is evidence over the past 20 years that clearly shows that the best indicator of success in school is the annual income of a child's parents. Since 1970, the Toronto Board of Education has been the only school district in Canada to regularly track the economic background of its students. In its 1988 survey, it found that 94 per cent of children whose parents were professionals ended up in the university-bound programs. But if parents happen to be manual or unskilled labourers, the child's chances are much reduced. Only 57 per cent of these children were in university-bound programs. The figure represents a noticeable improvement over the period in which the board has been keeping track. But heading to university and actually getting there are two different things. It has been well documented, particularly by Professor Paul Anisef of York University in Toronto, that a disproportionate number of Canada's university students come from middle-class or more affluent backgrounds. The elitist make-up of universities was revealed in a 1984 report to the Secretary of State called *Accessibility to Postsecondary Education in Canada*. In Ontario, for instance, the report found that 40 per cent of undergraduates and 50 per cent of graduate students in 1982 had parents with a university education. Yet people with a university education made up only 10 per cent of the Ontario population. In B.C., a 1977 report by the University Council of British Columbia found that while 50 per cent of those whose fathers were professionals enrolled at a university or college, only 15 per cent of those whose fathers were miners, loggers, fishermen, or farmers did so. Clearly, the advantages and disadvantages of the home environment are reinforced and perpetuated once children enter schools. Problems in the home and the environment at large are of course beyond the school's control. But when Brian, Medi, Judy, and others walk through the school's front door, they deserve better than a system that cowtows to inequality.

4

STREAMING

On the door of Principal Harold Doucet's office at St. Patrick's School in Halifax was a child's drawing: it was of a small blotch of glowing crimson next to a larger blotch adorned with a red halo. Across the top of the drawing was written: "I love you." Next to this was the name Latoya, the last three letters of which were written underneath the first three for lack of space. Suspended from the ceiling, in the far corner of the office, was a bird's nest made of grey papier-mâché with thin branches sticking out of it.

An overpass and a dingy stairway took me from Harold Doucet's office in the main building of St. Patrick's to the primary classes on the bottom floor of the annex. The stairway emptied into a dim hallway with classrooms on both sides. At one end, covering the walls from top to bottom, were huge sheets of white paper with small footprints smudged all over them. A sign read: "Even little people can make a big impression." At the other end of the hallway were large colour posters of a princess, a dragon, and Sleeping Beauty. Pinned to the pictures were about two dozen stories written by the children. Most ended with " . . . and they lived happily ever after."

One doorway in the hall led to Alice Moriarty's Four Plus class, what some call junior kindergarten. Doucet and I found Moriarty sitting on a small stool in the classroom's reading corner, surrounded by 17 four-year-olds.

"Hi Mr. Doucet!" the children burst out.

"Did I interrupt a discussion with, ahh . . . ."

"Mr. Pazoo!" they screamed, their eyes bulging to match those of the turquoise green puppet wrapped around Moriarty's hand. A girl jumped up and affectionately patted Doucet's stomach.

Doucet left and it was soon time for science. Alice Moriarty brought out a jar of water in one hand and a sweet potato in the other. The potato had been pierced with a ring of toothpicks used to suspend it in the jar. The idea was to have children observe as the potato grew roots during the next few days.

"If I put the sweet potato in the jar, what will happen?" Moriarty asked.

"It's gonna fall in the water!"

"It's gonna grow big."

"The skin's gonna come off."

Michael, a curly-haired boy with large beautiful eyes, said the water would spill onto the carpet. Moriarty removed the toothpicks, dipped the potato in the jar, and Michael discovered he was right. A quick lesson on volume and then back on track. It would have been easy to simply ignore Michael, and in many classrooms this would have happened. Alice Moriarty, however, is a good teacher.

Michael comes from a family in which he was sexually abused. At the start of the school year his most frequent expression was, "I'm bad." Next to Michael sat Aaron, who early in the year "wanted to rip the faces of kids off." In all, Moriarty said six of her pupils had serious emotional troubles because of abuse at home. With some, "lots of hugs and kisses" created a bond of trust that made the children receptive to learning. With others, the problems that arose from an environment of poverty were too deeply rooted to overcome in a classroom.

At the end of the day, parents came to Moriarty's class to pick up their children. On the way out the children grabbed cloth bags that had pictures of teddy bears and the words "Books Are Sweeter Than Honey" on them. The books inside were selected by the children and their parents, and the parents were expected to read them to their children. It was an attempt to get parents involved in their children's education. Studies have shown conclusively that children do better in school if their parents are involved. The same studies show that often parents with low incomes are too busy making ends meet to find the time. In the St. Patrick's program, homework had a new meaning. Parents were also expected to comment on the books after reading them with their children. Moriarity said she was interested in how the parents' writing skills had evolved through this program and how some had understood her teaching approach: that children should make sense of the story on their own terms. After reading the book *Don't Open the Box,* Aaron's mother wrote: "Even though the TV was on, Aaron paid very close attention. He told his version of the story. It's interesting."

Moriarty was thankful for her limited success but felt she was fighting a rear-guard action. While she tried to build the classroom experience based on what the children bring from their home environment, overwhelmingly the rest of the system does not follow the same route.

"There's a sense that [the children] need to sit and listen and be talked at. Whatever happens at home is supposed to be turned off when they walk in the door. That's asking them to be inhuman," Moriarty said. "Schools like ours should have full-time social workers and focus on developing thinking skills rather than on getting jobs. I think it's outrageous that at grade 9 we think we know whether the kid's going to be a brain surgeon or not."

Moriarty grew up in the neighbourhood. In her last year of elementary school, teachers advised her to become a hairdresser. So she was streamed into the general program, the lowest rung in Nova Scotia's secondary schools. "I wasn't stupid but I also wasn't loud or confident, so no one in school paid any attention to me," Moriarty said. "They assumed I wasn't bright enough, but the problem was I was never challenged or encouraged. It would have been nice if someone at school would have said, 'Alice could do more.' Children need someone to tell them they can do it."

The general program bored her. She wanted to drop out but was talked out of it by her parents. They were the ones who, after her graduation, insisted that she find a way to further her education. Moriarty turned out to be rare. Rather than settle for a future of limited potential, she called the ministry of education and insisted that she be allowed to write the advanced-level examinations. She passed with flying colours, entered university, and now does everything she can to make sure the children in her class aren't victimized in the same way she was.

Moriarty's class and her personal example make clear that the school is by no means neutral in determining a child's educational success.

Getting up each morning can be an opportunity for transmutation, but it takes some effort. It's easier to lie in bed for a moment and allow the mental threading of a film that is essentially a rerun of the previous day's feature. The projector rolls and a fuzzy storyline begins to appear: You stumble for the shower and then the coffee in a kind of routinized suspended animation – hot instead of cold water, milk instead of cream. Before you know it you're in the middle of a familiar story that brings a warm but tentative sense of security. All sorts of nagging questions, paradoxes, and ambiguities remain, but no matter. In the end they seem harmless, inconsequential, even silly. And besides, they were kicking around yesterday and the day before, so what's the rush in dealing with them today? After the second cup of coffee, with your defences in place, you pick up your briefcase, lunch pail, newspaper, squash racket, or whatever appropriate gear, and head out the door a fully recharged pack of stereotypes.

Study after study has shown that when teachers walk out of their homes and into the classrooms, many carry with them views and attitudes that may prove damaging to students from backgrounds different than their own. Part of the problem is that most teachers come from middle-class backgrounds. Tony Angiolillo, the grade 11 student at Toronto's Edmund Rice School, is convinced this means teachers have no idea what he and other students from low-income families face.

"A lot of teachers, they live in a lot of rich areas. Very few of them live where they don't have a great situation or whatever, so they don't understand a good percentage of the school. Like I live in this area and there used to be a serious drug corner, right? And the teachers, they talk about it like, 'If you do drugs you're bad,' this and that. But when it's being thrown in your face every minute of the day, like last year it was really bad, like they had thirty drug dealers there pushing every day at all times of the day. And like, the teachers don't know nothing about myself and that I live in that area and that when they're pushing it in your face and they're saying, 'Ten bucks but I'll give it to you for seven;

come on guys, take it.' I mean, they don't understand nothing, that's all I'm saying."

The principal of Edmund Rice, Brother Kieran Murphy, feels that Tony is right. I had asked him why teachers rarely discuss the roots of social injustices with students. "Teachers by nature are small 'c' conservatives. They're the kind of people who don't rock the boat," he said. "Look at where most of our teachers are coming from. Most of them are living a comfortable middle-class lifestyle. Ninety per cent of our teachers are not those who are largely familiar with injustice. If you come from a middle-class home with food on your table, the pressure is whether you get 90 or 85 on your exam. If you come out of that experience, it's difficult to have empathy for those who suffer injustice. Empathy is not an innate trait."

One of the most obvious signs of this cultural stereotyping is the low expectations that middle-class teachers have of children from lower-class backgrounds. These teachers fall into four general groups. Some expect less from the students out of a misguided sense of compassion, a feeling that disadvantaged children have enough problems at home without having to be challenged at school. Others, faced with large classes, simply don't have the time, energy, or training to push all students along. Slowly but surely they focus more on those students who are responding well. This helps to justify the teacher's self-worth, but at the exclusion of the rest of the class. The third group of teachers, when asked why disadvantaged groups generally remain disadvantaged, make clumsy suggestions about inherent stupidity or laziness. Of course some children are born with more potential than others, but unless genetics has a bias for money, this says little about why low-income groups keep getting the shaft. The fourth group is tormented by a sense of fatalism that turns their classrooms into sacrificial altars. They believe the systemic barriers against disadvantaged groups are insurmountable. "What's the point of spending each day banging my head against a wall? We may as well help those who have a chance," they say.

Lower expectations of inner-city children permeate Vancouver's Grace School like a stifling smog. Bill Barnes,* a long-time teacher

---

* Not his real name

there, put it this way: "I really get frustrated. I feel that as a staff and as a school, we don't set our expectations high enough. We accept mediocrity. We accept semi-garbage at times." But Principal Robert Penner believed the school's expectations aren't low, just realistic.

Penner, a tall man with wavy hair, square glasses, and the chiselled, wholesome features of an Ivy League, all-American quarterback, delivered his thoughts in a self-assured, rapid-fire manner, full of rhetorical questions. He was fresh from gaining a province-wide profile for his successful battle to give free lunches to children in inner-city schools. The cost of the lunch program was minimal, an estimated 65 cents a year per Vancouver taxpayer. But in then-Premier Bill Vander Zalm's free enterprise fantasy land, it was a matter for fierce debate, filled with all sorts of nonsense about the impropriety of feeding hungry children with public funds.

Penner was proud of his job and not afraid to provide a blunt assessment of what he sees as the poor potential of his students. In fact, his philosophy of education stemmed from this belief. During that school year, the staff at Grace had decided to stress five themes: manners, self-esteem, homework skills, school spirit, and recognition. The last one was an opportunity, as Penner put it, to go "out of our way to recognize each other." Each theme came with week-long events, and some teachers complained that the scheme took too much time away from the curriculum. Penner said he shot back with the facts. Grace, he reminded the teachers, had the dubious distinction of maintaining the lowest academic scores in the province. Penner said he told them, "Hey guys, don't give me the curriculum crap. You were never covering it anyway. I mean, you know, lighten up! We haven't had too many brain surgeons come through Grace yet."

Karen Riley said, "Oh the curriculum? Forget the curriculum. If you could see what excellent means for some of them, it would make you pass out, because, really, in this school we're a grade behind. The grade 4s are really grade 3s, and the grade 3s are really grade 2s."

"So what happens when they get to high school and they're a year behind everyone else?" I asked Riley.

"Only the strong survive, and the bright ones who get lucky," she said.

In this kind of educational Darwinism, why should the curriculum be important? Penner saw the mission of Grace as giving his children only the basic skills to "show up to work on time with their hair combed and their teeth brushed." In fact, he said, if the children end up working at McDonald's he would consider that to be a great success.

"You don't get too many kids deciding to become brain surgeons," he said again. "I mean, we're not talking that kind of change. What we're talking about is common value. What we're talking about is the ability to operate in this society successfully. The ability to go to the bank, to be able to go to the store, to be able to go to your job. You know, we're not talking about ripping people out of their class structure. We're talking about engaging them in the most limited possible way with their society. We teach them to swim, not to swim 45 miles."

Penner sat on a couch, still wearing the dark gray overalls he had donned earlier that day to help build props for the school play. In the middle of a rambling discourse on society's class structure, he got up, walked behind his desk, and underwent a social metamorphosis: He pulled down the long zipper of his overalls, freed his left arm, then his right, wiggled the overalls down to his ankles, worked some more on them to push them past his shoes, stood talking for a moment in a white T-shirt and grey jockey shorts, then reached for a white shirt with thin blue stripes, a yellow tie with black dots, and, finally, a suit. I asked him about his home life.

There's not much in common with the inner city, he said. For one thing, he estimated his own children had about a thousand dollars' worth of books. A regular headache was getting rid of the mountain of periodicals and daily newspapers – including the Manchester *Guardian* – that accumulated.

"You have a very consistent life, I imagine?"

"Remarkably so," he replied. "I try to break it up, but my wife is a fiend on that. From the moment the children were born she's had them on a routine." It included an early start on their schooling at home, playing on soccer and hockey teams, and weekly swimming and piano lessons. They hated the piano lessons, Penner said, and he simulated their reactions by banging the coffee table with his fists, stomping his feet, and screaming, "Aaahhh, nooo, nooo, I'm not going to play the piano!"

When he was principal of other schools, he would sometimes invite students to his home. With Grace students, this was out of the question.

"I'm a little paranoid about it. I have an unlisted phone number and I don't ever want to see some of the people I deal with here. They're too bizarre, way too bizarre," he said. He told me the story of Helen Hill, who beat up her husband with a hammer.

It was lunch time at Grace. Karen Riley and I walked out of her classroom and into the hallway, stopping in front of the children's paintings that celebrated good manners. Pointing to the school work, she said, "I guess the values are middle-class ones but they're the survival skills, aren't they? I mean, who are you going to hire, the guy in jeans who's grubby looking or the guy who's clean and has a smile? And even if the grubby guy is more intelligent."

Riley's description easily fits the definition of "cultural capital." It's a term popularized by French sociologist Pierre Bourdieu and widely used by critical pedagogists, an important group of educators with a growing influence. Its leading spokespersons include Brazilian Paulo Freire, Americans Michael Apple and Henry Giroux, and Canadians David Livingstone, Roger Simon, and Peter McLaren. (McLaren's 1980 book *Cries From the Corridor* was among the first to alert the public to the inadequacies of inner-city schools.) Critical pedagogy has been at the centre of a lively debate in North America for over 15 years. Its proponents argue that capitalist societies not only distribute goods and services but also reproduce and distribute cultural capital; that is, the values, norms, styles, attitudes, beliefs, and forms of knowledge that are defined as socially legitimate by the dominant and powerful groups in society.

When a group's cultural background corresponds to or forms part of the dominant culture, it becomes a commodity, something they can cash in or trade on. As the examples of Karen Riley and Robert Penner make clear, the cultural capital that counts in schools is that practiced by the middle and upper strata of society. The moment children from a middle-class or more affluent background enter school, their culture is worth something. It corresponds to the school's culture. This gives them an advantage over, for example, a working-class, black, or aboriginal child whose cultural background is not valued by the dominant society. From day one, disadvantaged children are forced to play catch-up.

The depth of this cultural bias is illustrated by the most commonly used IQ test in Canadian schools – the Wechsler Intelligence Scale for Children, Revised (WISC-R). Questions for the standardized test were selected from a representative sample, which necessarily means that most of the questions come from the dominant culture. For example, the WISC-R is based on a sample of 2,200 children. Of those, only 330 were non-white. Inevitably, then, the questions selected reflect the learning experiences of the dominant culture while denying those of minority groups. This is perhaps why one part of the WISC-R test asks children "How many pennies make a nickel?" and "Who discovered America?" and "How tall is the average Canadian man?" It is not surprising that children from a minority culture tend to score lower than other children.

Jim Cummins is director of the National Heritage Language Resource Unit at the Ontario Institute for Studies in Education (OISE) in Toronto and a consultant to school boards across the country on assessing children whose first language is not English. In 1984 he analysed 400 assessments of children from non-English-speaking backgrounds in a western Canadian city. His findings confirmed those of other studies: The average minority student's score was 15 points below the average of the other students.

These tests play a large role in placing a disproportionate number of ethnic minority students into non-academic programs that bar them from entering university. Teachers will often send children to a school psychologist because their academic performance doesn't match their ability to speak English. Yet Cummins' research again confirms that while immigrant children can speak English well within two years of entering school, it takes five to seven years before they can compete on an equal footing with their Canadian-born classmates in academic skills like reading and writing. The practice of most school boards, however, is to wait no more than two years before giving immigrant students IQ tests. All of this, says Cummins, is further evidence of the systemic racism that prevents disadvantaged groups from succeeding in schools.

Cummins believes the culturally biased testing of immigrant children is a violation of the Charter of Rights and Freedoms, and he predicts that Canada will witness court battles similar to those in the United States where, since the late 1960s, the courts have repeatedly ruled in favour of parents who have challenged such testing.

This kind of systemic racism is compounded by faculties of education that do little to prepare student teachers for the new cultural reality of classrooms. In addition, older teachers resist change, and a lack of provincial funding for retraining teachers guarantees the status quo. So blind is the provincial establishment to the need for change that the two most widely quoted reports on education in 1988 – the report of the B.C. Royal Commission on Education, *A Legacy for Learners*, and the Radwanski report for the Ontario government – virtually ignored the massive cultural transformations going on in Vancouver and Toronto classrooms. In Toronto, more than half of the students come from non-English-speaking backgrounds. In Vancouver, almost half of the 51,776 students speak English as a second language and, of those, 15,000 are in ESL classes.

As educators bury their heads in the sand, growing numbers of immigrant students are neglected by the schools. In a letter to the Vancouver school board in 1988, Bob Fitzpatrick, the social studies department head at Britannia Secondary School, wrote: "What exactly are we to do with the increasing number of students who can neither read nor write English well enough to pass the course, yet because of their age, are expected to move on with their classmates? At present . . . we are forced to either 'program these students to fail,' or to pass and graduate (them) unable to communicate in English." Either way, these students lose.

No small part of the problem is the general practice of placing immigrant students in special English classes where they are expected to learn the language by talking about Canadian images and concepts that are completely foreign to them. The federal government's policies have not helped. It refuses to fund ESL classes or any other programs designed to accommodate the diverse cultures filling the schools in large urban centres. Although education in Canada is a provincial responsibility, immigration is federal. It is therefore irresponsible of Ottawa not to support such programs.

Black parents have been especially vocal in saying that the school curriculum denigrates and even denies their existence. Mike Whitehead, the guidance counsellor at Nova Scotia's Coal Harbour High School, noted that black students are bussed in from communities where racial segregation is a fact of life. But the attitude they get from most teachers is, "I don't see black and I don't see white, I only see students." Blindness to Nova Scotia's racial differences is not, for most teachers, an exercise in egalitarianism. Racial myopia comes in handy for teachers who have spent their careers turning the classroom into a dull routine that excites like the hum of a refrigerator. To admit the existence of cultural differences would be a threat to their curriculum and teaching methods.

Whitehead said a black student once told him, "Sir, Martin Luther King is my hero and I've never once studied him." Whitehead could understand his alienation. "The curriculum is dominated by the white majority culture and their historical perspective. There's been no integration of black literature even though they've been screaming about it for 20 years."

Coal Harbour principal Angus McNeil recognized that white students could also benefit from a more culturally diverse curriculum. Living in segregated towns, the only images they have of blacks come from stereotypes. "A kid who's never been in an integrated situation, he walks into school and sees a great big black guy and that's all he sees," McNeil said.

Yet McNeil was hesitant to implement a more black-conscious curriculum. He argued that black history, or any cultural history, is best taught in the home rather than the school. That's how he learned of his Highland Scot heritage while growing up in Cape Breton. "I'm sure in the school it won't be done with the vigour parents would at home," he said. "I'm a history teacher but I'm not so sure I would be the best one to teach black history, and I don't teach Roman history as well as some guy from Italy would."

At Coal Harbour this cultural bias helped to ignite a four-day race riot between white and black students in January 1989. The riot made national headlines and ended with 18 students being arrested. The episode shook the province and mobilized the black community. Parents discovered a collective voice. Black activists, some of whom had been shunned by their own community, moved in quickly to channel the spontaneous sense of anger and awareness. They began to organize black parents and made school reform their main focus. McNeil said the school is open to changes. Rebellion can make a difference.

Textbooks offer students no reprieve from a middle-class world view.

Though they have improved in reflecting the multicultural nature of Canada, the subject of class remains taboo. In 1985, Satu Repo, a sociologist at York University, co-wrote a series of readers for grade 4 students with stories based on the low-income Toronto neighbourhoods of Regent Park and Kensington Market. Writers Margaret Atwood and Margaret Laurence acted as consultants to the series.

One story, *What's a Friend?*, tells of Fernanda, a Portuguese girl who tries to deny her culture while befriending Emily, the daughter of a young professional family that moves into a renovated home next door. The story explores the tensions that can exist between children from different economic and cultural backgrounds, and ends with Fernanda discovering pride in her culture while continuing her friendship with Emily.

The series went nowhere. It was largely shunned by teachers and school boards, primarily, Repo maintains, because it dared to clearly address the economic disparities in society. "The stories show that people from marginalized cultures must first embrace who they are in order to succeed in the larger society," she says.

In his 1980 book *Hard Working, Temperate and Peaceable: The Portrayal of Workers in Canadian History Textbooks*, Ken Osborne, a professor of education at the University of Manitoba, argued convincingly that school textbooks generally portray workers as happy and obedient when they're dealt with at all. In B.C., for instance, Frank Rodgers and Albert "Ginger" Goodwin – regarded as martyrs by the trade union movement – aren't even mentioned in history books. Rodgers was murdered by company goons on the Vancouver waterfront in 1906 for organizing a strike, and Goodwin was shot in the back by police in 1917 on Vancouver Island for opposing conscription. The shooting sparked a protest that led to B.C.'s first general strike. In 1977, the left-wing leadership of the B.C. Teachers' Federation (BCTF) tried to address this cultural bias but found itself outside the accepted bounds of thought.

The BCTF and its Quebec equivalent, the CEQ, are the most militant and socially progressive teachers' unions in the country. Their strong push for social change is unusual for teachers' unions in Canada. Most often, they are like the Ontario union where the emphasis has been on bread and butter workplace issues such as wages and workload.

Although they tend to pay lip service to issues of school reform, these take a back seat whenever they conflict with workplace issues.

Perhaps the most disturbing example of misplaced priorities in teachers' unions was the boycott of extra-curricular activities in the mid-1980s by Toronto teachers, to protest heritage language courses being scheduled into the school day. The Toronto board, dominated by the NDP – as was the teachers' union – was insisting on integrating dozens of heritage language programs into the regular school day. While this presented administrators with a big headache, the board argued that the benefits far outweighed the potential scheduling problems. For once, schools could address the reality of cultural bias, indeed, of "systemic racism," by sending out an important signal of its commitment to multi-culturalism. By providing the heritage courses to many of the 50 per cent of students who came from immigrant backgrounds, the school system was in effect saying "we value your cultural experience on a par with ours," according to former board chairman Penny Moss. But the teachers saw it differently. With the school schedule extended by half an hour, teachers lost some of their traditional free time – time they were expected to spend at school but that they had always considered their own. Eventually the boycott of extra-curricular activities ended and, despite considerable acrimony, a threatened strike by teachers did not materialize.

In contrast to the Ontario experience, British Columbia's teachers' federation evolved altogether differently. In the 1930s in B.C., a small group of socialists and communists challenged the leaders of the teachers' federation and elected some members to top positions. Although they failed to hold onto power, they provided ideological roots from which progressive teachers in the province drew sustenance for many years. In the 1960s, the left re-emerged in control.

"We elected people who realized that social issues and educational ones were tied together, people who knew that education didn't end in the classroom," said Jim MacFarlan, head of teacher training for the federation.

MacFarlan was a member of the Communist party until 1968 when he quit over the Soviet invasion of Czechoslovakia. In 1977, when he was president of the BCTF, one of its executive committees came out with a study called *Essential Educational Experiences,* or, as it came to be known, the "Triple E paper." Brimming with unabashed Marxist jargon, the study outlined how schools reinforced an unequal society. It said:

> Schools, in reproducing the kind of society in which we live, help to perpetuate the social class structure, the essential set of social relations in production. Not only do schools not help to create a classless society, they do not really facilitate upward mobility in the population. With very few exceptions, the formal curriculum of schools does not attach any validity to the lives of manual, clerical and service workers . . . . Textbooks, especially readers, literature and social studies texts, ignore their lives and the lives of their parents, even though it has been the labor of production workers which, literally, has built the Canadian economy. As far as the school curriculum is concerned, these are a people without a history, without a literature, without any form of social life. This kind of treatment, of course, is essential if schools are to produce submissive workers for the lowest rungs of the occupational hierarchy . . . . Thus a great many children in schools are trained to be nobodies.

Among its many recommendations, most of which have become part of accepted rhetoric, the study recommended that schools give students the knowledge and skills to "transform the society. Power as used in this context means organized energy . . . . At present, in schools, many students and many teachers lack power and control over their own lives."

The media and politicians quickly branded the Triple E paper a piece of communist propaganda. By the time the federation's annual convention came around, the Cold War rhetoric had become province-wide commie bashing. At the convention, the whole executive, including MacFarlan, was voted out of office and replaced with a conservative crew.

MacFarlan now says that while the study's analysis was correct, its language was unacceptable. "The average teacher says, 'What the hell is the social relations of production?' It was part of the rhetoric of the

1960s except it was now the middle 1970s and people weren't prepared for it." Rhetoric too can be cultural capital.

The amount of evidence indicating that the game of school is skewed to give middle-class families a better deal is voluminous. In their book *Schooling and Work in the Democratic State*, Martin Carnoy and Henry Levin examined grade 1 classes in two schools in the U.S.: an upper middle-class school they called Huntington and a lower middle-class school they named Smith. Both are in a San Francisco suburb. On the issue of classroom control, the Smith teacher relied heavily on commands and orders, what the researchers called "external" controls. The Huntington teacher relied on an "internal" control system – placing responsibility on students with phrases like "use your time wisely" or "use good judgement." While there were also external controls on the children's time and space, the dominant mode at Huntington was to appeal to an internalized set of values, asking children to think for themselves and decide what to do.

At Huntington, children were constantly being reminded of the future implications – either in work or in higher grades – of their classroom performance. The teacher also frequently mentioned how work would help them in future professional occupations. At Smith, the less affluent school, the researchers found that the emphasis was on the present. The future consequence of activities was rarely mentioned.

Huntington put a much greater stress on cognitive academic skills and gave its children more opportunities to verbalize ideas and give lengthy and complex responses to questions. The Smith teacher, on the other hand, was much more likely to accept one-word answers. Carnoy and Levin concluded, "The educational interactions in the two first-grade classrooms reflected a socialization pattern in which the Huntington students were being prepared for roles at the top of the work hierarchy and the Smith students for roles in the lower and middle portions of the job spectrum."

Jean Anyon's detailed and widely quoted study *Social Class and the Hidden Curriculum of Work* arrived at similar conclusions. She looked at grade 5 classes in five schools – two working-class, one middle-class, one upper middle-class, and one made up of children whose parents were top corporate executives. Anyon, a sociologist at Rutgers University, found that the teaching methods used in the various schools were preparing students for future roles similar to those of their parents.

At the working-class schools, work was done in a sequential fashion involving rote behaviour and little decision-making or choice on the part of students. The teachers rarely explained why the work was being assigned or how it connected to other assignments. They spent much of the school day controlling the time and space of their students and giving commands. "Their present school work is appropriate preparation for future wage labor that is mechanical and routine," Anyon wrote.

At the middle-class school, work generally involved following directions in order to get the right answers. But the directions often called for some figuring, some choice, and some decision-making. "In this school the work tasks and relationships are appropriate for a future relation to capital that is bureaucratic . . . . Such work does not usually demand that one be creative, and one is not often rewarded for critical analysis of the system."

The fourth school, which Anyon called the "affluent professional school," had children working creatively and independently. Through their work, children were expected to interpret and make sense of reality and get self-satisfaction. And the teacher's attempts to control the class involved constant negotiation. "In their schooling these children are acquiring *symbolic capital*: they are being given the opportunity to develop skills of linguistic, artistic, and scientific expression and creative elaboration of ideas into concrete form. These skills are those needed to produce, for example, culture (e.g., artistic, intellectual, and scientific ideas and other 'products')."

Finally, work in what Anyon called the "executive school" stressed the development of analytical and intellectual powers. Discussion on social issues was common, everything from "Why do workers strike?" to "Why do companies put chemicals in food when the natural ingredients are available?" It was the only school where bells were not used to begin and end periods. This school "gives its children something that none of the other schools do: knowledge of and practice in manipulating the socially legitimated tools of analysis of systems . . . . Their schooling is helping them to develop the abilities necessary for ownership and control of physical capital and the means of production in society."

At the high school level, the research is no less extensive. Probably the most widely quoted study on the effects of high school streaming was written by Jeannie Oakes, a social scientist with the Rand Corporation, a respected think-tank in California. In her 1985 book, *Keeping Track: How Schools Structure Inequality*, Oakes examined 297 classrooms and found that high schools continue the practice Anyon and others have documented in elementary schools. Students in the higher streams, Oakes found, learn how to write thematic essays, how to think critically, and how to solve challenging problems, while lower-streamed students focus on rote learning. Also, teachers in high streams devote more classroom time to learning, are more enthusiastic, and less apt to use strong criticism or ridicule, and have higher expectations of students than teachers in low streams.

Furthermore, labels like Ontario's basic, general, and advanced not only strongly influence how we perceive the labeled, but also influence how the labeled see themselves. Oakes quotes two American studies to show how streaming appears to actually retard academic growth. One study documented how the intelligence quotient scores of senior high school students *decreased* after their placement in lower streams. The other showed how students placed in higher streams did better than those in lower streams, even if they had similar backgrounds and did as well in elementary school before being streamed. In other words, when everyone around you tells the story of a world view and your place in it, you start living that story as if it were natural.

In Canada, the study that most highlighted the problems with streaming came from the 1987 Radwanski report commissioned by the Ontario government. Although his recommendations have been criticized as contradictory, George Radwanski's arguments about streaming are persuasive. After an extensive review of the literature, Radwanski concluded: "The evidence is overwhelming that streaming is a social injustice, a theoretical error and a practical failure . . . . Doing away with streaming must lie at the heart of any strategy to address the fundamental need for improvements in our education system (and) to significantly reduce the drop-out rate in the long run."

Students relegated to grossly inferior programs, Radwanski said, can't see why they should keep studying. If you're going to be dead-ended, you may as well head out and try it on your own, and many do.

In Ontario, figures released by Radwanski and which are still applicable indicate that an astounding 79 per cent of those in the basic vocational level drop out, 62 per cent of those in the community college-bound general stream drop out, while only 12 per cent do so in the advanced, university-bound stream. Overall, 33 per cent leave before getting a high school diploma, a figure that generally corresponds to the national average. Radwanski also found that a disproportionate number of drop-outs come from low-income homes. While 37 per cent of all Ontario students come from low-income families, these students represent 51 per cent of drop-outs. Conversely, while 36 per cent of students come from professional and managerial homes, they make up only 22 per cent of drop-outs. Streaming, Radwanski concluded, is perpetuating poverty.

Those against streaming say it's morally repugnant to segregate 14-year-old children according to deemed ability. Put everyone in the same class, they say, and then use "co-operative" methods where students work in small groups. Brighter students can then help slower ones – they may not be absorbing as much new academic content but in helping weaker students along they not only learn about co-operation but also about the process of learning. Those who support this idea point to studies that show the brighter students are not held back.

Those who question the effectiveness of co-operative groups say it's only common sense that brighter students will do better in a classroom of their peers. This group says that if you think students are bored today, wait and see what happens when brighter ones have to wait for slower classmates to grasp basic concepts in the curriculum. And several principals in segregated vocational schools like those in Toronto have said that if slower students are placed in a class with highly motivated and competitive students, they would first be ridiculed and then devoured. They insist that slower students need to be segregated for their own protection. There is some truth to this fear. But most of the fear comes from the fact that the game of school instills many high-achieving students with the values and temperament of mercenaries. For those placed on the bottom rung, streaming takes a stiff whack at their self-worth. To contain rebellion while severely limiting human potential requires the deceptive subtlety of a magician. Those condemned must accept illusion for reality, injury for justice. The victim greases the guillotine with his own sense of guilt.

■

The limits schools impose on many students are legitimized by the principle of meritocracy. In meritocracies, talent, ability, and effort ostensibly determine social mobility and status, instead of birthright or privilege. This principle has taken firm hold in Western societies in the twentieth century and, if applied fairly, is certainly an improvement on more nepotistic times. Unfortunately, there's nothing divinely ordained about our meritocracy. The criteria used to judge students do not come from the heavens, although many pretend that they do. In fact, meritocracy is a myth.

The social and economic changes of the 1960s saw the school system expand virtually overnight as high schools opened their doors to children from low-income families. In a true meritocracy, over time, this educational expansion would reduce the advantages of privileged children and increase those of disadvantaged ones. This would mean that for lazy or untalented middle-class children, money and status would no longer buy automatic access to society's privileges. Likewise, talented and hard working children from working-class backgrounds would rise to the top.

Christopher J. Hurn, a sociologist at the University of Massachusetts, said a society that is becoming more meritocratic must satisfy three propositions:

1. The correlation between educational and occupational status will increase over time.

2. The correlation between parents' social status and the social status of their children will diminish over time.

3. The correlation between parents' social status and the educational achievements of their children will diminish over time.

After an extensive review of educational studies, Hurn concluded that while the first proposition is valid, the other two are not. Statistics on who goes to university and who ends up in non-university-bound streams show the continuing link between parents' social status and a child's educational performance and future status. And while there are many examples of individual social mobility, the chances of moving from one class to another have not increased. For instance, one U.S. study in 1978 estimated that about 20 per cent of the sons of manual workers reached professional or managerial positions – a percentage virtually identical to that of the 1920s and 1930s.

"Educational expansion," wrote Hurn, "and the expansion of higher education in particular, has not resulted in a *dramatic* reduction in the relationship between social status (of parents) and school success (of their children). Nor, it is apparent from the data on social mobility, has it resulted in any substantial reduction in the ability of parents to pass on their status to their children. Education has not proved to be the great equalizer."

For one thing, the middle class again has got the upper hand. Many of its members achieved success in school and at work by mastering linear, sequential thinking. Consequently, linear thinking is another form of cultural capital that middle-class parents pass on to their children, who then cash it in at school. Students who master mathematics and the sciences are deemed intelligent. But what of the children who show a raw awareness of intuitive knowledge? Whose understanding of the world around them has nothing to do with math and science and everything to do with the experience of their emotions? Likewise, what of those with artistic talent or a dexterity in making things? Carpentry skills are valued in high school vocational programs, but by then those students more than likely have been judged failures in elementary school. And courses like drama and music, which in the hands of a good teacher may bring out the less valued forms of knowledge, are relegated to the status of options. The message is clear: They are secondary in importance. Certainly, the values placed on different kinds of knowledge and skills are dictated to a large extent by forces outside the school. It is the school's uncritical reflection of those forces, particularly in the elementary years, that narrowly defines the ability and success of students.

If the meritocratic principle has not created a more socially fluid society, what purpose does it serve? The very idea of a meritocracy predisposes us to looking up. "A school with a strong meritocratic ideology is inevitably implying that there is something *wrong* with being working-class, for this is a state that any sensible pupil will work hard to escape from," writes British educator David Hargreaves. But what of those who can't escape? If society, through its schools, claims to use independent criteria to determine who wins and who loses, then who is to blame when someone loses?

Students at Toronto's Brockton High School have felt the weight of losing. Brockton is a strictly vocational school in a working-class neighbourhood in the city's west end. Among a group of 15 students in a grade 11 and 12 auto body class, all but two had failed a grade or more in elementary school. More astonishing is that *all* of them blamed themselves for their failure.

"I just became lazy," said Joe, echoing the response of his friends during a group discussion. "I didn't like all the homework they gave me so I stopped doing it."

In their book *The Injuries of Class*, American sociologists Jonathan Cobb and Richard Sennett argue that schools dispense "badges of ability" to pupils who rise above the masses in classrooms. To dissociate oneself from the group by scoring highest on tests is to be acknowledged as an individual and awarded dignity. But what about students who make up the mass? What about Joe, whose individuality has not been officially recognized because he hasn't risen above the crowd? Who can Joe blame for this? His teachers, after all, assume the role of independent judge and jury, an act reinforced in Joe's mind by the fact that some students around him succeed. No one has explained to him the biases of the hidden curriculum. Perhaps Joe can best protect his dignity by simply not trying. This way, he reassures himself that failure was a matter of choice and not a question of innate stupidity. But if it's perceived as a matter of choice, what right does Joe have to ask for a greater share of the economic pie later in life? The more a society claims to be meritocratic, the more likely its victims are to blame themselves.

By the time many of these students reach high school and are placed in low streams of study, the inner damage is great.

"Our whole program is based on addressing and helping kids who have been wounded," said Ken Hanson, Brockton's vice-principal.

"The kid walks in the door and, on the whole, he or she feels like a loser," added Elinor Gower, the head of Brockton's history department.

Often, they'll also walk in reading at a grade 4 level, which raises serious questions about the education they received in elementary school. With such poor skills, instilling the obedient work ethic needed to hold low-paying jobs gains a forced validity. Better the most basic of skills than nothing at all. High schools like Brockton try hard to go beyond this type of band-aid education, but their position at the bottom of the educational system ensures that the stigma of failure remains a heavy burden on their students.

It's not uncommon for students in Toronto's vocational schools to get off the bus before it reaches their schools to avoid being recognized as basic-level students. "If someone asks you what school you go to, you lie," said one student. "You tell them you go to Danforth Tech," a school with higher streams of study.

Schools use dignity as a commodity that they bestow on some and not others. Fortunately, they don't succeed in completely stripping students of their dignity. Students will find dignity outside of school in sports, music, with friends, or with lovers. Likewise, workers toiling in monotonous jobs that obliterate the line between humans and machines will find dignity in activities off the shop floor. Furthermore, students who recognize they've been shuffled out of the schooling game don't transfer their self-worth to those on the winning path. In fact, they often ridicule academic students for being "browners." Students in basic-level courses demand respect and take an almost fierce pride in their work – whether it is cutting hair or patching up the body of a car. The battering of dignity they endure in and out of school sparks resistance that, coupled with self-blame, turns into a kind of elastic bitterness that is at once directed at others and themselves.

Streaming has much to do with the aphorism "knowledge is power." At one level, school is about giving valuable skills and "high-status" knowledge to some students while withholding it from others. The fact that the winners are from the middle and upper classes should be no surprise because it's their parents that either make up the system or at the very least know how to manipulate it. While the home environment is a factor in reproducing inequality, schools themselves are working hard to teach children at the bottom how to stay there while teaching those at the top how to hang on to what their parents already have. The process is skewed by a cultural bias that permeates schooling – from teachers to textbooks – and it is legitimized by the myth of meritocracy. Invisibly they combine to shape the self-image of young people, a messing with the soul that spares no one, including the middle class.

5

FEAR OF FAILURE

The hidden curriculum is relentless. In a society that lives and dies by competition, children learn very early about winning and losing. Alan King, a sociologist who has done extensive studies in education for the Ontario government, recalled asking one elementary school child how he felt about failing a test. "Someone has to fail," came the quick reply. This rule has been preset, of course, by an economic system that is suspicious of anything that isn't a product of competition. And with the global economy being used as both carrot and stick, competition's socially assigned place is unthreatened, as unquestionably accepted as gravity.

It's believed that competition is the best way to sort the bright from the not-so-bright. Indeed, schools begin sorting as soon as children walk through the door. In grade 1, it's not uncommon for children to be placed in reading groups with names like "the bears" and "the tigers" to separate the slower readers from the faster ones. By grade 2 those judged to have low IQ scores or labeled as having behavioural problems are streamed into special education classes. Most elementary school teachers do everything they can to protect students from being sorted out of the game, but the pressures to judge are obstinate and, in the end, their resistance is futile.

Rituals that pit one student against another permeate the classroom and run much deeper than the obvious competition for marks. Seated in straight rows, children spend most of their time staring at the backs of other pupils' heads. There's certainly value in learning how to be alone in a crowd, but coupled with incessant rituals of competition, the lesson taught is that it's "everyone for themselves." And teachers actually do everything they can to make competition fun.

At St. Patrick's in Halifax, I watched a primary class during French period sing "Je suis une pizza," and then play a game called Five Buzz. The young children stood by their desks and one after another counted in French. The trick was to identify all numbers that could be divided by five or that amounted to five when their digits were added. Children who missed suffered the judgement of television game shows – *buzzzz* – and had to sit down. The game progressed quickly and, with two children left standing, the others sat on the edges of their seats, cheering quietly for one or the other. A boy named Christopher won. For his efforts he received a candy and five points on a blackboard scorecard. The loser thrashed the air with his hand as if to say "shucks," and his face flushed with wistful embarrassment. In his loss I remembered my childhood in a Montreal elementary school.

The year Pierre Trudeau was first elected prime minister, I was selected by my grade 4 teacher to be the captain of one of two teams. I named my squad Apollo and felt rather self-satisfied for reflecting the technological spirit of the times. The captain of the other team was Donatina, a girl who lived around the corner from me. The game was ostensibly designed to teach us the multiplication tables. Every morning the teams lined up facing each other, Donatina and I at our respective helms, with the teacher standing at the front of the class. She would then flash a card: $8 \times 4 = \underline{}$ and the game was to shout out the answer before your opponent did. As captains, Donatina and I squared off first.

I distinctly remember my reaction to the first flash card because it was similar to the hundreds more that followed. With my optic nerves still dutifully carrying the message to be processed and synthesized by my brain into a comprehensible image, my eardrums vibrated with Donatina's answer. It was a matter of synaptic timing, and mine just happened to be slower than Donatina's. In any case, each morning I was usually left with my finger pointing and my mouth slightly open, as if I'd forgotten something important I wanted to say. A month of this taught me not only to despise math, but Donatina as well. Then one day, I did it! I beat her to the draw! Everyone, including the other team, erupted into a wild cheer. But as I walked to the end of the line to await my next turn, I knew Donatina had let me win.

In his book *Culture Against Man*, Jules Henry described an everyday classroom scene many of us have experienced. It is not unlike the moments during the Five Buzz game at St. Patrick's or the multiplication drill of my grade 4 classroom. Henry, an American anthropologist, watched a student named Boris struggling to reduce $12/16$ to its lowest common denominator. The teacher quietly encouraged Boris to "think" while several students began waving their hands wildly, eager to give the answer. At this point Henry described young Boris as "pretty unhappy, probably mentally paralyzed." After a minute or two of further encouragement the teacher turned to the class and among the "forest of hands" called Peggy, who told Boris the right answer.

Boris, surely not for the first time, was picking up the background noise of the hidden curriculum and learning a powerful cultural lesson. For Peggy to win, he had to lose; it's as simple and brutal as that. Henry described this as a classic example of the fear of failure instilled by the school's hidden curriculum. He wrote: "Such experiences imprint on the mind of every man in our culture the *Dream of Failure*, so that over and over again, night in, night out, even at the pinnacle of success, a man will dream not of success, but failure.

"The external nightmare is internalized for life," Henry added. "It is this dream that, above all other things, provides the fierce human energy required by technological drivenness. It is not so much that Boris was learning arithmetic, but that he was learning the *essential nightmare. To be successful in our culture one must learn to dream of failure.*"

Probably the most fear-stricken group today is the middle class. Despite all their privileges, they are feeling squeezed to the point of panic. Economic statistics for both Canada and the United States indicate that wealth is becoming more polarized between rich and poor. In July 1990, a research group, the Centre on Budget and Policy Priorities in the U.S., released a study based on an analysis of congressional budget office data on income and taxes. It found that the total after-tax income of the richest 1 per cent of Americans was almost as high as the total for everyone in the bottom 40 per cent. The bottom 40 per cent received 14.2 per cent of all the after-tax income in the U.S. in 1990, while the top 1 per cent received 12.6 per cent. "This marks a sharp change from 1980, when the top 1 per cent received half as much after-tax income as the bottom 40 per cent," according to the report by the non-profit organization, which specializes in issues affecting poor people. It also found that wealthy Americans paid a smaller percentage of their income in taxes in 1990 than in 1980, while lower income households paid a larger portion. In the end, the richest 2.5 million Americans have nearly as much money as the 100 million with the lowest incomes. As for middle-class Americans, the report concluded that they were getting less of the total share of income than at any time since the end of World War II.

It's much the same in Canada. A survey by Statistics Canada found that the 20 per cent of Canadians with the highest incomes increased their share of total income to 41.9 per cent in 1989 from 39.9 per cent in 1981. The gain came at the expense of the middle class, which had 52.8 per cent of total income in 1989, down from 54.9 per cent in 1981. Poor people kept their puny share of 5.2 per cent of the income pie during the same nine-year period. In other words, many in the middle class are either slipping from their social rung or holding tight, fearing the fall.

Middle-class parents are eager to pass on their status to their children, and part of this involves stratifying the school system as much as possible to isolate their children from those they believe will lower standards: In practice, this amounts to most people outside their economic or cultural background. There are no consciously wicked intentions in this. In fact, it is their singular love of their children that drives them. The goal is to create as direct and clear a path as possible to success – the point where the intoxicating troika of money, power, and status culminates in a single job description. It comes down to old-fashioned turf protection, not unlike what gangs do.

Middle-class parents try to segregate themselves on three fronts: by neighbourhood, by schools, and within schools. Terry Symonds had seen this phenomenon in the inner-city neighbourhood of North Halifax where he grew up. Symonds was director of the North Halifax Library on Gottingen St. "This area has gone from a whole community to pockets of communities," he said. A stocky, friendly man, he ran what could truly be described as a community library until his death in 1991. It worked closely with the local grade school, St. Patrick's, and local teenagers used it for a drop-in centre as much as a library.

"White and black used to be a community here," Symonds said. "There was a bond; we were all working poor and we all knew each other. If I went up the street and got into trouble I'd get hollered at by someone who knew me. Everyone looked after each other. There was a discipline on the street, there was respect. Man, old ladies in the neighbourhood were always giving me grocery lists – and I'd do it too." But that was then.

Since then, the arrival of young professionals has sent house prices soaring, forcing long-time residents with relatively good jobs and the desire to own a home to buy outside of the community. What's left is a noticeable split between the poor and the affluent. For instance, the new professionals don't enroll their children at St. Patrick's. Instead, they send them to French immersion schools outside of the neighbourhood. The result is that as parts of the community go upscale, St. Patrick's remains an inner-city school, stigma and all. In fact, since moving into North Halifax, these professionals have worked hard to make sure no one confuses them with "those" people. They even lobbied city politicians to change the street names. Now the affluent parts of Maynard, Creighton, and Gottingen streets have been renamed Fuller Terrace, Northwood Terrace, and Novalea Drive.

"No, I don't know the spelling of Novalea because I don't care," said Symonds, visibly upset. "It's Gottingen Street, man. That's what it's always been and that's what it is. This is just another attempt to isolate us, to cut us off from our own community."

Vancouver's Granville Street is another example of social segregation. The street divides the city into east and west, rich and poor. Working-class neighbourhoods and inner-city schools are all on the east side while the upper-class communities and the advanced schools are on the west side. Until 1988, the west side was the exclusive home of the city's two Mini Schools, facilities devoted entirely to those students believed to be extraordinary. Entrance into these publicly funded schools is by selected application and, after individual interviews, only students with high academic averages and "leadership qualities" get admitted. Once selected, they go through a program that has them finishing high school in three years instead of four. Physical distance alone was enough to discourage east-side students from applying, although after years of criticism that Mini Schools were little more than publicly funded perks for the rich, one was finally opened on the east side.

French immersion programs are another example of middle-class stratification. As valuable as these programs are, they are offered mostly in upscale neighbourhoods. Vocational schools, on the other hand, are located mainly in low-income communities. In Toronto, for instance, vocational schools are all south of Bloor Street, the east-west thorough-fare that divides traditional working-class neighbourhoods in the south from the more affluent ones in the north. The world of money and power, unlike that of daily existence, offers few coincidences.

Middle-class muscle flexing continues within the schools. In addition to the established streams – those that lead to university and those that don't – provinces have the "gifted" programs in Ontario, the "honours" classes in Nova Scotia, and the "challenge" courses in B.C. These programs are a result of lobbying from affluent parents.

In Ontario, middle-class groups fought hard for Bill 82, which became law in the mid-1980s. It is usually associated with requiring schools to provide special programs for children with disabilities, but it also created the gifted stream. Parents must convince a tribunal that their child is gifted. A senior administrator at the Toronto Board of Education said the criteria for admission were flexible and middle-class parents pushed hard to get their children accepted. "Being in a gifted class today is a status symbol. It's like having a BMW. It's become part of the yuppie syndrome," she said.

In B.C., "challenge" programs emerged in the early 1980s. At New Westminster Secondary School, the parents of challenge students have their own organization separate from the school's parent-teacher committee. They use their clout to screen teachers assigned to the courses and to get extra funding for the program. "I've had challenge classes every year," said English teacher Rick Boudell, "and you don't get too many kids from poor families in there, and yet they're not chosen on the basis of money."

As the economic disparities of the 1980s became more acute, middle-class parents redoubled their efforts to segregate their children from those they deemed less able. Not surprisingly, most of these parents were firmly against any attempt to get rid of streaming. In the summer of 1988, a group of Toronto parents from schools in the city's most affluent neighbourhoods made this clear to an Ontario legislative committee reviewing the school system. They demanded standardized tests at the end of grade 8 to weed out undesirables who they said were somehow entering the advanced streams and holding back their children. Dreaming of failure, the middle class stakes out its turf.

Maple Grove Elementary School is on tree-lined Cypress Street in Shaughnessy, one of Vancouver's wealthier neighbourhoods, where parents can afford to do more for their children's education. In 1985, for example, the school grossed $28,000 at a wine and cheese party. Tickets sold for $60 each or $100 a couple, with 70 per cent tax-deductible. This kind of financial reserve – and the political clout it speaks of – is one reason schools in affluent neighbourhoods inevitably have more and newer computers, nicer playgrounds, more music and theatre programs, more library books, more field trips, and more of everything else schools can use. But school Principal Al Garneau says the intense commitment to education by Maple Grove parents has its drawbacks. Garneau, a tall man with broad shoulders, has a finely tuned understanding of the contradictory forces tugging at the school system.

According to Garneau, many Maple Grove parents function on two beliefs: first, they're convinced that their children are brighter than they really are, and second, they believe success for their children as adults rests on them being given as big a head start as possible. Garneau blames the first illusion on television. He believes children pick up vocabulary from television that allows them to talk about all sorts of things without understanding the full significance of what they are saying. He compares it to a child who can read the numbers on a digital watch without understanding what constitutes time. The second belief comes from the parents' own background. "A lot of them are very successful and they want that same success for their kids," Garneau says. The result is a drive to create super children. Parents mesmerize their children with flash cards, enroll them in cooking, fitness, music, skating, dancing, and all kinds of other programs, all by the age of three. Children are pushed to read long before they are ready and placed in preschool programs where they're taught to "decode," which is the ability to sound words on the page. This method, however, does little to ensure that children understand what they are reading.

For Garneau, early formal education stifles imagination and curiosity and puts children in a spoon-feeding mode, where they become dependent on others for their learning. "They're programmed to death," says Garneau, who quotes widely from the works of respected educators and psychologists such as David Elkind and Bruno Bettelheim. "Children have not been given the time to play and be children. So what I see are the burn-outs."

Some parents, for example, won't allow their children to believe in legends or fairy tales. "No, Virginia, there is no Santa Claus." As a result, children pick up the message that play is something childish and therefore resist taking part in it. They walk into Maple Grove suffering from play deprivation, a symptom of which is depression.

"What do I see here? I see the depressed kids," Garneau says. "I see kids buckling under pressure, under unreasonable expectations, kids who can't make it. C pluses aren't good enough, it's got to be a B or an A. They figure they failed if they get a C plus, and I see kids that have not been able to be children."

It usually catches up to children sometime between the ages of 8 and 12. Then, Garneau says, they "are like tired old businessmen because they've been on such a routine and they haven't been allowed to play. Life has all been work, work, work, drudgery, produce, produce, speed, and they finally run out of steam. I really believe that modern society is placing totally unrealistic expectations on our children. We're not allowing them to be children and I see childhood disappearing everywhere. I mean, when you've got six-year-olds going to birthday parties in three-piece suits, it tells you something."

Garneau thinks the community has come around a little since his arrival at Maple Grove in 1987, when he began warning parents about the effects of unreasonable pressure on children. But some attitudes are deeply rooted. "My teachers here can hand out a test and one of the kids will ask, 'Does it count?' Well, what do you do with a comment like that? What does that tell you? So we're working at the other end with our kids, 'Hey, listen, not everything in life has to produce results. Sometimes you can do something for the sake of accomplishing it and not worry about whether it gets you somewhere else or whether it gets you an A or a B on some report.'"

But, Garneau's best efforts aside, the competitive angst that lies behind the floral gardens and stately homes of Shaughnessy is being exacerbated by other pressures. Until the mid-1980s, few immigrants lived in Vancouver's affluent neighbourhoods. Then along came wealthy families from Hong Kong with the economic clout to buy into the neighbourhoods and send their children to the local schools. Before 1987, there were no ESL classes on the west side of Granville and so immigrants were forced to go to schools on the east side. One ESL class was finally started at Maple Grove in 1987. At that time, only 12 per cent of Maple Grove's children were ESL students. By 1989, they numbered more than 25 per cent and some white, success-driven parents did not approve.

The tensions in the neighbourhood began with the building of so-called "monster homes." Developers buy up homes in Shaughnessy, tear them down along with the surrounding trees, and build mansions on the whole lot, almost to the sidewalk. It's a style that seems to suit prospective buyers from Hong Kong who, accustomed to a crowded little island, must see front lawns as a horrible waste of space. Shaughnessy residents maintain that the massive slabs of shiny marble and white columns are out of place among the stately old homes set back from the street. But aesthetics are not the only concern.

Shaughnessy residents don't believe the real estate statistics indicating that the massive influx of baby boomers into the home-buying market – many coming from other provinces – is the real reason for Vancouver's housing prices going up. The residents claim the monster homes are driving up housing prices to the point where some long-time residents can no longer afford to live in the neighbourhood. Suddenly, the high value of their homes stopped being a protective barrier and, for the first time, threatened the status quo.

The animosity in the neighbourhood has crept into the school and much of it has focused around its ESL class. There's the usual, unproven complaint – ESL students will lower standards and slow down the rest of the class – but Maple Grove teachers Mike Northy and Lori Duncan believe the anger is a result of racism. In fact, Lori Duncan said that racism is blatant. During the two-and-a-half years she's been the school's ESL teacher, she has tried to foster understanding towards the new Asian members of the community, partly by setting up a multicultural committee made up of teachers and parents. So far it hasn't worked, and the resistance hasn't only come from parents.

"This is a very traditional school," Duncan says. "There's a core group of teachers who have been here for a long, long time and in order to fit into this school, there's a lot of pressure put on you to assimilate to their ways. I've heard this said, 'If you don't like it, transfer or leave.' That's the attitude. It's almost a policy at Maple Grove. In fact, I get the feeling the majority of teachers would prefer we (the ESL class) didn't exist."

There were 20 students in Lori Duncan's ESL class when I visited. Hanging from strings on the ceiling were cards on which the children had written and drawn what their lives would be like at ten-year intervals. An abridged version of one girl's life cycle went like this: "One year old I was just eating, crying, and sleeping; 20 years old I would go in to Harvard to work and to be famous and rich; 30 years old I would marry and have kids then I am a mother; 50 years old I would be happy that my kids will go to Harvard like me!" From the stories the children told, that trip to Harvard may turn out to be a rough one.

"They say f-words because they hate Chinese," Stephen said during a group discussion. "They say to me, 'Why do you come to Canada, why you not go to other country?'"

"Why do they say these things to you?" I asked.

"They don't like we come here because they say we make expensive the houses," he said. Stephen was ten years old and had arrived from Hong Kong two years earlier.

"Do they really say that?"

"Yes," the group shouted in a chorus.

"Sometimes, other kids treat us like monsters," Elsa said. "They say, 'Crazy Chinese, your hair is black.'"

"Do you think Canadians will do this to you when you get older?"

"No," said Edmond, "because I will make some money for Canada and they won't laugh at us then."

The children said the older boys in the school were responsible for the verbal assaults and for pushing them around at recess. Paul, a frail looking ten-year-old from Hong Kong who had been in Canada for three years, was one of their victims. He injured his shoulder one day and some time later, while it was still tender, he was playing in the schoolyard. An older boy approached him, tugged hard on his jacket sleeve and, as Lori Duncan described it, pulled Paul's shoulder out of its socket.

"They say 'slime ball' and then they pull my jacket," Paul said meekly.

Principal Al Garneau explains the incidents this way: "We've got our share here of kids who like to tease others. I call them social predators. They're kids who go around looking to find out where someone is vulnerable and then ride them. They push buttons on kids. When it happens to someone who's fat or who has red hair, we call it teasing or bullying. When it happens to someone who's Chinese, we call it racism. I have difficulty with that. I've known situations where kids are teased if their parents are merely renting the house that they're in instead of owning it, or if they're not wearing the neatest runners with the right labels."

Teacher Mike Northy, who spent his childhood in West Vancouver schools fighting a barrage of slurs about being Jewish, believes there was more than just bullying involved. "There's been a traditional tolerance in this province for racism," he said. British Columbia, according to Northy, has a frontier mentality that upholds all individuals' right to make as much money as they can. Anyone perceived as being in the way of that goal is asking for trouble. Armed with the economic clout to buy into an establishment neighbourhood, Asian immigrants are playing by middle-class rules and messing up the game. With its reputation for high academic achievement, the Asian community poses a threat to an established group of people trying to secure at least an equivalent rung on the social ladder for their children. The number of Asian students entering the University of British Columbia has so alarmed some people that it has spawned an insipid and racist play on the letters UBC – the University of a Billion Chinese.

Needless to say, fear of failure can become pretty ugly. The parents of some of the Maple Grove children leave little doubt that, as a collective dream, the fear extends far beyond the school walls. It's not uncommon, as principal Al Garneau pointed out, that children from middle-class and affluent homes enter school already full of fear. But despite the best efforts of educators like Garneau, the rituals of competition that permeate schooling ensure that the fear is implanted even deeper. Schools toy with the very dignity of people; those streamed high get it stroked, those streamed low get it trampled. The myth of meritocracy performs this relentless judgement as though with the blessing of God. For those stamped "losers," rebellion and resignation are their lot. Those under intense pressure to succeed, those for whom the fear of failure feeds off their central nervous system, those who risk burn-out by the age of 12, we call "winners."

Andrew Kishino was a grade 13 student when he and I lived in the same neighbourhood in Toronto and bumped into each other a lot. One day we met in our neighbourhood mall while I was on the telephone, somewhat perturbed, asking a bank employee how a money machine could possibly eat up my card and leave me with one dollar after the banks had closed. Andrew had just returned from Virgin Records, where he had dropped off a tape of rap songs in the hopes of getting a record contract. He had taken a year off school to pursue his music career, and to survive he worked as a bank teller. As he and I talked, two teenage women, both Asian, stopped to say hello.

"Hey, Kish, what are you up to?" one asked Andrew. She was petite, with full black hair flowing over her shoulders.

"I took a year off," Andrew replied.

"Finding yourself?" she asked, smiling.

"Yeah, finding out about the real world. And it just sucks, man. Give me high school life any day," Andrew said.

"What's so horrible about the real world?" I asked.

"You get these people who are having a bad day, right, and they come in and figure, 'I'm going to let this bank teller have it,' as if that's going to fix anything. God!

"So it reminded me of this song," he continued, launching into a tune by Kool G. Rapp and DJ Polo:

> *I was sort of a porter, taking the next man's orders*
> *Breaking my back for a shack or headquarters*
> *All my manpower, for 4 bucks an hour*
> *But I took my time and wrote rhymes in the shower.*

I had first met Andrew when he attended North Toronto Collegiate Institute, an academic school, offering only university-bound courses. It has long seen itself as a training ground for Canada's professional and technical elite, a mandate the school makes very clear to its students. "I tell them, 'look, it's your ballgame. It's going to be you who will set the pace in the economy and be the future leaders.' And they're aware of that," said James Hogarth, the school's principal.

The school's academic success rate is phenomenal. Every year, 80 per cent of its graduates enter university, compared to 18 per cent province-wide in Ontario. Most of the students are from middle-class and affluent families. As Hogarth put it, "They come from good stock." And their parents work hard to make sure they stay that way. "The parents know what marks are needed for their kids to get into university," Hogarth said. "If they see them slipping, they're down here in a second and they want to know what's wrong. Second best isn't good enough here." After all, students have their sights set on the more prestigious universities, such as Queen's in Kingston, Ontario, where entrance requirements are high. In a few cases, they're unable to handle the stress. One of the school's guidance counsellors said that about 40 students a year suffer from serious emotional strain due to the pressure for high marks. For students like Andrew Kishino, it can all get a bit troubling.

Kish, as he was known, was the only b-boy in the school – a sub-culture of one. His Nike running shoes had no laces and complemented a black track suit highlighted by rainbow stripes. His ornaments? A black cap and a large clock that hangs from his neck. Andrew led a rap band, the music of preference for b-boys that has captured the imagination of black working-class youth since the early 1980s. Above all, Andrew wanted to rap his way to musical fame and fortune. But the competitive forces that drive North Toronto Collegiate lured him towards the corporate world.

"A good job is one that's high paying, that has status and lets you buy a BMW," Andrew explained during a group discussion in class, generally echoing what is perhaps the number one answer when teenagers are asked to define success. "Something like an executive job where I can wear three-piece Italian suits and have the power to lay off hundreds of people. But that's in no way what I really want to do," he quickly added.

In 1989, Andrew was in the final year of his university-bound program and the pressure was getting to him: "It's really cutthroat here. My music's a real safety valve from all the pressure at school." The following year, still short a few credits for his diploma, he attended school part-time and worked at launching his rap career.

I had walked into North Toronto after doing almost two months of research, gathering the views and observations of students across Ontario's basic, general, and advanced streams of study. I was interested in everything from their schooling experience to their views on life in general. I interviewed North Toronto students and sat in on classes over the period of a week. I also read David Hargreaves' book, *The Challenge for the Comprehensive School*. It seemed to crystallize much of what I had heard over the two-month period. It described the school system in England as one that batters the dignity of most students and leaves them with little choice but to rebel.

I wrote a four-part series of articles that the *Toronto Star* published in a package in June 1989 under the headline, "The Hidden Curriculum: Students get the message when they're sorted into winners and losers." Basically, the series can be summarized by one paragraph: "Schools are organized like factories, sorting students for the best and worst jobs. Education experts say the system uses the wrong yardsticks to determine who wins, puts too much pressure to perform on even the top students, and strips the losers of their self-esteem." The articles also clearly stated that this was mainly due to a school system that reflected the demands of an economic system based on competition.

Before the articles were published I showed them to a class of English students I had interviewed at North Toronto. The students were in what Ontario calls an OAC course, the equivalent of the former grade 13 class in the advanced, university-bound stream. Andrew Kishino was a student in the class.

Most of the 15 or so students were deeply disturbed and offended by the articles, although Andrew concurred with my conclusions. Comments ranged from "You made us look like a bunch of neo-Nazis" to more specific complaints. For instance, I had quoted Betsy, one of the top students, as saying, "My family always says, 'Make up your own mind,' but I'm not allowed to screw up. People are telling me what I should be instead of letting me figure it out on my own." During the discussion of my articles Betsy said, "You made it look like we got where we are on the backs of others." Her tone was calm and she sounded deeply hurt. My point that students with her economic and social background had an unfair advantage over less affluent students had the effect of tainting her achievements. Whether or not Betsy deserved her success – and I had no reason to believe she didn't – I argued that it was attained by playing according to imposed rules that leave no alternative: In a competitive system winners can't exist without losers.

One student raised his voice in wounded indignation. "The poor and working class," he shouted, "have only themselves to blame for being where they are. We've got equal opportunity for all and those at the bottom of the social heap are there because they're lazy!" He shook with rage, as though my analysis had offended his very sense of being. He utterly rejected the argument that the race to the top is cooked from the start and has much to do with economics and political clout. Unfortunately, he is not alone. The belief that society offers everyone equality of opportunity is firmly held by most students. This myth is the consequence of the meritocratic principle.

The harsh reaction to my articles shook me because, rightly or wrongly, the students believed I had shown a lack of compassion. To them, I turned out to be just another adult exercising the power of judgement.

Their English teacher, Bruce Reevely, said to me later,"What they're saying is, 'How can you hope to reflect the group if you're not able to reflect the individual?'" While I argued that his students received an automatic sense of dignity simply by the way society perceives those in the advanced streams, Reevely emphasized that even North Toronto students did not escape the relentless judgement of school. Some are stamped failures while others survive, only to face another hurdle and more pressure. Reevely didn't say so, but he seemed to be describing a game where even when you win, you lose. It sounded very much like a high school version of what the students at Vancouver's Maple Grove School experienced.

"Cultural elitism," Reevely said, "is alive and well at this school." In English courses parents want the so-called classics taught, and more generally teachers "are under horrendous pressure to go back to the 1960s" form of rote learning. But he added that many North Toronto teachers resist this push backwards. As individuals they choose to opt out of the system and adopt a set of values and teaching methods that develop thinking skills.

He has a point. To categorize people with homogeneous labels like "middle class" is to overlook the human complexities and contradictions of individuals acting within those groups, and to perpetuate the error, as I understand it, of traditional Marxists. Individuals, however, don't act in a vacuum, nor should they. They can't shed their environment as though throwing off an overcoat. For individuals to effectively revolt against rules that dehumanize, those rules must be named and given a face other than that of a deity. When human structures such as hierarchy are glorified as absolutes, the sense of powerlessness they create breeds nihilistic revolt or resignation.

In the middle of my conversation with Reevely, three former students, all young women, walked into his office to say hello. They used to be three of his top students and were now in their first year of university. Reevely invited me to ask them about their five years of schooling at North Toronto.

"High school's a game, basically, and I had just two or three teachers who taught me something," said Michelle, her friends concurring with a nod. "The rest of the time I was trying to do as well as I could on as little work as possible."

"What do you mean, school's a game?" I asked.

"Well, some teachers depend on kids to show up, so you do, and you get your marks; others want you to talk, so you do, and you get marks for that," Michelle said. "Like in math last year, I never did homework, I just did class work and I got 90. There's something wrong with a system that lets you do that. You just have to figure out what buttons to push." In other words, the game of school encourages a Pavlovian response that teaches conformity.

That game also has an ironic conclusion. Competition is about getting credentials and marks that are high enough to get into university. The students who have been shuffled out of the game stop working because they see no point to their efforts. Those still on track – the winners – learn about the kinds of behaviour that will elicit the most rewards. In a school system that works on a one-way transmission of information from teacher to student, knowing when to swallow and regurgitate proves fruitful. Of course there are always students who make the most of their high school years; they are likely to be in the more affluent schools, which stress creative thinking skills. But the very nature of the school game makes getting the right score more important than learning. There are also teachers who try to instill a passion for learning, but it comes off sounding rather hypocritical when the rules of the game are so patently cynical. During a class discussion at Toronto's Brother Edmund Rice School, grade 13 student Olavo Cordeiro put it simply: "Schools, you know, every now and then they like to stress that marks aren't everything, but when you come down to it, they're the *only* thing. What they're really doing is teaching you to compete. When teachers look at you, they look at your mark."

"They're preparing you for competition because that's what life's all about," said another student in Olavo's class. "You can't have financial success if you can't compete."

Edmund Rice is made up mainly of students in the basic and general programs, in courses leading to community college or work but not to university. The school does have a small university-bound program and Olavo was one of its students. The competition these students face to enter university is so fierce that some teachers say they water down their courses to make it easier for students to get high marks. And the students know it.

"The academic kids don't come here because they see this as a general and basic level school," said an Edmund Rice math teacher. "But the ones that are here, I mean, if I don't water down my course, 70 per cent of them are going to fail. You can't teach them the way you teach kids at Lasalle [an academic school]. I think many teachers in a lot of schools are giving kids higher marks to push them through."

As the stakes get higher, the fear of failure becomes more haunting and the means to survive more desperate. One group of Edmund Rice students described several methods of stealing or copying tests, all of which they try regularly, with success. "Look," one student said, "I have to submit a 71 per cent average to get to York University. I'll do anything to keep that average up. I've never stolen anything in my life like in a store or anything, but when it comes to something as important as your future, when you know you won't get caught, you don't think twice about cheating. You just do it."

It's an attitude Montreal students put to practice during province-wide, standardized examinations in the spring of 1990. Somehow, students got a copy of the tests for grade 10 history and grade 11 economics. Quebec's department of education discovered the scam and annuled the test results of 1,400 students in nine schools. Jim MacKinnon, the principal of Lindsay Place, one of the schools involved, said it was "ludicrous" to think that the exams had only made their way into the hands of students in the nine schools. "There are bound to be some other youngsters beating the system," he said.

So the game of school twists its way into a paradox. Business leaders believe competition is the most efficient way to sort the bright from the not-so-bright. As they push to have more of what they see as natural selection in schools, the stakes get higher and students do whatever they must to get the credentials that keep them on the winning path. Rote learning gets rewarded, some teachers water down their courses, and, in the end, credentials are devalued. Add to this the battering of dignity suffered by "losers" and the intense pressure placed on some "winners," and the clearest victor in the game of school is the fear of failure.

6

PUNCH PRESS EDUCATION

Math teacher John Major,* a tall hulk of a man, slowly paced the front of the classroom with the authority and suspicion of a foreman surveying his workers. His grade 11 students at Coal Harbor High School in Nova Scotia were tightly packed into five straight rows, their backs to the large open windows behind them. It was the last period of the day and it was hot. In the open fields surrounding the school, students hung out in groups enjoying the sun. Classes sat half empty and the English class next to Major's was cancelled because only one student showed up. But Major's class was full and quiet, except for the scratching of pens, the odd sigh, and, for a moment, the shrill sounds of Def Leppard leaping through the windows from a radio outside. Major waited until the musical shrieks faded and then gave another exercise. For almost an hour, Major had his students going non-stop. The timing, the beat, was as regular and sharp as a punch press: matrix, transposed matrix, orthogonal matrix; question, answer, question, answer. Then a quick exercise and on to the next round. "I want to get all the loose ends of this chapter finished today," he said to the class.

"Nothing ever stops here," he told me as the students worked in silence. "We have too much material to cover. The key is to keep on

* Not his real name

driving them, to step on them. I let them know where they stand. If they can't hack it, they shouldn't be in here."

This, after all, was the honours class, the select group of teenagers who next year, if they passed, would be in the advanced math course. "If you think these kids are good, wait till we weed more of them out," he said.

Major, considered one of the school's top math teachers, had a particular fondness for the image of crushing people. "If you don't control them at first, you don't control them at the end," he said. "The first two months, I step on them, no one speaks out. I control them, simple as that. It's like training a dog."

"School makes you feel like a robot," said Laura Zazulak, a student in the advanced academic program at Toronto's Central High School of Commerce. "The bell rings, we file into class, we do our work, then the bell rings and we leave. It's like beginning of story, end of story. They talk *at* us and we're expected to sit there and digest it all and then spit it out for the final exam. And that's suppose to make us a better person? I don't think it does."

Students often use mechanical metaphors to describe their schooling experience. This is not surprising since so much of school functions like a machine. Its rigidly hierarchical structure, its sorting and slotting process, and the dominant teaching method in classrooms are all essentially mechanical forms – the major nuts and bolts of the hidden curriculum. Schools use these forms to try to preserve and reproduce the existing culture. Preservation, as far as schools are concerned, requires order and order means hierarchy, sequence, and control; hence, the factory model. There is nothing evil in wanting order. Without it, survival would be precarious. But the kind of order imposed by schools is one that tries to grind students down into clumps of meat. The order flows from the top down and is intended to keep everyone in their allotted place along as straight and narrow a line as possible. To stray from this linear obsession is to be branded a rebel. And yet to remain in the approved slots, to perform in keeping with the linear flow, is alienating to both student and teacher. "Form follows function" is an architectural axiom that in one sense applies to schools. If the function is to develop

students who "fit" into a stratified society without kicking and screaming, then the linear grind of schools is generally effective. But if the stated goals of schools are to be taken seriously, if developing critical and
questioning thinkers is their objective, then we're in big trouble. The
factory model of schools rejects students and teaching methods that
don't fit, the way a compact disc player spits out a warped disc.

The pillar of this linear structure, the element that makes it seem
"natural" and defeats attempts to tamper with it, is the way Western
culture perceives time. Principals of inner-city schools, such as Harold
Doucet and Robert Penner, typically complain that their students have
no respect for the time clock. Children from inner-city communities,
they say, tend to come and go as they please, disregarding the school's
schedule as though functioning on a different clock. Indeed, Robert
Penner of Vancouver's Grace Elementary School sees as one of his
main duties the task of wrenching children out of their "circadian
rhythms" and planting them firmly on a linear track of time. Circadian
rhythms are a problem for principals and teachers because they get in
the way of an early step in the socialization task of schools: getting children to internalize the clock's tick as a pulse in their central nervous
systems. More than anything else, that's what Karen Riley's math drill
with the tape recorder was all about: training children to work to the
linear beat of the clock. The punch press beat of John Major's classroom indicated that his students had learned this lesson of the hidden
curriculum.

In his book *The Silent Language*, American anthropologist Edward T.
Hall argues that Western societies are locked into an assembly-line view
of time. He calls it monochronic time: tasks are performed one at a time
and sequentially within a set schedule. According to this system, value
lies in getting the job done by following set procedures; nurturing relationships among people is of little importance. It's a mode that Hall says
characterizes the world of business, the professions, and large bureaucratic organizations. Not surprisingly, it's the frame of mind preferred by
men. Hall contrasts monochronic time with the polychronic: a time frame
in which people concentrate on doing several things at once. Here, meeting a schedule takes a back seat to developing relationships. There's more
sensitivity to the context in which the work takes place, and workers have
more freedom to decide when the task should be completed. According

to Hall, it's a concept of time found in North American Indian and Latin cultures and, generally speaking, more often in women than in men.

In another book, *The Hidden Dimension,* Hall notes that the way we see time has much to do with how we structure our space. With our minds thinking in straight lines, we build along straight and narrow models, constructing roads and towers on tight right angles, as if by a god of perpendicularity it were a law decreed. The Italian piazza or Spanish plaza, on the other hand, is an architectural example of a society that sees life in a more polychronic way. By their very nature, city squares encourage people to come together in a collective, singular whole.

Despite the rule of the straight line, people can't help relating in a polychronic fashion, even though such scenes are, at the very least, cause for discomfort, if not police action. The polychronic was alive and well during a basketball tournament at St. Patrick's School in Halifax while I was visiting. The tournament was a yearly event that brought together a dozen or so teams from Ontario, the Maritimes, and New York State. As far as the black community was concerned, it was much more than a sports event. People came and went throughout the day. They gathered as much outside the gym as they did inside. Someone had parked a Cadillac with tinted windows, spoked hubcaps, and a polished, warm, brown gleam in front of the gym's entrance. It acted like an anchor, gently holding together the whirl of human activity that surrounded it. A man with sunglasses used the shade of the car's bumper to shield his case of beer from the mid-day sun. He offered drinks non-stop, sometimes giving them away, sometimes selling them. Beside him, a man was drinking. He was thin, slightly hunched, with a cap, round wire-rimmed sunglasses, a goatee, and slacks rolled up above his ankles. He held a can of beer while cooing over the smiling baby of a tall, stunning woman who leaned on the Cadillac, posing for pictures. She was joined by another young mother and her twins, whose eyes were eagerly taking in all the activity around them while their Daddy followed them with a movie camera. The toddlers caused a slight sensation with their silver and black tracksuits and matching caps. The sight of these baby rappers seemed to please an enormous woman bopping to rap music, a motion that originated from a pronounced twitching of her shoulders sending waves of flesh crashing down her thighs and back. Her sweatshirt proclaimed: "I may be fat but you're ugly and I can diet . . ." Everyone seemed wrapped in a soft sensuality, a celebration of the body that is socially unacceptable unless objectified to sell consumer goods. Nothing was sequential, nothing was linear; it was whole.

The same could be said for students hanging out at the street corner at Pelham and Hugo avenues in a working-class neighbourhood of west Toronto. Situated in front of a corner store directly across from Edmund Rice High School, it is the exclusive territory of about 25 young men and a handful of young women. Here, they usually congregate before school starts, during lunchtime, and for about an hour or so at the end of the day. School administrators see them as troublemakers. To some students, they're "the rockers," as defined by the broad category of music they prefer. To most, however, they're simply "the gang that hangs out at the corner store." For those doing the hanging out, the attraction is obvious: "Everything happens at this corner, you know, this is where it's at," one student says.

The scene on one spring day is typical of most sunny days throughout the year. Several teens lean against a Camaro, its passenger door open, distorted rock sounds blaring from the car stereo. A row of students sit on the storefront ledge, smoking and occasionally jostling each other. A few others stand talking to a man from the neighbourhood who is walking his dog. Spilling from the corner onto the street is a group of guys, their jean or black leather jackets having replaced maroon pullovers as incongruous additions to their Catholic school uniforms: white shirt, maroon tie, grey slacks, and black shoes. The alteration complements the roles they've carved for themselves on the street. One teenager, a member of a local gang called the "Lost Boys," seems intent on refining a macho strut. Several others jump from group to group. They're the floaters. "You know, they float around and take advantage of you, like they bum smokes, things like that," says Paul Perreira, an 18-year-old student. A sexuality charges the corner like an electrical current, surging with the passing of girls or the screech of Camaros taking the S-curve of the street at Formula One speeds.

"If you look at everybody over here," says one student, "they're all smoking and they're all talking to each other. It's a place where people come and show off. It's like they come with their cars, you know. That's all it is, it's a show." But on another level, much more is happening. In his book, *Schooling as a Ritual Performance*, Canadian educator Peter

McLaren provides a detailed ethnographic study of the unstructured street culture of working-class youths. These youths are immersed, McLaren says, in the ethos of play; they are acting in a profoundly polychronic way reminiscent of their childhood. This sets the stage for a clash of time frames when they enter the school, where they're required to perform "hard work" in a rigid and sequential nature – that is, in a monochronic mode. For the students, it amounts to a relentless assault, a wedge driven between mind and body that to varying degrees they all try to resist.

The clash of a polychronic culture with a monochronic system is one reason working-class students don't do as well in school as those from more affluent homes. The middle class is more in time with the beat of the clock and therefore more able to fit into the school's sequential structure and approach. It's another example of the kind of "cultural capital" that counts in schools, even though it has more to do with the beat of machines than the rhythm of humans.

At St. Patrick's School in Halifax, teacher Neil Hudson was about to begin his grade 9 English class. He handed me a poem from one of his students, Bobby Conrad, and then started dictating notes on how stories are constructed. "The theme is expressed through plot and characters . . . it transcends time and place . . ."

"Sir, are we going to take notes all class?"

"Yes, note-taking is a skill that you'll need in school."

"But we'll be so tired we won't be able to write next period."

There were only a dozen or so students, spread out in pairs, mostly at desks against the side and back walls. In the front and middle of the class were empty desks.

"Sir, how many more subtitles do we have to take down?"

"Lots, Jamie. Just be quiet and take it down."

Bobby Conrad sat near the door. His poem, which he had written on his own initiative, was entitled, "The Nations fool":

The time has come!
Death is on the way.

My mind is clouded by a dreary haze of
fear,
Bodies lying everywhere,
It's like the nation went out to play and never returned for
supper.
Once we believed in god, now it's sad
to say that we only have tomorrow.
Politicians hide them selves away from
reality.
Why should they go out and fight.
At one time people listened to the
pleasant sounds of the nations music
station.
Now they're listening to the roar of the nations fool.

The pessimism is disquieting, but it reflects the fatalism that shrouds most teenagers today. Bobby Conrad was thinking in engaging images, even though his punctuation was a bit off and his handwriting was almost illegible, making his life in school precarious.

Bobby was soft-spoken and inclined to break out into a shy smile. "I'm kind of a quiet person. I don't say too much. I like writing. It was back in grade 1 or 2 when the trouble started. Because I was so quiet, the teacher didn't pay too much attention to me." As he spoke, I heard the voice of Alice Moriarty, the St. Patrick's teacher who had suffered a similar fate as a student.

Bobby had failed grades 3, 4, and 9. He was 17 years old and in grade 9. In his poem, he said, he had tried to imagine a nuclear holocaust – the result of politicians high on power. His solution was simple: "I think they should take all the politicians, put them in a big wrestlemania and have them fight each other."

Growing up in Halifax's inner city had taught Bobby about the realities of life. "Life's about pushing and getting pushed," he said. "The problem with the guys in power is that they do all the pushing and they don't know much about being shoved." Ironically, but perhaps not surprisingly, Bobby Conrad, a kid who had a problem with authority, wanted to become a narcotics officer. But his teacher feared he might never graduate and instead end up as one of those people stamped "loser" by the system.

"Unfortunately he's the square peg and he doesn't fit into the system. It's unlikely he'll succeed," Neil Hudson said. The following year Bobby was due to enter a full-fledged high school and Hudson believed the kind of assembly-line program that John Major practiced would spit him out.

"At some point there's going to be too much emphasis on form, on structured format, on regimented exercises, and assigned writing topics," Hudson said. "Bobby's not good at that. He fits the holistic language approach. He needs total freedom to choose his own material. He's the type who likes analysing things." Analysis requires looking at the world right side up, upside down, and sideways, John Polanyi's "inspired groping." But it is an unpopular mode of thought in a school system obsessed with sequence. Yet, as much as he hates it, Hudson believed schools didn't have a choice. "I see the workplace as being confining and I feel to a certain degree we have to prepare students for that atmosphere."

The way teachers conduct their classes goes a long way towards preparing students to do as they are told in the workplace. Bernard Shapiro suggests that the complexities of a modern technological environment require a "radical rethinking" of teaching methods. As Ontario's deputy minister of education, Shapiro spent a day each week observing classrooms. He was not impressed. "They're the classrooms I myself attended and they're being taught the way I was taught," he said. "I think perhaps we might have overdone it on the stability side."

Teachers talk at students as though they are talking into a tape-recorder. Being talked at by teachers comes a close second to being bored in the long list of complaints from students. Of course, being bored is often a result of being talked at, a practice that dates back to the establisment of the earliest Canadian schools in the eighteenth century. Studies have found that up to 80 per cent of the talk that goes on in classrooms comes from the mouths of teachers. *The Teaching Experience*, a 1988 study of almost 6,000 Ontario high school teachers by Alan King, a sociologist at Queen's University, found that advanced-level courses were dominated by the lecture method of teaching or by the Socratic method. Students are unequivocal about their reaction to these forms of teaching: the lecture mode is especially conducive to daydreaming, and the question and answer format of the Socratic method is an exercise in giving teachers the answers they expect. "The trick is to figure out what the teacher wants," said a high school student in Alliston, Ontario, echoing the words of Michelle, the North Toronto pupil who described school as a game. "You do that and you get the marks." In the general and basic streams, King found that teachers tended to have students do seatwork independently, usually filling in the blanks on worksheets.

These different teaching styles are based on control and "transmission." The transmission method of schooling amounts to spoonfeeding; teachers acting like Moses unveiling the Ten Commandments while students sit passively, mouths open out of habit and necessity, not willingness. "All they want to do is give us facts," said Debbie Maheras, a grade 13 student in the university-bound program at York Collegiate in Toronto. "We memorize them and as soon as you finish the test, you forget about it."

"There's not many people here who remember what they learned in grade 10 science. All you remember is your mark," added Steve Carty, a student in the same class as Maheras.

The transmission method of education is at the structural and pedagogical heart of virtually all public schools in the Canadian system. Certainly elite schools, aware of their mandate to develop social and economic leaders, are far more likely to stress creative thinking skills. But there are few of these schools in the public system. As well, the creative thinking they encourage is exercised within the context of a strong, vested interest for both the school and the student in maintaining the status quo. That, after all, is what parents expect from elite schools and, in this sense, transmission reigns.

Schools dispense content: isolated and sequential bits of information enshrined in provincial curriculums. Getting the right answer is more important than knowing how to solve the problem. In science, for instance, duplicating the results of experiments that countless others have performed is more valued than understanding the process that achieves the results. "It's like following a recipe," admitted Peter Everett, the former head of the Science Teachers Association of Ontario. A highly critical report in 1984 by the Science Council of Canada concluded that in high schools, "the right answer counts most and therefore, answering questions the 'right' way takes precedence over inquiries into real problems." Education professor Gordon Wells was more blunt: "Schools have got it wrong for decades. They're organized around teaching whereas, of course, they should be organized around learning. It's bizarre that somehow or other we got this idea that knowledge and truth and bodies of facts and theories exist out there somehow, and if only we knew how to parcel them up and sequence them and deliver them, then every kid would be able to just accept them."

Despite repeated testimonials from students and evidence from numerous studies, teachers bristle when accused of acting like glorified pablum plungers. That's understandable: There's little dignity to be had for anyone who sees themselves that way. And most teachers honestly don't believe that's what they are doing. By now, the practice seems to have become natural. Teachers themselves went through many years of spoon-feeding. Learning when and how to swallow brought success, the sanctifier of crippling behaviours. In his book *The Meaning Makers: Children Learning Language and Using Language to Learn*, Gordon Wells writes: "Perhaps the most insidious influence of all is our own previous experience. Most of us have had many years of being talked *at*, first as pupils and students and, later, during our professional education, both pre-service and in-service. As a result, we have probably unconsciously absorbed the belief that a teacher is only doing his or her job properly when he or she is talking – telling, commanding, questioning, or evaluating. And, in many cases, that is what we see when we look to our colleagues for a model of successful teaching." In other words, few of today's teachers are equipped to do anything else but spoon-feed children while trying to keep control.

Many of today's teachers were hired when the post-war baby boomers were entering the system between 1960 and 1970. During this period in Ontario, the number of teachers almost tripled as more than 20,000 were hired. Huge enrolments sent school boards scrambling. A common joke among educators was that anyone with a pulse could end up in front of a class. Many of the new teachers, especially those in the elementary grades, were straight out of high school themselves and given only one year of training before being certified. A senior school board administrator in Toronto recalled how some principals cruised these one-year teachers' colleges as though they were singles bars. During this period, wages increased rapidly as teachers' unions became larger and more powerful. (The average salary in Ontario in 1990 was $42,000.) During the 1970s, as enrolments began to decline, this huge bulge of teachers settled into long careers. It's not surprising then that 60 per cent of Ontario teachers are over 40 years old. This makes the establishment of a rapport with students even more difficult than it already is.

Poorly equipped and poorly trained, most teachers faced large classes full of baby-boom children as soon as they started their new jobs. Keeping control of students became a matter of survival. By the late 1980s, little had changed. A 1987 report commissioned by Ontario's ministry of education concluded that "students are being short-changed" by training programs that fill classrooms with new teachers who are unable to teach properly, even though those training programs are more extensive than ever. After completing a three-year university degree, prospective teachers apply for a one-year degree program at faculties of education. But they receive only eight weeks of training in school classrooms. The Ontario report, written by OISE professors Michael Fullan and Michael Connelly, said that this amount of classroom training for student teachers is grossly inadequate. It recommended that after graduating from the one-year program, student teachers should go through a four-year apprenticeship where they would spend much of their time in the classroom. They would receive their teaching certificate only after successfully finishing the apprenticeship. Teachers' unions were fiercely opposed to this idea, arguing that the lengthy apprenticeship would dissuade many from becoming teachers. Faced with this opposition, the government backed off. It decided that teachers would first get their certificate and then enter a one-year apprenticeship program. So regardless of how poorly they perform during their apprenticeship, teachers retain their certificate to teach students. This, Michael Connelly said, "makes a mockery of the certification process."

Currently, applicants to the faculties of education are judged primarily on the basis of marks. According to the Fullan-Connelly report, experience with children is considered important at only a handful of universities in Ontario.

In *The Teaching Experience*, Alan King found that 56 per cent of Ontario high school teachers – including 63 per cent of male teachers –

did not choose teaching as their first career. They were originally drawn to professions such as law, medicine, and engineering and for various reasons – including not having the marks necessary to enter those university programs – settled on teaching. Once a candidate is finally accepted to a faculty of education, the chances of developing a passion for teaching are slim.

Universities have been widely criticized for not taking their faculties of education more seriously. At a speech to Canada's university presidents in 1987, the Ontario deputy minister of education, Bernard Shapiro, described the contribution of universities to the education of Canadian teachers as a "public scandal." In fact, in times of budget cuts a favourite target for university administrators is their faculties of education. At the University of Toronto, for instance, 19 staff positions at the faculty of education were left unfilled for several years until hiring began again in 1988. This kind of stagnancy has major repercussions. Professors in faculties of education have been criticized by teachers' unions, among others, for not keeping up-to-date with new research on education. Their courses continue to separate theory from practice and treat knowledge as isolated bits of information to be mastered and transmitted rather than as fluid, socially constructed stories made up of personal experiences, empirical observations, historical accommodations, and accepted morality. Faculties have also done little to train teachers for the new realities of the multicultural classroom or to deal with sex-stereotyping in the curriculum. In fact, training that attempts to provide new teachers with the ability to understand the social practices that reproduce inequalities is virtually non-existent. "New teachers by and large either don't have a broad social vision or if they do, it gets stunted" by the bureaucratic nature of schools, said Michael Fullan, who became dean of the faculty of education at the University of Toronto after his report on teacher training. Said one principal: "How much social awareness are they taught in university? None. They come out as socializers, not as transformers of society." In short, many become what critical pedagogist Henry Giroux called "clerks of the empire."

Becoming "clerks of the empire" is no great crime in an institution with a mandate to preserve existing culture. Once in the classroom, teachers, like students, are constrained by the school's linear tick, the beat of patriarchy.

In a 1989 study, OISE professor Andy Hargreaves noted that schools function according to monochronic, assembly-line time frames because that pattern is "the prerogative of the powerful" and not because it is more educationally effective or efficient. In schools, as in all other major institutions, those with the power are men. In 1987, there were 269,800 elementary and high school teachers in Canada. Almost 60 per cent of them were women and most of these were in the elementary grades. This percentage hasn't changed much since the early 1980s. Women have fought hard to end the discrimination that has kept them out of administrative positions. So far, they have little to show for it. In 1977, 14 per cent of principals were women. Ten years later, only 16 per cent were women. And the higher up the administrative ladder you go, the bleaker it gets. In Ontario, in mid-1989 for instance, in a province which likes to see itself as being at the forefront of innovative pedagogy, only three of the 120 directors of education at school boards – a position akin to chief executive officer of a corporation – were women.

There's nothing mysterious about why so few women are at the top. For instance, until the mid-1970s in Toronto the old boys' club of principals, which called itself an association, appointed principals virtually free of outside scrutiny. Qualifications were of secondary importance. "It would all depend on whether you had your cottage on the right lake," said Dan Leckie, a former school board chairman. The principals had it their way until a group of reform trustees, which included Leckie, was elected to the Toronto school board in 1969. Most were members of the NDP and they kicked off a decade-long series of reforms that continue to have an impact on schools across the country. Hiring practices were an early target, and the reformers began by instituting a practice of advertising job openings. They also insisted on having a say in the hiring of individuals for key school board positions. One case in particular in 1970 drew the collective ire of the principals' association.

After an extensive search, the board had decided to hire John Bremer as the new director of education. Previously, Bremer had run the school system in Philadelphia and the trustees were impressed by his innovations. He had pioneered a curriculum that incorporated the out-of-school, everyday experiences of students, providing a sense of relevance in the classroom that was previously absent. The fact that Bremer was an American became the focal point of enraged opposition from Toronto principals in their fight with the reform-minded trustees. They took their case to education minister William Davis, who eventually stepped in to veto the appointment on the grounds that Bremer did not hold an Ontario high school principal's certificate.

For women teachers who wish to become principals, the old boys' network remains a formidable barrier. Seeing little hope for progress, some have left the system. While there are a few affirmative action programs around, it will be years before they start to make a difference – if ever.

While men vastly outnumber women teachers in Ontario high schools, half of those under 30 years of age are women. This provides a glimmer of hope for the researchers who in 1988 conducted a survey of the members for the high school teachers' union. "Women give greater weight to items about fairness, caring, and concern for students as individuals," their report said. "Perhaps when women outnumber men these traits will be slightly more evident in schools because policy and programs will reflect the female viewpoint more than they presently do." As many women have found, however, the road to the top is like being funneled through a filtration plant that has been programmed to break down what it defines as impurities, including a view of time (polychronic) that clashes with the patriarchal (monochronic) one.

Traditionally, elementary schools have been a ghetto for women. In his study *Teacher Development and Teachers' Work*, Andy Hargreaves notes that the world of the elementary teacher is deeply polychronic in nature, becoming less so as children move to the higher elementary grades. In the less structured classrooms, children float from one learning centre to another: from painting, to reading, to puzzles, to manipulating clay, to writing, and so on. The teacher moves from one group to another, sometimes working with several children, sometimes one-on-one. The environment is unpredictable and constantly changing, with the teacher's priority being to help children successfully complete the task-in-hand while getting them to co-operate with each other. Her male bosses are not likely to think that way. Their tendency is to impose change according to an assembly-line schedule, without regard for the peculiarities of the elementary classroom.

Hargreaves believes this is a prescription for failure, particularly when trying to implement new programs or reforms. Teachers are often left trying to figure out how to squeeze a new program into their day while still juggling the complex nature of the elementary classroom. Inevitably, the pace of change falls behind schedule, which results in administrators putting more pressure on teachers to meet the timelines, which results in teachers becoming more bogged down in fulfilling their duties, which results in more pressure from bosses. In the end, everyone simply settles for the appearance of change.

Time, normally an invisible source of conflict in schools, became the central issue in a 1987 strike by elementary teachers in seven Metro Toronto school boards. The strike was about equality. Elementary teachers were tired of being treated like second-class citizens, compared to their mostly male high school colleagues. The issue that galvanized the teachers was their demand to have time off during the school day to better prepare for classes. Although some elementary teachers had "prep-time," it wasn't guaranteed in their collective agreement. In contrast, high school teachers had 200 minutes a week to prepare lessons. This discrepancy had everything to do with political clout and nothing to do with workloads. The strike was partly successful when elementary teachers won 100 minutes, but ultimately it seems only to have placed them more firmly under the control of their male bosses.

Teachers are inclined to use their free time in flexible ways, as needed, whether preparing classes or relieving stress. In his study, however, Hargreaves found that administrators did not appreciate this approach and instead sought to control the teachers' preparation time. Most principals demanded that teachers meet with colleagues during this free time, often in specified rooms, regardless of necessity or importance. This Hargreaves sees as part of management's "colonization" of the private space and time of teachers. Instead of treating them like professionals, management seems to be perpetuating the traditional view of the Western capitalist workplace in which employees are inherently lazy and eager to fritter away their time unless there is a rigidly structured, controlled, and supervised environment.

What Hargreaves calls "the culture of fragmented individualism" in schools makes it difficult for teachers to overcome this hierarchical control. Many retreat behind the closed door of the classroom for protection from the judgement of colleagues. Who knows what goes on behind closed doors? Indeed, even for teachers with open minds, the isolation of the classroom presents few opportunities for them to discuss with their peers ways of improving and assessing their performance. Lacking support and faced with students who would rather not be there, teachers feel like soldiers waging a lonely war. They often talk, for instance, of being "on the front lines," or of "the troops acting up." This isolation is fostered by a centralized structure that, since the days of Ryerson, has used teachers as supervised cogs designed to instill a curriculum over which they have little control. How they interpret the curriculum in the classroom is another matter. But the rigidly bureaucratic nature of schools makes it less likely that teachers will rock the boat. Those who try to spark a social conscience in students recognize they are jeopardizing the progress of their careers in a system in which administrative efficiency paves the road to the top.

"If you stand out on the front lawn and start calling for change, you're going to be viewed as a wild-eyed, semi-crazed sort of person because you're going to be questioning some fundamental values in society," said Edmund Rice principal Brother Kieran Murphy. "Sometimes it means your job if you're going to talk about the injustices of society or the fact that you're living in a system that's hypocritical. Those kinds of things follow you right through your career. They're not going to put the disturbers in positions of authority, they want corporate people." Alan King's study suggests Murphy's belief is accurate. Teachers most likely to seek administrative positions, King found, are those who did not choose teaching as a first career.

Spoon-fed by schools and teacher-training programs, faced with students who would rather not be in class, isolated by a bureaucratic structure that promotes passive efficiency and shuns the creativity that flows from questioning, the transmission model of teaching serves as comforting practice for many teachers. Being workers, it's not surprising that teachers are under the same assault of time and space as their students, creating the grounds for solidarity between the two. Dominated by male administrators and locked into an assembly-line system of time, schools alienate both students and teachers. But as with many a natural alliance, power has come between them. Students are the only group below teachers in the school hierarchy and, in their own words, they have had it with the "power trips" of teachers. It all breaks down into an environment where everyone seems to be pushing and being pushed at the same time, creating a kind of petrified frenzy. Anthropologist Edward Hall believes organizations locked in monochronic time tend to lose sight of their original goals and inertia takes over. Such is the case with Canadian schools. Through their assembly-line time frame, schools foster disconnectedness; today is completed in sequence, on schedule, but with no relation to yesterday or tomorrow, creating an education without context.

Structured and operated according to the industrial model, schools and their assembly-line transmission modes are quite simply out of step with their environment as Canada moves from an industrial to a post-industrial society. In post-industrial societies, as McGill University professor Norman Henchey notes, the central activity is "the generation, control, organization, and distribution of information, the forming of patterns of information into knowledge, and the search for perspectives on knowledge, what used to be called the pursuit of wisdom." In his essay prepared for the Canadian Teachers' Federation, "Education for the 21st Century," Henchey states, "Communications replace production and transportation as the key industry and mode of organizing economic activity; the chip replaces the gear and the car as the new social metaphor."

The transmission mode of teaching flows from the linear, sequential structure of schools which, as noted earlier, partly reflected the development of the printing press. In print cultures, information is centralized and flows from the top down, a pattern dramatically altered and undermined by the advent of electronic media. The new methods of communication, particularly television, have restructured social relationships in no less dramatic a way than the shift from an oral to a print culture.

Like all technologies – except of course those designed solely for killing – television enslaves and liberates at the same time. While it's zapping us with white noise, television also undermines the very status quo it essentially tries to maintain. In his book *No Sense of Place: The Impact of Electronic Media on Social Behavior*, Joshua Meyrowitz argues that authority rests on control of information. Electronic media such as

computers and telephones make information accessible to more people
than was the case in print cultures. They allow people to share information without having to adhere to the "proper channels" of an organization's hierarchy. Perhaps the best example is computer "hackers" – often
they are teenagers – who can break into secret government programs or
infect whole systems with killer viruses. Authority is undermined still
further by the way television removes the lustre from traditional positions of power. It has forced politicians out in the open and, like the
Hans Christian Andersen fairy tale, shown children that the emperor has
no clothes.

With television, youths get a front-row seat to adult hypocrisy.
Politicians, for instance, are regularly exposed as fumbling dolts inspired
not by principles but by backroom wheeling and dealing. One example
of this was a documentary aired on CBC's *The Journal* on the NDP leadership convention in November 1989. Using cordless microphones and
other electronic gadgetry, the documentary captured the secret deals that
are the stuff of politics. To hear leadership candidate Simon de Jong
apparently agree to a deal behind closed doors to support Dave Barrett
in return for a $7,000 raise and the job of party whip confirms what
every schoolchild learns early: in politics, the lust for power runs
roughshod over the dignity of principles. Seconds after making the deal,
de Jong met the press, and, when specifically asked, he flatly denied it.
We then watch the sorry but not unusual sight of reporters spreading
the denial to viewers across the country. In the electronic age, privacy
enters the realm of nostalgia, dirty laundry hangs everywhere, and, for
those who know how to "read" television, hidden agendas are revealed.
"One of the ironies of the electronic age," Meyrowitz states, "is that new
media have made completely centralized control technically possible yet
socially unacceptable."

Even the most conservative television shows, such as *Father Knows
Best*, have played a role in weakening traditional relationships of authority. The television series showed children that parents are adept at
assuming different roles for different occasions. In the presence of children, parents are seen as cool, calm, and completely in control. Away
from them, they are shown filled with anxieties and doubts. Television
has taught children that adults consciously conspire to hide things from
them and has exposed what Meyrowitz calls the "secret of secrecy." By

unveiling adult secrets, television blurs the line between adulthood and childhood. This is further illustrated by advertising that depicts child models in provocative adult poses and clothing. Spawned by one technology, the printing press, childhood is being obliterated by another, television.

Print cultures allowed adults to control passage into their world and the grade school system helped regulate that passage. The grade system slowly unveils adult secrets as children became more proficient readers; fifth graders are told more than fourth graders, who in turn are told more than third graders, and so on down the line. Television bypasses this linear sequence. "Through television news and entertainment, children learn too much about the nature of 'real' life to believe the ideals their teachers try to teach them," Meyrowitz says. The myth of the all-knowing teacher is pierced, yet schools continue to function as though it were not. When children walk into the classroom, they bring in an image of society that differs from that held by children of earlier generations. The age-graded curriculum flounders in "culture lag." For students, schooling becomes a waste of time, an experience to be endured, like a jail sentence. Meyrowitz states: "The current difficulty maintaining school discipline and of teaching students reading and other subjects may lie more in the antiquated *structure* of the school than in a sudden change in children's basic abilities or willingness to learn."

Hopelessly impaled by hierarchy and rigid linear sequences, schools are seen as increasingly irrelevant by a youth culture profoundly plugged into the electronic age. This linear obsession fuels resistance and reinforces the biggest crisis in Canadian schools today – a crisis of literacy.

7

LITERACY

Developing literate students is the professed aim of all groups trying to reform Canadian schools. It seems everyone is jumping on the literacy bandwagon. Literacy, or rather the lack of it, is a national concern. In a speech on education in August 1989, Prime Minister Brian Mulroney lamented that "17 per cent of Canadian high school graduates are functionally illiterate." To be functionally illiterate is to be unable to do things like read and understand the right dosage to take from an ordinary bottle of cough syrup, recognize the long distance charges on a telephone bill (although given the puzzling makeup of the latter, one has to wonder who the illiterates are), or follow instructions for a household appliance. Mulroney's 17 per cent figure came from a definition used in a 1987 Southam national survey on literacy. The survey, the first of its kind in Canada, concluded that 4.5 million Canadians were functionally illiterate. In the summer of 1988, after the Southam survey was released, Mulroney announced a total of $110 million in funding for programs to develop functional literacy.

The fact that so many people can't do these "functional" things is tragic indeed. More tragic, however, is the consequence that functional literacy has become the goal – for some, more like the mission – of the most dogged and influential groups steering school reform into the grim looking-glass of the twenty-first century. Essentially, groups fighting for functional literacy have coalesced under the back-to-basics banner. Business groups are its most powerful members. Back-to-basics supporters proudly cling to the puzzling position that students who can think creatively will be developed by making the school system more rigid and mechanistic than it already is, hence their push for such items as standardized examinations. They emphasize the traditional way of teaching literacy through repeated drilling of the cherished three Rs: reading, writing, and arithmetic. In reading and writing, the stress is generally on "decoding"; that is, the ability to sound words on a page.

The other camp vying for dominance in the literacy debate supports what's called holistic language. The ability to sound words on a page, it maintains, does little to ensure that students understand what they are reading. This camp stresses a complex process in which children learn to arrive at their own conclusions, rather than accepting what they read as gospel.

The back-to-basics movement has managed to make functional literacy the national objective. Indeed, it fits well with the Progressive Conservative Party's campaign to further shackle schools with the spirit of "international competitiveness." From this point of view, a nation that can follow instructions is a nation prepared to compete.

Back-to-basics supporters have créated the misleading impression that they alone uphold the three Rs. Presumably, if the other side has its way, it would turn children into philosophers who could somehow think without knowing how to read, write, and count. In fact, the aim of holistic language supporters is to achieve mastery of the three Rs while taking literacy far beyond the functional realm. It all comes down to how one defines literacy. If functional literacy is the definition, then drilling children will suffice. If more is expected, then a completely different classroom approach is needed. In the end, the difference is between empowering students to think creatively and molding them into fatalists who passively follow instructions.

Essentially, functional literacy means more of what now dominates in schools – a Karen Riley-style of drilling. The more blanks students fill in, the more likely they will be to memorize it. Vancouver educator Frank Smith derisively calls this the "rabb_t method." It begins immediately, in kindergarten. Here's a simple example documented by Toronto education professor Gordon Wells: The teacher had just finished reading, without interruptions, the picture storybook, *Little Black Sambo*, to a group of five-year-olds. Then the drilling began:

Teacher: What did the first tiger take off Little Black Sambo?

Child 1: Shirt. (Teacher does not respond.)

Child 2: His coat.

Teacher: His coat that his mummy had made. Do you remember when his mummy made it – what colour was it?

Children: Red.

Teacher: Red, yes. What did the second tiger take?

Children: Trousers.

Teacher: His trousers. What did the third tiger take?

Children: Shoes.

And so on. Question, answer, question, answer. The story is treated as bits of information to be recalled on demand. The teacher leads and the children follow, spewing forth appropriate answers that test their recollection of facts. What the children individually get out of the story is utterly unimportant, as though the written text and its interpretation were carved in stone. This, according to Wells, is the dominant mode of interaction with texts in school. It falls far short of any meaningful kind of literacy.

Wells' 15-year study of schools in Bristol, England, published in his 1986 book *The Meaning Makers,* established him as an internationally recognized expert in literacy. He left England to escape Margaret Thatcher's axe on university budgets and went to be a professor at the Ontario Institute for Studies in Education, where he continues his work in Toronto classrooms. In his research he identifies four levels of literate behaviour that everyone, regardless of age, is capable of using: performative, functional, informational, and epistemic.

The performative level is a simple understanding of what's needed for reading and writing to occur: a recognition that a letter written on paper conveys a meaning. Of course, it's a prerequisite for all higher forms of interaction with texts. The functional level uses texts as a means for action. Reading the instructions for a household appliance falls into this category. The informational level is used when gathering information and communicating it. Completing a questionnaire or using a reference book to find out facts is an example of informational literacy. The emphasis, for instance, is on obtaining knowledge from a science textbook and recording what has been found. The validity of the knowledge is not questioned. The knowledge is simply transmitted from textbook to student. Reading is believing. Wells says it is the dominant mode of schooling. Finally, the epistemic level – the most sophisticated level of literacy – recognizes a text as a work in progress, a provisional attempt by the writer to capture what he or she currently understands about an issue. Putting it down on paper provokes the writer and other readers to work further on the idea, interpreting and refining its meaning. As Wells puts it, when readers ask, "Does it make sense in relation to my own experience?" they are engaging with the text epistemically.

Wells' classifications point to a dangerous irony in the present debate on literacy. Schools are now stuck in the informational mode of literacy, the transmission of knowledge as unquestioned truths. If the back-to-basics people got their way, schools would regress to the functional mode. Once again, we seem intent on looking forward and falling back.

Vancouver's Grace Elementary School provides a graphic example of the back-to-basics approach to literacy and its corollary of spoon-feeding. Like most schools, Grace teaches reading and writing by using thick workbooks bursting with blanks to be filled in. One such workbook for level 6 students was published by Ginn and Company in 1977. The following are some sample exercises with the skills they're intended to fine-tune in parentheses:

(Comprehension) Make sentences from these words. Write the sentence: trees Men cut tall

(Comprehension) Read each question. Put X on the lines by the two sentences that tell how the people or things are alike: How are computers and people alike? ___They both can work. ___They are both machines. ___They both can give answers to questions.

(Decoding) Circle the word that completes each sentence: Will the doctor (chips check) the men?

(Vocabulary) Underline the word that completes each sentence. Then read the story: In the morning, the children walked in the (soft noise) snow.

The workbook is 126 pages long and is likely to keep Grace students sitting quietly at their desks for many hours. Another motivation for teachers to use it is that it takes up little time and energy to mark. But after children write, "Men cut tall trees," what do they really comprehend aside from the cold logic that turns the muddled words into an unquestioned act? And if computers and people are alike in how they work and answer questions, then why aren't they both machines? And how many children circle "soft" even while knowing that footsteps in the dead of winter can sound like the grievous creaking of a wooden boat fighting the insistence of the sea? These points may seem minor, but it's likely that these and many more questions will jump into children's heads when they are sitting alone, fumbling with the exercises and being bombarded by isolated bits of information. Yet, fully aware of the nature of the game, they will circle the words they know the teacher will mark as being right. The transmitted lesson is that students should do as expected.

Also popular in the traditional mode of teaching children to read and write is the use of "SRA labs." They're the colour-coded series of stories that test children with multiple choice questions on plot and vocabulary. When I visited, Bill Barnes' grade 5 and 6 class at Grace was hard at work on the SRA stories, which were written at an institute in the U.S. in 1957. If students were on the series of blue stories, they needed three perfect or near-perfect scores to advance to the brown series. The students read the stories, answered the questions on the card, and then gave it to Barnes for correction. Barnes and I sat at a table at the back of the class.

Barnes to a student: "You'll never get on to the next card if you keep making mistakes like this. Seven (mistakes), that's 21 off, that's 79. You had better be up in the 90s next time."

To another student: "Oh, you do the same thing he does – read it 60 miles an hour."

To the class: "You guys just whip through these without understanding what you're doing." To me: "They just blitz it but they don't take it in. They read the words but they don't think about what the words mean." This, of course, is exactly the problem with the SRA series and similar drills. They teach speed instead of reflection.

The *pièce de résistance* in the traditional mode of teaching reading and writing is the Basal reader, a standardized text for students at various grade levels. Karen Riley offered that these readers have been criticized for using formal language, such as "with that he departed." But no matter, she said, it does the job. She quickly flipped through its pages, and the reader seemed a carousel of pristine middle-class images.

This ooze of suburban mores is a big reason the reader is so highly valued by Grace's teachers.

Principal Robert Penner saw it as a kind of anti-anarchy device. "If we develop a society where we don't have common values, we're in deep shit. And that's coming. The growth industry in this town is steel bars and shotguns for homes. That's because of the lack of shared values. Plus, in a multicultural society like Canada, probably the most you and I have in common is the Basal reader we had in grades 1 and 2. Those are the linkages that we have and if we don't keep them going . . . . Sure, you're saying the school is a socializing device. You're damn right it is, there's no doubt about it. The socializing process of school is *the* process!"

This middle-class bias, shared by the comprehension workbook, raises the question of what the images say to Grace's inner-city children. What does it tell them about where the "right" answers are found? Certainly not in their highrise apartments or in their single-parent families or anywhere in their ghettoized community for that matter. The answer, the "truth," lies in that two-storey home, in that modern kitchen, in that family with the pasted-on smiles, in that lawn that's permanently manicured, that picket fence that never peels, and all the other forms of mom's apple pie deceptions. It's *there,* so shut up and open wide. In the end, the back-to-basic accoutrements of Basal readers and workbooks impose a passivity on all students, regardless of class. And with some, the transmission comes replete with a pistol-whipping of their dignity.

The SRA series and the Basal reader are both colour-coded. Through the colours, learning to read is transformed into a competition and used more as a way of streaming students than anything else. Both Bill Barnes and Karen Riley used reading groups. Barnes said he began each year by giving the students a standardized reading test to decide where they belonged. He had three groups: the Lizards, Sky A, and Sky B. The reading level, according to Barnes, ranged from a low of grade 2 in the Lizards to a high of grade 7 or 8 in Sky A. They read from a Basal reader twice a week, once to Barnes and once to a teaching assistant. The goal, of course, was to move up to the next group. Karen Riley said: "The kids know, it starts at a very young age. They know they're going to be in the pink reader or the orange reader and they look forward to moving into the next group. Like my grade 3s, right now I'm calling them grade 4 minuses and that makes them think that they're really big shots because they think they're grade 4s."

"I'm not on blue yet," said Jason, fumbling his SRA story. Jason was in Bill Barnes' grade 4 and 5 class. He looked down at the table, embarrassed.

"Blue's the good one," said Barnes, ticking away sententiously at Jason's answers: right, wrong, right, wrong, wrong.

"I can't wait to get to blue."

"Why?" Barnes asked.

"Because everybody's on it. Is anyone on orange?"

At the front of the class, on the blackboard, was written "BAD PEOPLE." Underneath it was the name "Jason."

Jason, of course, was learning much more than the limited kind of reading skills the SRA labs teach. He was learning one of the tougher lessons of the hidden curriculum – for others to win, he's got to lose. Jason wanted to progress in the reading series not because he was interested in becoming a better reader, but because he wanted the same badge of dignity the teacher gave to those students at the higher levels. This is how the natural enthusiasm and curiosity of children get beaten out of them at an early stage in their schooling. The most basic function of schooling, the teaching of reading, is turned into an attack on the children's self-esteem. Can anyone blame Jason if he learns to detest reading? Somewhere in their earnestness to drill the basics into children, schools have forgotten that reading and counting have little to do with being a sensitive and kind human being. Shouldn't that be as much a function of schooling as teaching children how to read?

Barnes believed that children want to compete. "Whether you have competition or not, they make it among themselves. Especially around report card time. You give them their marks and you don't advertise it to anybody else. Well, they're always checking up on each other to see who's got As, you know. I mean some of them get money from their parents for a B or an A; you know, their parents bribe them. They use it as an incentive, as a reward."

Barnes might have been suggesting that competition is innate or that it begins in the home, but he did his share to sustain it. Every Friday the students had a spelling test. If they spelled all 18 words correctly they got $1 million in play money. But each mistake cost the students $100,000. At the end of the year they could use their money to buy games and comic books from Barnes. "Some kids already have $20 million saved up," Barnes said.

Like so many teachers, Barnes also gave students marks for neatness in their notebooks. "The cleanest notebooks are not too hard to spot," he said. "Some of them have drawings all on the outside of them, or they'll put out only two of them when you know they've got five. Some they just don't want you to see." A girl gave Barnes her notebook for correction and he added, "Some of them use colour like this, I don't know why." The girl had underlined her answers with six red lines, in the shape of an inverted pyramid. She had a smile on her face.

Schools operate under the false assumption that rewarding children with prizes will encourage them to work harder. According to child psychologist Margaret Donaldson, a substantial amount of evidence has indicated that if an activity is rewarded by a prize that has nothing to do with the task at hand, then the activity is less likely to be performed in a voluntary manner when prizes are absent. It is also less likely to be enjoyed.

One of the several experiments Donaldson wrote about in her book, *Children's Minds*, was conducted in a nursery school. One group of children was given drawing materials and told they would get prizes for drawing. Another group was given the same materials but prizes weren't even mentioned. Some days later, both groups of children were given an opportunity to use the same drawing materials along with other toys. The expectation was that those children whose drawing efforts had been "reinforced" by prizes would spend a longer amount of time drawing. But the opposite happened: Those who had received the prizes spent a smaller portion of their time drawing.

The buzzer rang to end the period. It was the same sound you hear in old war movies when submarines are submerged. Bill Barnes asked me what class I was going to visit next.

"Karen Riley's," I replied.

"Oh, her class probably works on remote control by this time of year," he said.

Moments later I walked into Riley's tape-recorded drill and realized that Barnes was serious.

■

Grace's traditional approach to reading and writing is repeated in schools across the country. But there is a contradiction. Officially, Grace has adopted the holistic language program as part of the Vancouver school board's attempt to improve the performance of inner-city students. In Barnes' class, for instance, the children are asked to do several drafts of stories before settling on a final one. Barnes also allows them to come up with their own ideas, telling them they should write from what they know and feel. This forms part of the holistic writing process but, judging from the way Barnes conducted the rest of his class, the overall impact of the holistic program was minimal. Clearly the school was still entrenched in the back-to-basics model. As far as Karen Riley, for one, was concerned, more drilling was needed, not less.

"I've gone right back," she said. "I've gone through the phase where it's inherent in the child, you let the creativity come out, you just give him a piece of paper and he'll write reams and reams. That can work, but how can you write reams and reams if you don't know the words and if you're incapable of writing it down? So basic skills are very important. So I'm kind of a reactionary, I guess."

The situation at Grace says much about the holistic movement's predicament. Its method and goals have been generally adopted by several provinces in curriculum guidelines, but its use in the classroom has been uneven at best. And as its supporters try to convince more teachers of the program's value, they're fighting a rear-guard action to fend off the back-to-basics onslaught.

The word holistic comes from the Greek *holos,* meaning whole. It refers to an understanding of the universe as complete and interrelated, unable to be broken down into the sum of its elementary particles. This is in complete contradiction to the dominant Cartesian view of the universe as machine. The holistic approach is also at odds with the assembly-line style of sorting and slotting students into boxes. This clash with the traditional, linear structure of school helps to explain the limited growth of the holistic movement.

In Canadian schools, holistic language programs have been growing in prestige since 1965, and one of their most influential proponents is Don Rutledge, a brilliant educator who retired as associate director of the Toronto Board of Education in 1988, after planting and nurturing the seeds of what he has described as a revolution. It began on a hot August day in 1965 when James Britton, one of Rutledge's mentors and an internationally renowned linguist, gave a talk on "Language and Learning" to a group of teachers at the Toronto board. At the time, Britton was in the vanguard of what has become the holistic language movement. Britton told the audience: "If man symbolizes experience, the representation is something which lasts in time, which doesn't disappear when the phenomena disappears, and therefore can be worked upon. And since it lasts in time and can be worked upon, it can be worked upon jointly, and this seems to me to be the key to it."

In Toronto, holistic language was first seriously considered in the late 1960s, after the school board came under intense pressure from parents who believed their children were getting a raw deal. In elementary schools many students were being streamed into courses for handicapped learners, and those lucky enough to make it to high school were placed in dead-end vocational programs. Inner-city parents formed a group called the Trefann Court Mothers and, with the help of community activists, demanded changes from the school board that made headlines for weeks. In the end, they simply wanted what more affluent parents take for granted: a school that at the very least would teach their children to read, write, and count.

Leaders of the group included three women: Noreen Gaudette, Barbara Dawson, and Lisa Guiren. Among them they had 22 children, none of whom had made it to university – most had never finished high school. The women now say that their children were promoted through the grades even though they had difficulty reading and writing. Teachers never bothered telling them that their children were struggling until the kids were about to enter high school, and by then their educational fates were sealed. Most of them were streamed into vocational programs.

The women described coming up against an education system that, at every turn throughout their unsuccessful push for change, tried to put them in their socially ordained place. One conservative trustee said at the time that expecting immigrant or poor children to compete equally with white middle-class children was like racing donkeys with horses.

"That's the way they made me feel, that there was a deficiency or something and that it was hereditary," Lisa Guiren said.

"They had a meeting at Park School and they told us our kids were slow because they didn't walk until a certain age, they didn't get their first tooth until a certain age and I thought, 'What the hell has that got to do with my child learning how to read?' " added Barbara Dawson.

We were sitting in Barbara Dawson's kitchen, and the women were describing the attempts by some teachers and board officials to blame the low achievement of their children on their failure as parents. "They said it was our whole environment, it was downtown, inner city, you know, we didn't know anything so how could we expect our kids to know anything. And that we never had any books or newspapers in the house," Guiren said.

"Oh, I hate that so much!" Noreen Gaudette said. "Did you ever hear the one, 'These poor children never saw a cow, only on the baking soda box.' My God!"

Outside of school the attitude was also less than hospitable. In the early 1960s, parts of their neighbourhood were being razed to make room for subsidized housing projects like Regent Park. People went from being homeowners to living in subsidized housing, and Mayor Phil Givens' response was simply: "You can't make progress in a growing city without some people getting hurt." Part of the progress involved labeling the neighbourhood a slum area in order to justify demolishing it.

"I lived here all my life and I had never heard our neighbourhood called that. All of a sudden we were considered trash," Gaudette said.

The area became an attraction of sorts. Schools from the suburbs would organize walking tours so the children could get a first-hand look at the slums. Gaudette said she almost died of shame one day when her grandson was taken on one of the tours. While standing in front of her home he was told, "This is where the poor people live."

"I've always been ashamed, I guess, and I was born and raised here," Guiren said. "For 32 years I worked at the post office and I never told anybody where I lived, I'd say downtown or The Beach." Guiren's reaction is not unlike students in segregated vocational schools who are ashamed to admit they attend such schools. The weight of labels has sunk deep inside to shape how inner-city people see themselves. Even though they clearly rebelled against the school system, some of the mothers couldn't help feeling like they were stepping out of line.

"I felt inferior," Lisa Guiren said, recalling meetings her group had with teachers and principals. "Yeah, I always knew my place and I still do."

The battles of the Trefann Court Mothers pressured reform-minded trustees to give more resources to inner-city schools. In 1975, at the urging of Don Rutledge and others, the school board agreed to officially implement the holistic language approach at Dundas Street Public School in the city's east end. Rutledge invited James Britton to help out.

Holistic theory has five central tenets: 1) build on the abilities and experiences each child brings to the classroom; 2) consider the desires of the child for writing and other exercises; 3) let children work together in small groups; 4) expose them to good literature, especially poetry; and 5) these features should form the basis of all subjects and not be restricted to English classes.

Building on what the child brings to school takes the accepted theory that learning should match the child's level of development a step further. Schools test children on what they can do independently. This determines what psychologists call the "actual" developmental level. However, to grade children exclusively on what they can do on their own is to stunt their potential. It does nothing to help them expand the horizons of their development.

Russian psychologist Lev Semyonovich Vygotsky identified what he called the "zone of proximal development," a mental area consisting of those immatured functions that children can perform with the help of others. It is common for children who have the same actual development to have very different zones of proximal development. So to advance their development it is far more important to test what children can do with the help of others than to test what they can do on their own. In his book *Mind in Society*, Vygotsky wrote: " . . . what a child can do with assistance today, she will be able to do by herself tomorrow."

This is one reason group work is an important part of the holistic approach. By talking in groups children guide themselves through their infinite zones of budding development. Through talk, children use their own experiences and prior knowledge to clarify and refine their interpretation of information: the essence of literate thinking. This is what

James Britton means by his oft-quoted phrase, "shaping at the point of utterance." The mind exists in a perplexing wave of images that forms a continuous story. The second we utter a word, we free it from a wave of symbolic thought and give it a clarity that demands contemplation. We press on with our utterance, somewhat tentatively, not completely sure of the full shape of the thought, secure in the knowledge that we've succeeded before, yet hesitant about what we're going to come up with this time around. Inevitably, we reach a natural conclusion, a period, where we catch up to the full meaning of what we have said and make instantaneous adjustments as we launch into the next utterance. How many times have we stood on street corners, caught in an impassioned debate with ourselves, only to be snapped out of it by the leery gaze of a stranger? Don Rutledge puts it this way: "The little girl who says, 'How can I know what I think until I hear what I say,' is exactly right." To straighten things out is to talk them out.

The students in Ann Maher's class provide a good example of this. Maher teaches a combined grade 4 and 5 class at Kensington Community School in downtown Toronto. She has an acute understanding of holistic language, and her classroom expresses that understanding. It is filled with pets, drawings, models, plants, books, and many other objects that capture the eye's attention. When I visited, the children arranged themselves into small groups as I stood in the middle of the classroom, my eyes moving from one thing to another. At the front of the class, some children were reading to Maher one at a time while others worked on projects. I was surprised at how quiet and engaged they all seemed to be. That's when Gregory Campbell and Cory Marcus approached me. "We're making an F14 Tomcat."

Gregory was a large boy with thick lips and big round cheeks. He was 11. Cory was tall and wiry. He was 10. Gregory wanted to be a "robot scientist and make a car faster than the fastest car in the world." Cory wanted to design airplanes. Both were in grade 4, both had failed a year, and both had figured out a lot more about our global predicaments than many adults. We stood in the middle of the class talking and were soon joined by two other students, Son Ngo and Sergio Dasilva. The big news at the time was the catastrophic Exxon oil spill off the coast of Alaska, where the captain of the tanker was charged with being drunk. We had the following exchange, which I think illustrates how many times a combined story can be modified as children help each other out by sharing what they know.

ME: What do you think about that oil spill in Alaska?

CORY: Well the captain is stupid, trying to deek icebergs, 'cause the Titanic tried to do that and it sunk.

GREGORY: I think they should get fined. Well, they already have them but most people don't pay.

SON: The garbage gets in their bodies [fish] and they can kill other animals that eat them.

GREGORY: Like that animal, ah, you know . . .

CHORUS: The whales! . . . A shark! A tiger shark! . . . Dolphins!

GREGORY: Yeah, the dolphins, they're dying. And the whales too.

ME: So do you think people are going to smarten up?

CHORUS: Noooo!

CORY: This might go on for another 50 years or something.

GREGORY: No way! By the year 2000 *everything* is going to be wiped out.

ME: What do you mean wiped out?

GREGORY: Like all the garbage, some of it they don't know what to do, some of it they recycle, some of it they just put in a *big* garbage dump . . . Oh yeah, at my camp they have recycling and I recycle my own stuff.

CORY: Some kids in school, they make paper airplanes and they throw them around the schoolyard and then it goes in the mud and they kick it around.

SERGIO: Yeah, they should recycle.

SON: Plastics are the worst, right?

SERGIO: Yeah, they're the worst.

ME: Why do adults do this?

CORY: They're lazy.

SON: They want cash. They want to make money.

CORY: They want *money*, they're *lazy* and they don't *care*!

ME: What do you mean they want money?

GREGORY: Like in the United States, the government, they give more money to the army, you know, to build more airplanes so they could fight more.

CORY: I'm not sure but I think they jumped into Vietnam.

SERGIO: Yeah, they just jumped in.

James Britton and Gordon Wells would say Gregory and his friends took part in "collaborative talk." It is also an example of what Britton means by an education that works on symbolic representations. Language, both spoken and written, is the most powerful way humans symbolize their experiences. In trying to make sense of the oil spill, Gregory and his friends had symbolized it to themselves in various ways. In the conversation, they jointly worked on connecting their understanding of the spill with other stories floating around in their heads. Together, they constructed a tale of people devastating their environment for money and power. In short, the children manipulated symbols to construct a meaning that made sense to them. They shaped them into the form of a story which then became part of their continuous inner stories, only to be refined and rewritten the next time around.

Ann Maher structures much of her class around such talk. For instance, for a project about winter she began by reading Robert Service's ballad, *The Cremation of Sam McGee,* to the class. They then discussed what they found intriguing about the ballad. The children decided they wanted to explore the Yukon so they broke off into groups to investigate its location, climate, and wildlife. In all cases, Maher encourages students to determine for themselves both the questions they want answered and how they will answer them. She expects the children to work without direct supervision, but will regularly discuss with each group how far it has progressed. She also makes sure they have books and other materials to use for research. Working in groups, the students resolve differences by sharing information, listening to each other's suggestions, and incorporating them much the way Gregory and his friends did. Throughout the process, Maher helps students focus on the problems they encounter in searching for answers, but she never provides solutions.

"It's important for them to reflect on the fact that this is how *all* people learn," Maher said. "It helps them to understand that everyone has something to contribute. When they realize that, their confidence grows. It gives them dignity."

Students are more apt to construct stories, holistic theory says, if they are allowed to write about what is important to them. Alice Moriarty's class of four-year-olds in Halifax provides a simple example.

The classroom looked like the inside of a child's head that had exploded: children's drawings and paintings of animals, cutouts of trees touching the heavens, giant birthday cakes with the names of children on candles, and dinosaurs, plants, Plasticine, building blocks, and books everywhere. All of it hung from ceilings and walls or lined shelves and tables. To observe things one piece at a time was difficult, like trying to isolate the colours of an iridescent oil blotch on a wet pavement. By the door stood an easel holding a large sheet of paper. On the sheet the children had written their names, something they did every morning. The letters quaked with determination. In September only two children had been able to write their names, while the others copied from name cards. Four months later, no one was copying. "They still don't know the alphabet, but they know about letters that have a value to them," Moriarty said. Making writing meaningful for children, arousing an intrinsic need in them, is one of the pillars of the holistic way Moriarty teaches language.

Each child also had a journal that he or she filled with drawings. Underneath the drawings were squiggles that indicated the children were aware that writing is used to tell stories. To adults the wiggly lines and circles are nothing more than wiggly lines and circles; to children, they represent the world. The only way to figure them out is to ask, and that's what Moriarty was doing every day. As the child related the story, Moriarty wrote a sentence under the drawing, describing what the child said. Inevitably, the children use those words and others pasted around the class to describe future drawings.

Holistic language theory is as complex as it is ambitious. This complexity alone has scared off many teachers. It's not uncommon to find teachers practicing mutant versions that defeat the holistic objectives. For example, many teachers set up students in groups only to have them work individually rather than co-operatively. As Don Rutledge said, "Some teachers are more in the swim than in the know."

Holistic theory has made significant inroads at the top of the educational hierarchy, but it is struggling in the classroom. This threatens the program's survival. Change from the top down has a poor record in education and is often resisted by teachers as just another passing bandwagon, especially when the messages from the top are contradictory. As students enter the higher elementary grades, the public clamour for

accountability through standardized examinations increases the pressure
to spoon-feed content. By high school, the assembly line is in full swing
as students shuffle from one class to another receiving isolated bits of
information. Biology has no connection to chemistry, which in turn has
no connection to physics, and so on, as if the world were divided into
45-minute periods. Finally, many teachers simply fear giving responsibility to students. As one teacher who recently began using holistic
methods said, "Teachers are afraid of losing control. I know I was."

Schizophrenia has set in. Grace School in Vancouver and St.
Patrick's in Halifax both suffer from it. Alice Moriarty said St. Patrick's
is divided between holistic and "drill and kill" methods. A child will be
taught holistically from junior kindergarten to grade 1, get drilled in
grade 2, placed back on a holistic cycle in grades 3 and 4, only to be
thrown back on the assembly line for grades 5 to 9. "It's pathetic,"
Moriarty said.

Perhaps the most telling example is at Dundas Street Public School
in Toronto, which in the mid-1960s was one of the first to experiment
with the holistic language approach before adopting it in 1975. From the
beginning of the project, hiring was restricted to teachers who upheld
holistic language theory. But Carol Howell, a Dundas Street School
kindergarten teacher well-versed in holistic ways, says the policy is no
longer observed. The stigma of working in inner-city schools tended to
keep teachers away from Dundas. Over the years, as teachers left, it
became impossible to replace them with others who understood or
accepted holistic language. So the requirement was unofficially and quietly dropped. "The system has broken down even in this school," Howell
says. "A child will go from one class to another and come across a completely different philosophy."

Supporters of the holistic language approach face the massive contradiction of trying to fit this program into a rigidly linear and sequential school system that sorts and slots. Unless the contradiction is
resolved, the application of holistic language may forever remain spo-
radic and erratic. The Toronto school board hopes to overcome this barrier by taking advantage of the educational aphorism that what is tested
is what is taught. Under the auspices of Don Rutledge, the board has
designed a system of "benchmarks" for grades 3 and 6 that describe how
well the average student can read, write, count, reason, listen, solve

problems, understand poetry and art, and make oral and dramatic presentations. Students will be evaluated against the benchmarks, and Rutledge hopes this will lead teachers to give up their spoon-feeding ways and adopt holistic methods that foster the kind of independent thinking the benchmarks try to evaluate. While the benchmark testing will help foster holistic methods, it is doubtful that it will be enough to sustain them. As long as private industry dictates the overriding mandate of schools, the development of people prepared to take control of their environment will remain the preserve of a powerful few.

Holistic language is an essentially democratic exercise that aspires to turn people into molders of history. It is an attempt to unify all knowledge into a continuous pattern of stories and to make children aware that every day they are engaged in a process of constructing reality.

8

MECHANICAL MIND

Awed by the beauty and mystery of the heavens, we demand unity with nature. Determined to make everything familiar, we long to link the known with the imagined. We dream of our place among the stars, and a myth is born. In his essay "Mythology," Robert Graves wrote that myths have two functions. First, they answer those questions that children embarrass adults with, such as, "Who made the world?" and "How will it end?" Second, they serve to "justify an existing social system and account for traditional rites and customs." In that sense, they serve as essential consumer products, a kind of social DNA. Myths are the narratives that reconcile the deep and mysterious inner world of intuition with the dazzling outer world that we see and touch, yet can't comprehend. They form the beliefs we take for granted and rarely question, acting like a frame for everything we see.

Myths have held societies together for millennia as people refine them, debunk them, and create new ones, according to circumstance. Graves noted, for example, that the Akan people of Ghana used to have a matriarchical society with an all-powerful moon-goddess who created the world. But their reverence was of their own making. In the early Middle Ages the male-worshipping Sudanese invaded the Akans and over time forced their captives to accept the authority of a sun-god and a patriarchal social system. Myths are influenced by social realities but remain uniquely human products. In short, they are a way of constructing reality and living our collective dreams. They are the symbols we use to represent the world to ourselves, an exercise in abstraction, guided by our intuitive interaction with nature. Once in place they seem to come alive, charming us down a path like the plot of a good novel. Indeed, myths are like mental social scripts whose tales can deceive the senses.

John Polanyi tells a story of being stopped on the street by a stranger and asked to read a certain word. The word was misspelled – it had a letter missing – but Polanyi says he didn't notice and simply uttered the full word. Asked if there was something wrong with the word, Polanyi said there wasn't and read it again. The point of the story is that he was fooled by his own mind. His eyes were, in a sense, blinded by what he called the "cultural picture" in his head. This cultural picture, or inner story, automatically inserted the missing letter to make what the eyes saw "fit" the running script in his head. Myths are the images, beliefs, values, and habits that make up the cultural picture in the mind.

"All experience is subjective . . . our brains make the images that we think we 'perceive,'" writes American epistemologist Gregory Bateson.

Child psychologist Margaret Donaldson notes that the building of this cultural picture is a natural process that begins virtually at birth. Donaldson is a renowned psychologist who spent years studying under the world-famous psychologist Jean Piaget. In her book *Children's Minds*, she argues that Piaget underestimated the potential of children. Piaget said children existed in an "egocentric" state until the age of six or seven. Egocentric people are unable to adopt another person's point of view, unable to recognize that people with experiences and beliefs other than their own will interpret the world differently. In children this theoretically means that they can't figure out simple problems. Piaget's child is supposed to think that if water from one jar is poured into another jar of a different shape, the amount of water changes.

Donaldson shows that the poor performance of children in Piaget's experiments was due to a breakdown in communication and not an inability to decentre. Essentially, the children simply misunderstood what the experimenter instructed them to do. Children who were asked to perform tasks similar to those in Piaget's experiments succeeded when given different circumstances and explanations. Since the 1960s, however, the theory of the egocentric child has had a considerable influence on primary education, from kindergarten to grade 3. If children can't decentre, then giving them some control and responsibility over what they learn seems pointless. And what good is giving children high quality literature, such as poems, if they can't understand someone else's point of view? The child is seen as a passive, helpless receptacle of information, which is ironic because it contradicts Piaget's overall conclusion that infants are actively trying to make sense of their worlds. Here, Margaret Donaldson concurs.

"We do not just sit and wait for the world to impinge on us," she states. "We try actively to interpret it, to make sense of it. We grapple with it, we construe it intellectually, *we represent it to ourselves.* Another way to put this is to say that we are, by nature, questioners . . . . These questions and these strivings imply some primitive sense of possibility which reaches beyond a realization of how things are to a realization of how they might be."

From our earliest moments, we are dreamers. Like scientists, we make predictions about our environment and test them. In a sense, we are born storytellers.

In *Growing with Books,* a ministry of education resource guide for Ontario teachers, Gordon Wells argues that the earliest experiences of a baby involve elements of narrative structure: cause and effect seen in actions and their consequences; intentions formed and achieved or thwarted; pain, hunger, and loneliness alleviated through the love and care of others. By making connections between events, by recognizing patterns, children build ever-changing stories inside their heads, and they use these stories to try to explain their presence in a dazzling and threatening world. In constructing their stories, children are symbolizing the world to themselves.

Gordon Wells, like Margaret Donaldson and other child psychologists, relies heavily on the pioneering work of Lev Semyonovich Vygotsky, the brilliant Russian psychologist whose ideas form the cutting edge of child development theory. This is impressive, considering Vygotsky died in 1934 at the age of 38. His work, however, wasn't translated into English until the mid-1960s, and one of his most important books, *Mind in Society,* wasn't discovered until 1978. Vygotsky's writings are rather cryptic, filled with powerful concepts thrown out in a condensed manner. In general, he saw the learning of language, and all higher psychological processes, as a dialectic between individuals and their social environment. Here is an example: Picture a baby trying to grasp an object beyond reach, a bright red rattle in the shape of a monkey. Initially, the gesture is nothing more than that – a movement aimed at an object that designates forthcoming activity. The baby's hand is poised in the air, grasping helplessly, and a whimper turns into a slight hacking as the effort is frustrated. But when a parent comes to the rescue, a fundamental change occurs.

"Pointing becomes a gesture for others," Vygotsky wrote in *Mind in Society*. "The child's unsuccessful attempts engender a reaction not from the object she seeks but *from another person*. Consequently, the primary meaning of that unsuccessful grasping movement is established by others."

Only later does the child make sense of the situation by piecing together the pattern involved. The child then comes to recognize the unsuccessful grasping as pointing. In other words, the gesture has been turned into a symbol laden with meaning. With this awareness, the gesture's function changes from a movement aimed at an object to a movement aimed at another person, "a means of establishing relations."

Language seems to develop the same way. The infant makes sense of the social context first and then picks up the words used to describe actions and objects within that context. Words like "milk" and "cake," for instance, are usually generated first around mealtime. The meaning of words, like that of objects and gestures, is decided socially through common consent. In making the connections, in building the inner story, the child is also learning the cultural significance of actions. Outside of their own culture, educated people can perform stunning acts of miscommunication. In Canada, waving someone towards you may involve holding the palm of your hand skyward and repeatedly folding your fingers. In Malawi, Africa, this means, "I want to have sex with you."

Context, then, is everything. In his book *Mind and Nature: A Necessary Unity*, Gregory Bateson states: "Without context, words and actions have no meaning at all. This is true not only of human communication in words but also of all communication whatsoever, of all mental process, of all mind, including that which tells the sea anemone how to grow and the amoeba what he should do next." Context is an aggregate of relationships, a subsystem of what Bateson calls the "metapattern"; that is, a pattern of patterns that unites the universe – a story that tells all stories.

Within any given context, individuals attempt to make sense of the relationships that form the pattern, much like the child coming to know what pointing means. Within the same context, however, each person is likely to interpret the message differently. The story told by quantum physics suggests that absolute definitions don't exist.

Quantum physics discovered that the universe is not, as Descartes and Isaac Newton believed, a set of building blocks, but rather a complex set of relationships that enlace. By observing particles in the nucleus of atoms, physicists found that electrons, protons, and neutrons – the essence of all matter and life – do not have a solid, single, or independent state of existence. In fact, they seem to be in a constant state of transformation from a particle to a wave. Furthermore, the electron cannot be isolated from other particles or analysed independently. It is inextricably related to other particles. Finally, the only way to observe the properties of an electron is through the filter and biases of the observer.

"If I ask it a particle question, it will give me a particle answer; if I ask it a wave question, it will give me a wave answer. The electron does not *have* objective properties outside of my mind," physicist Fritjof Capra states.

Nothing is real, it seems, outside of relationships. Individuals make sense of these relationships according to their past experiences and biases. Human consciousness – the continuous story or cultural picture we carry around in our heads – is built collectively through interaction between the culture and the individual. In this manner, knowledge and truth are constructed. None of it comes from the heavens. The myth of progress is no exception. Over the past 400 years, the subjective interaction between humans and their environment has imprinted the myth of progress as the dominant cultural story in our minds. We use it to interpret, indeed construct, reality the way John Polanyi's "cultural picture" constructs a word that doesn't exist. Yet schools and much of society act as though this human-made myth were God-sent. We have let our myth-making machines get the better of us.

■

It takes tools to build myths. One of the earliest and most powerful is the symbol. *The Bullock Report*, a 1975 British government-commissioned study on education, described humankind as being "essentially a symbol-using animal" and said that this helps explain our "individual, social, and cultural achievements."

> What makes us typically human is the fact that we symbolize, or represent to ourselves, the objects, people and events that make up our environment, and do so cumulatively, thus creating an inner representation of the world as we have encountered it. The accumulated representation is on the one hand a storehouse of past experience and on the other a body of expectations regarding what may yet happen to us. In this way we construct for ourselves a past and a future, a retrospect and a prospect; all our significant actions are performed within this extended field or framework, and no conscious act, however trivial, is uninfluenced by it.

With such immense power, imagine how mind-blowing the invention of the first symbol must have been. It's a story best left to literature. Italian storyteller Italo Calvino spent a lifetime trying to weave transcendent paths with an ingenuity, precision, and human warmth rarely matched by other contemporary writers. Until his death in 1985, he wrote extensively about the power of language and was admired by linguist James Britton, who played a key role in writing *The Bullock Report*, and psychologist Jerome Bruner.

In his short story *A Sign in Space*, Calvino introduces the reader to Qfwfq, an ageless single-cell organism, "a mass of protoplasm like a kind of pulpy dumpling with a nucleus in the middle." During one of his spacial orbits, Qfwfq makes a sign, just so he can find it again on the next go around some 200 million years later. It changed his existence:

> I thought about it day and night; in fact, I couldn't think about anything else; actually, this was the first opportunity I had had to think something; or I should say: to think something had never been possible, first because there were no things to think about, and second because signs to think of

them by were lacking, but from the moment there was that sign, it was possible for someone thinking to think of a sign, and therefore that one, in the sense that the sign was the thing you could think about and also the sign of the thing thought, namely, itself.

For Qfwfq, that first sign was the story of him and the story of everything else. It was the beginning of a story that would tell all stories, achieved with the invention of a tool to manipulate and understand the environment, a way of breaking down a mass of infinite connections into comprehensible segments. In this sense, we're all like Qfwfq. Simply put, signs give us the ability to separate *this* from *that* and to think about *this* and *that* separately. With signs we name, classify, and assign meaning to the world. When Descartes proclaimed, "I think, therefore I am," was he not exalting the technology of symbols?

It's believed that the need to record quantities gave rise to written language. Lev Vygotsky gave the example of the early counting system of the Papuas of New Guinea. They would start with the pinky of their left hand, move through the fingers, then add the left hand, forearm, elbow, shoulder, right shoulder, and so on, finishing with the pinky of the right hand. When they ran out of body parts they used sticks, shells, or other objects – objects that then took on a new meaning. From symbolizing things, humans evolved to symbolizing speech through the invention of writing. Suddenly, as Gordon Wells puts it, "Meaning could be preserved beyond the point of utterance." Time, space, and the limitations of human memory were conquered with the stroke of a hand.

It's not difficult to imagine people as overwhelmed as Qfwfq making the first sign. In a sense, it was like falling in love with oneself. Suddenly, those symbolic animals could permanently enshrine their dreams. The pictures in their heads became pictures on paper. Those who mastered the technology could manipulate these self-images to new heights, until the marks on paper slowly began to form a story of their own. With the invention of the printing press in the fifteenth century, the printed page became the first completely standardized product. Its straight lines, sentence structures, paragraphs, numbered pages, and chapters had a symmetry that mesmerized. Within 50 years of the invention of the printing press, more than 50 million books had been printed. In her book *The Printing Press as an Agent of Change: Communications and Cultural Transformations in Early Modern Europe*, historian Elizabeth Eisenstein argues that the layout of books influenced how academic disciplines structured their knowledge and organized their arguments. Linear, cause-and-effect thinking fit nicely with the flow of the written page. As the page flowed, so did people's myths. The more powerful the technology, the greater the chances it would immolate its creator.

All societies adopt many myths, but the most fundamental myth in Western society has to do with the god of progress. It is very likely a god and not a goddess, because the notion was invented by men. A dictionary defines progress as a forward motion, "to develop a higher, better, or more advanced stage." Up, up and away!

Self-gratification is one of the strongest human drives. To satisfy dreams, humans developed tools, which in turn helped shape their dreams; one influencing the other until it became difficult to tell what was doing what to whom. What is clearer is the result of the interaction, the product. Today, the product is a culture that toys with extinction. We invented technologies that accelerated our powers of abstraction, our powers to create myths, but in the process forgot that we are the dream weavers. "Myth transforms history into nature," states French sociologist Roland Barthes.

The story of how Western thought and civilization incorporated the myth of progress in its collective mind to the point where that myth seemed "natural" is far too complex for even a brief overview here. But the development of one of the West's most deterministic inventions, the mechanical clock, shows how the relationship between humans and their technology has evolved. The clock, counting the seconds, ticks like the collective heart of society. We've internalized its beat in a way that makes submission to it psychologically gratifying.

In his seminal work, *Technics and Civilization*, historian Lewis Mumford argues that the idea for the mechanical clock grew out of the desire for order and power that ruled in European monasteries. By the decree of Pope Sabinianus in the seventh century, monastery bells had to be rung seven times in a 24-hour period to mark the seven daily periods of devotion. A way had to be found to keep track of when to ring them. The mechanical clock was eventually devised, first appearing in the cities of the thirteenth century. Less than a hundred years later, the hour was divided into 60 minutes and minutes into 60 seconds. An abstract division of time had developed that increasingly became the point of reference for both thought and action. By the end of the sixteenth century, the clock had found its way onto mantlepieces in England and Holland. The upper classes were naturally the first to become enthralled with this latest technological wonder, with all its mechanical wheels that seemed to turn with the perfection of the universe. "Time is money," they dreamed, and another cliché – "as regular as clockwork" – was an ideal promoted by the bourgeoisie, for whom ownership of a watch was long a symbol of success. "The increasing tempo of civilization," Mumford says, "led to a demand for greater power: and in turn power quickened the tempo." The pace has left us breathless.

The clock changed our perceptions of reality. It changed the structure we have in our heads, the one that acts like a frame for everything we see. Until the fourteenth century, time was measured against eternity, a consequence of people interacting with nature and its seasons, a relationship that was severed by the clock. As a machine producing seconds and minutes, the clock created a sense of immediacy which previously had not existed. Time became a mathematical equation, an absolute, immovable force whose trajectory is as straight as rain. The mechanical clock put time on a plane independent of human consciousness, changing the way we visualize our world and the way we represent it to ourselves.

In the Middle Ages, the symbols and values that guided people, part of the structure in their minds, reflected the power of the church. Space was divided arbitrarily to represent the ten commandments, the twelve apostles, or the Holy Trinity. The highest point in the city, for example, was the tip of the church spire. Then, between the fourteenth and seventeenth centuries, a new perspective was discovered, and art changed. The canvas was divided into squares and for the first time depth emerged in paintings, guiding the eye along streets, buildings, and alleyways. It didn't take long before the world was wrapped in a grid as cartographers laid down the invisible lines of latitude and longitude that helped Columbus and others set sail. Space was conquered and our love affair with progress began.

"Movement became a source of value: movement for its own sake. The measured space of the picture reinforced the measured time of the clock," Mumford states.

Swept away by movement, framed and guided by squares, the world began to look radically different to the people of the Enlightenment. The new attitudes towards time and space began to govern how people worked and lived. In business and timekeeping, men counted numbers until, out of habit and what poet Wallace Stevens called the "rage for order," only numbers counted. For instance, the change from a barter economy to a money economy had its origin in northern Italy in the fourteenth century. To go from placing value on a cow or a piece of land to a piece of paper took a giant leap of abstraction. By the middle of the sixteenth century merchants were already working with the stuff of stocks and bonds, and bookkeeping had become a crucial occupation. The accumulation of pieces of paper had created a new appetite: the quest for power by means of abstractions. "The power that was science and the power that was money were, in final analysis, the same kind of power: the power of abstraction, measurement, quantification," Mumford says. With this passion for numbers, men turned their eyes to nature and embarked on the Scientific Revolution. By the end of it they had managed to view the universe as a machine.

Objectivity and certainty were elevated to the status of gods. Cold and calculated, they guided humanity towards the absolute truths men themselves were defining. In that sense, men couldn't miss; it was a fool-proof way of gratifying the desire to know all. Each new invention – writing, the clock, the printing press – made an indelible impression on their minds. Machines shaped what people valued by providing the framework they used to understand the world. Like the invading Sudanese, machines refined and changed the collective mythologies of civilization. They influenced the questions scientists asked and therefore the answers the world provided, each answer reinforcing the kinds of questions they asked and the method used to ask the questions. In short, they stealthily guided behaviour until intuitive knowledge seemed primative and uncivilized. The way people interacted with nature, the way they had survived for millennia, went out of fashion. The body was seen much like a machine, powered by an omnipotent mind obssessed with quantifying, grading, and categorizing. This mechanical narrative seemed to satisfy the lust for progress, the drive to weave a story with *the* conclusion, the definitive ending where everything is familiar.

A more recent technological purveyor of the myth of progress is television. The impact of television on human activity is at least as significant as that of the clock or the printing press. Teachers are almost unanimous in blaming television for practically every change they've witnessed in students over the years. Rick Boudell, English department head at New Westminster Secondary School in B.C., believes a full range of electronic media – television, VCRs, computer games – is stunting the imaginations of his students.

"I mean, they're used to 'turn me on *now*, excite me *now*, or I'm tuning you out. I'm shutting it off,'" Boudell says.

"Every teacher you can find will say that students read less now because they're used to it just being presented to them. And I think that reading less affects their imagination. You know, on television it's just being shown to you; you don't have to imagine what the character looks like or what they're thinking. You know, when I read a story I was always the protagonist; I always got right inside the head of the protagonist. That's how I really got into literature. And I ask kids now and only a few of them do and they're generally the better readers. The rest of them, they just read a story. They don't get into any of the characters. They're less creative, and it frightens me."

Media critic Neil Postman, in *The Disappearance of Childhood* and later in *Amusing Ourselves to Death*, details how the invention of the telegraph and the photograph slowly replaced the printed word as the dominant way of understanding our world. The electronic media changed the dominant form of public interaction from one of words to one of images. In other words, the technology we use to symbolically represent the world to ourselves has been transformed.

The medium disseminates information in two ways. On one level, it provides consumers with ready-made packages of meaning to be swallowed whole like TV dinners. On another, it destroys meaning by doing away with context. We witness this lack of context every day on the news when items flash by rapidly like isolated bits stripped of history, until a continuing war in El Salvador or Lebanon has no more meaning than a running soap opera. These flickering images without context turn much of television into the ultimate in twentieth-century distraction – a medium of white noise. For some students, the white noise of television and the white noise of the classroom elicit the same response. During a grade 13 class discussion on technological determinism, Christine Panayotou, a senior student at York Collegiate in Toronto, said television was training people in a pattern of thought that reflected commercial breaks. "It's like that when I'm in class," she said. "I concentrate for about eight minutes and then I clue out for a couple of minutes, just like when a commercial comes on." With television, as with schools, this apprenticeship in the mechanical transformation of the mind begins early.

It takes no expertise to watch television, and this largely accounts for its success. All viewers need to do is to recognize the unchanging patterns of its shows, the visual jolts that occur every few seconds. In *The Disappearance of Childhood*, Neil Postman quotes a study by Daniel Anderson of the University of Massachusetts that found that children begin to watch television with systematic attention at the age of three. By then, they have favourite programs, and can sing along with commercials and ask parents for the products advertised.

Unlike print media, television does not segregate its audience. Its format makes no distinction between child and adult. Indeed, studies indicate that children prefer to watch adult shows rather than shows produced for them. Postman notes that an estimated three million U.S. children under the age of 12 were watching television at 11 p.m. *People in Society*, a high school text in Ontario, gives the most widely accepted statistics: By graduation time the average high school student has spent 22,000 hours watching television, twice as many hours as spent in the classroom. In that same period, the student has witnessed 18,000 TV murders.

A kindergarten teacher in Toronto tells a story about the day she gave her pupils "Big Wheel" bikes. She first had the caretaker jazz up the bikes with stickers. Immediately, they launched into a smash-up derby routine, which the teacher quickly put an end to. She took one child aside and asked why everyone was being so rough. "'Cause it's the

A-Team," the child said, referring to the graphic on the stickers the caretaker had placed on the bike. The "A-Team" television series, filled with car chases and violence, seemed to have determined the rules of the game. What else could the children do but play accordingly?

This raises perhaps the greatest concern about television: Does it induce children to commit violent acts? Bruno Bettelheim, one of the towering figures in child psychology, says no.

In *Recollections and Reflections,* his last book before his death in March 1990, Bettelheim argues that the child's own personality – formed in the home under parental influence – is the decisive factor in the reaction to violence on television, and not the violence itself. A lesser factor is the child's emotional state while watching a violent scene. Children are more prone to acting out if they are highly anxious or angry while watching. Violence on television, according to Bettelheim, provides children with a cathartic outlet for their emotional tensions. "They need material for aggressive and retaliatory daydreams in which they can vicariously act out their hostile feelings without hurting close relatives."

Bettelheim finds that adults have historically been suspicious of new forms of mass entertainment. "It usually becomes accepted once people realise that life goes on in the same haphazard way as before." Movies and comic books raised concerns similar to those now expressed about television.

Children have always harboured violent fantasies, Bettelheim argues. Their lives are full of the disappointments and frustrations that come from wishing for so much, but having so little control. This creates a need for daydreams, and television provides the material for such dreams. Children watching television "are neither bored nor stultified," Bettelheim states. Instead, they're simply participating in fantasies of success that make their frustrated existences more bearable.

Bettelheim recognizes that television becomes dangerous when parents use it as a babysitter for their children, or as an excuse for not spending time with them. The problem, then, stems from how people use television and is "not one inherent in the medium," he says. Without the necessary teaching from parents, the danger is that children will passively accept the TV dinners of packaged meanings they see – a form of illiteracy that is widespread.

At New Westminster Secondary School I met a self-described "popular group" of students for whom televison set the superficial standards by which they compared their own lives. Consumerism, that element of the myth of progress most heralded by television, held them captive. The popular group was a subculture made up of a dozen or so students. They were popular, they said, because they threw the wildest parties, dressed in the latest *GQ* fashions, and were pretty much the kind of people everyone else in the school wanted to be. The day we met, their biggest concern was trying to come up with the $2,000 each one would need for their graduation celebrations in a month's time. This sum didn't include a trip to Hawaii that was also in the works. They weren't, by any stretch of the imagination, rich kids. They came from lower-middle-class families and they worked long hours in part-time jobs to keep themselves in the latest labeled clothing. Looks were very important.

"People always say, 'Looks don't count' and everything but if you look at someone and he's totally gross, you're not going to say he has a real good personality when you don't even know him," said Christine, one of the students. "If they're wearing a big Metallica shirt and jeans with holes and stuff, and they're walking around with long hair, you know, you're just not even going to consider talking to them."

"Like in our group, no one's fat," said Mike. "It's weird when you think about it. Like, you can't be fat and go to the beach in a bikini. Imagine a girl who's really, really big and she goes to the beach with all these girls. They would really feel bad."

"Do you sometimes wish you were somebody else?" I asked one of the young women.

"Like that girl in the 7-Up commercial. She's absolutely gorgeous and the guy's incredibly hard," said Sloane.

"She has a stereotypical body," Tony said. "She has the body of how you should look. This is hypothetical, but I bet you if they had fat models, everyone would want to be fat."

Of course, Tony's analysis is correct. During the Renaissance, the standard beauty had a plump figure. Now she's the bikini-clad woman in 7-Up commercials. It all depends on the image of beauty that dominates the collective mind, and nothing sells images like television. The trouble arises when people buy those off-the-rack consumer images on sight, like some divine apparition.

However, the impact of television is anything but black and white. As noted in chapter 6, television decentralizes control of information and reveals adult secrets, thereby undermining the very status quo it tries to maintain. Television also exposes teenagers to the darker side of the myth. The tale of consumer heaven is difficult to swallow when poverty and environmental collapse are nightly television fare. Hypocrisy is revealed as a central value for authority, and with power seemingly out of reach, cynicism runs rampant. The materialistic tale that drains beauty of its spiritual essence also rationalizes the lust for power that fuses at the point of a nuclear missile. In this context, it becomes far easier to think of bikinis than absolute nothingness.

"It's too much to think about, you know, the whole world blowing up," said Tony. "It's just so bad now that there's not much you can do anymore, unless you do it as a whole. But how are you going to get people to do it as a whole?"

When the world was a neighbourhood, change seemed an arm's length away. In the global village, change seems as close as the stars and best left to the powerful.

The myth of progress is society's collective hidden agenda; hidden because it lives in harmony with our minds, making acquiescence to its messages seem natural. With its narrative we build the structures and the institutions that guide our lives: abstractions drive the economy and the school system. Those abstractions are only one version of the truth, and the inability to recognize this is endemic in our society. We have evolved a series of myths – involving competition, patriarchy, hierarchy, linear thinking – that explain, indeed excuse, the way power is exercised. For the better part of two centuries, for instance, it has been perfectly natural to accept the excesses of industrialization. Only the threat of a global environmental cataclysm seems equal to the myth of progress. Sometimes it takes a nightmare to wake us from our collective dreams. Students recognize the horror that looms, but feel powerless. The difference is this: We can let it fester in our minds until we are resigned to its dark inevitability, or we can understand how the horror becomes commonplace and recognize it as a social creation with no divine right to exist.

Schools should help people understand how this warped social tale was manufactured. But the factory model of schools is a structure void of context. The separation of knowledge into sequential bits, the hierarchical flow of authority, the spoon-feeding of information: All of it preaches a tale where submitting to the status quo is prized and rewarded. It's a hidden curriculum that severely limits the ability of people to manipulate symbols. This is particularly apparent in the traditional method of drilling students in reading and writing. Students are taught to abdicate the process of building a retrospect and a prospect. Meaning is transformed into a value dictated and accepted rather than something woven consciously by individuals and the community. Symbols are petrified with the weight of "truth," and the skill of writing becomes a technology that enslaves rather than liberates. When writing becomes a process of passivity, the child's natural process of trying to make sense of the world, of weaving it into a story, becomes skewed. The interaction between the child's personal tale and the collective story is thrown off balance. What should be a process of constant refinement becomes one that embraces, in a rather clumsy and reluctant way, the dominant tale or myth.

One program that tries to address this human myth-making is the media literacy courses that have been part of the Ontario high school curriculum since 1989. The aim is to help children understand that television presents ideologically laden lifestyles, subjectively chosen and carefully produced to seem natural. When the boys are throwing back a "cool one," life is less than complete if tall shapely women aren't somewhere in the vicinity. The curriculum guide to the media literacy program says children should learn to "decode" what they see. In the case of a sitcom that portrays a squeaky clean, full of understanding, all-American family, it may be a simple matter of asking students to compare them to their own families. The curriculum stresses a hands-on approach to learning. By writing their own commercials, for instance, students can experience for themselves the subjective decisions that go into creating an image that will sell a product. Media literate persons are those who make sense of what they see only after assessing the situation with what they know and what they have experienced. They construct their own personal meanings instead of passively accepting television's images. The kind of literacy taught in this media progam is essential for any school system concerned with developing people who can think for themselves. Its goal is to develop students who can "read" the myths that form the cultural picture in the mind and in society's hidden curriculum.

The holistic language approach to reading and writing tries to foster this kind of literate behaviour throughout the curriculum. It maintains that the process of consciously manipulating symbols to construct personal meanings lies at the heart of literate behaviour. It tries to transform the transmission model of schools. After all, what is there to transmit when the only certainty is uncertainty? On this point, science and literature embrace. With *Don Quixote*, Cervantes gave birth to the modern European novel and advised us to embrace what has been called the "wisdom of uncertainty." The perfection of the stars will forever elude science and inspire poetry. If scientific history has proven anything, it's that science proves nothing. Scientists once thought the sun revolved around the earth, the weight of a ball determined how fast it fell, the universe was made up of small indestructible particles of matter, time was absolute, and the continents were always in their present place. Then came Copernicus, Galileo, Einstein, and the discovery of continental drift. All of them changed what was held to be the "truth." In other words, scientists approach the world the way everyone else does – with a fictitious script in their heads. They call it theory, conjecture, presupposition, and probability. This is not to say that scientific information is useless. The scientific method of inquiry is one of the more valuable tools for the construction of stories that help explain our universe. Its logic gratifies the intellect. In the end, however, scientific findings are simply plausible stories pieced together in much the same way children write their inner tales: by making predictions and waiting for incongruities to rewrite the script. Truth is a matter of social consensus, and the truths of science are no exception. More than 300 years after Cervantes, physics acquiesced to literature and formulated the "uncertainty principle."

If everything is relative, then all opinions are valid, but not all are well-informed. Survival demands literate children who understand how society's collective story is an aggregate of individual inner stories. The holistic language program does this. It sees literate people as those who understand how they came to know what they know. They do not act like marginal characters swept away by a history of supermen and cataclysmic events – the history told in school textbooks. History is theirs to shape. Myths such as progress are theirs to modify or banish. Fatalism is anathema to them. A literate person is a person of action.

9

LOOKING FORWARD, FALLING BACK

In March 1988, Ontario's government and the teachers' unions sponsored a conference to discuss ways of reducing the 33 per cent drop-out rate. The conference was called "Mission Possible." By that time the global economy and international competition had achieved the mythical status of a new evangelism. Governments and businesses geared up to take on other governments and businesses in the world arena, and the pre-game warm-up involved a ritual dance obsessed with efficiency. Social services, portrayed as bleeding entrepreneurial spirit, became targets for cutbacks. The Canadian Manufacturers' Association, one of the country's most powerful business lobby groups, was at the forefront of this assault. Corporations developed merger mania, gobbling up smaller companies at home in order to gobble up others abroad. It all boiled down to a massive realignment, a leaner and meaner time that ruled the day with cold solemnity.

In education a common word for this kind of adjustment is "retooling," as though the classroom were no more than an assembly line in need of new parts. The pressure was on to retool, and schools, given their task of reflecting society, had little choice but to comply. The Toronto conference on drop-outs gave a disturbing example of just how far the retooling was going.

The conference was held at Toronto's Convention Centre, and Bob Keech, a vice-principal from Windsor, conducted one of its workshops.

The room was crowded, with maybe a hundred people, most of them teachers. Keech immediately shifted into high gear, preaching a populist brand of educational fundamentalism. His booming voice, his flailing arms, his intense gaze, his whole manner suggested revelation and salvation. His performance was a mix between television evangelism and Rambo. On the one hand, he wanted to wipe out teachers' colleges – "bomb them, burn them" – because he said they produced academic snobs unable to communicate with anyone but students heading to university. On the other hand, he suggested greasing up the system for the more efficient production of automatons. Near the middle of his talk, he introduced his parents, thanked them for his success, and said they had sat through his performance several times before. The white-haired couple beamed. Strangest of all perhaps was that Keech's act was funded by Ontario's Liberal government. It was paying to send Keech on a road show to schools across the province in order to sell his program.

Keech's program was appropriately called "teach-to-pass," and schools in Windsor, Ottawa, Thunder Bay, Waterloo, Lincoln County, Acton, and Cambridge were already using it. Passing was made simple. It boiled down to being obedient and docile. The bulk of marks in courses came from the social behaviour, work ethic, homework, and attendance of the students. Understanding the academic content accounted for only 40 per cent of the grade. As Keech explained it, a student could miss out on all the skills needed in a math course, for example, and still pass. "A kid can pass my (math) course but fail math," he said. Keech's program was designed for students not heading to university. Schools, he said, have to face facts: Some students simply *can't* learn. It seemed, then, that the goal was to create the illusion of learning while preparing them for life in a factory. Keech said that this is done partly by "inflating the marks."

Keech had some classroom tests on display. One test evaluated students by asking them questions like: "Do you have neat work habits (you do not doodle or scribble in texts or notes)? Do you get to work quickly and work until the task is finished?" Another asked students to respond to statements: "I am courteous to others in class/ I do not interrupt others by talking out of turn/ I do not abuse the property of others." The program also emphasized incentives, such as coupons worth five bonus marks for being on time for a whole week. As the teach-to-pass newsletter said, "Ford, Chrysler and GM give rebates or option packages for a penny," so why not schools?

Attendance is mandatory. Students who miss more than 15 classes are "thrown out" of the course and have to spend that period studying. "It gets rid of those kids in the classroom that don't want to learn," Keech said. He couldn't say how many students had left his Riverside Secondary School in Windsor this way, but the school population had declined by about 100 in the eight months the program had been in place.

Keech's methods were grounded in a desire to give employers what they wanted. During the workshop, he distributed an article from a professor at Butte College in Oroville, California. It listed the top five employee traits which, according to bosses, would lead to success on the job:

1. Be honest and dependable.
2. Be reliable and punctual.
3. Get along well with people.
4. Co-operate with supervisors.
5. Accept and handle responsibility.

Another handout was the *Teaching-to-Pass Newsletter*, Volume 1, Issue 2, from January 1988. It provided this rationale to students: "The teacher is boss; it must be done his/her way, not your way. In the work world, things are done the company way not the employee way."

The degree of success depends entirely on how success is defined. In Riverside's math courses, the failure rate dropped from 60 per cent to 10 per cent since teach-to-pass was brought in. Students who otherwise would have had their self-esteem destroyed by failure, Keech said, now felt good about themselves. He made no apologies for the fact that his program did not develop students who could think for themselves. He was on a mission, spreading salvation. He had fine-tuned the assembly line at his school and was now helping dozens of others do the same – all with government funding. The Liberal government, after all, had defined success as a reduction in the drop-out rate. The government had gone as far as to promise that it would cut the rate by one-third over five years, and teach-to-pass was one way to do it.

It all seemed quite ludicrous. I walked out of the seminar in a haze of disbelief, and in that sense probably felt much like teenagers do. Teenagers spend much of their time confronting absurdity by being forced to spend five days a week in institutions that make absolutely no sense to them. The subjects, the content, the discipline, the scheduled time-table: They find all of it incomprehensible and irrelevant. In the bitter-sweet dance of life, schools try to teach the minuet to children who want to do the monster mash. Perhaps that's how institutional absurdity thrives. It depends on people's intuitive awareness that life is prepos-terous. Life is absurd, ergo, school is absurd.

Teach-to-pass has no difficulty fitting into the school system, and this, of course, is its strength. It is quite compatible with the kind of tape-recorded drilling that went on in Karen Riley's elementary class at Vancouver's Grace School.

Later the same day I met Bob Buckthorp, an organizer of the con-ference and an executive member of the Ontario Secondary School Teachers' Federation. He described teach-to-pass as a "Pavlovian" pro-gram that satisfied the demands of many employers for "obedient little servants." He said, "This scares the hell out of me. If this is all society wants, then this program says we'll meet those needs."

But what exactly does society want? This is what Buckthorp wanted to know. As usual, the government was sending mixed messages. "On the one hand they want independent, creative thinkers, and then in the next breath they say we want them to fit neatly into slots in the work-place. Society is going to have to make up its mind. Does it want wid-gets or does it want independent, critical thinkers?"

The teach-to-pass bandwagon was being propelled by a societal anxiety that hadn't been experienced since the Russians launched Sputnik and took a lead on the Americans in the space race. In the 1980s, the fear caused by Japanese Hondas and cheap Korean clothing replaced the "Red Menace" as the latest frenzied force pushing educational reform. The changes were taking place within the context of the gloomiest peri-od of Western conservatism since World War II: Ronald Reagan, George Bush, Margaret Thatcher, Brian Mulroney, and fans of the "new right" presiding.

In February 1983, a Carnegie Conference in New York left no doubt that as far as the attendees were concerned, the goal of education was economic well-being. The conference brought together 50 high-level policy-makers from business, government, universities, education groups, and trade unions. Their report, *Education and Economic Progress: Toward a National Education Policy,* said: "In 1957, Sputnik and national defense issues drew forth massive public interest and support. In the 1960s, the Great Society and social justice became the incentive for reform and support. Today, the needs of the economy are paramount. The economic challenge from Japan and other countries is the modern Sputnik, a powerful lever for the reform and support of education. Indeed, the conference concluded that the present economic challenge is more profound than Sputnik and as fundamental as the change from an agrarian to an industrial economy after the Civil War."

Also in 1983, the United States, which at the time paid its teachers an average of less than $20,000 a year, faced a report by the National Commission on Excellence in Education called "A Nation at Risk." It hit Americans right in their manifest destiny: "Our once unchallenged preeminence in commerce, industry, science, and technological innovation is being overtaken by competitors throughout the world . . . . The educational foundations of our society are presently being eroded by a rising tide of mediocrity that threatens our very future as a Nation and a people." The nation reacted immediately. State politicians rushed to implement the report's recommendations. Within a year of its release, 41 states had made it harder to graduate from high school, 37 had introduced new and stricter standardized testing programs, 20 had increased the number of hours students had to spend in school, and 19 had toughened school discipline policies. By the end of Reagan's term in 1988, his secretary of education, William J. Bennett, had called for a "leaner and meaner" high school curriculum, and New York principal Joe Clark was glorified on the cover of *Time* magazine, posing with the baseball bat he used to keep the students in line.

Margaret Thatcher went further. Unhindered by the division of powers that Reagan had to contend with, she remade the British school system in her image. A 1985 British government white paper, "Better Schools,"outlined what the change was all about: "The Government believes that the standards now generally attained by our pupils are neither as good as they can be nor as good as they need to be for the world of the twenty-first century. School education should do much more to promote enterprise and adaptability and to fit young people for working life in a technological age." How does one "fit" young people into future jobs? It's simple. As the white paper said, you "encourage the qualities, attitudes, knowledge, understanding and competences which are necessary to equip pupils for working life." With that, Thatcher radically changed a school system that, a few years earlier, had been radically changed by the Labour Party. The Labour Party had set up "comprehensive" schools partly as an attempt to make education more democratic. These apparently did not work. On the surface, they removed the physical segregation that reflected Britain's rigid social-class structure. Middle- and upper-middle-class students in exclusive grammar schools were placed in the same schools as poor, working-class, and visible minority children. But nothing else changed. The schools kept the same rigid, academic curriculum and examination system that historically was used to restrict access to university. The results were the same, but the elitist nature of the system was less visible. The process of schooling, however, runs much deeper than what lies on the surface.

Thatcher ploughed ahead with her reforms. She imposed a national, "common" curriculum on schools. All students must study mathematics, English, science, history, geography, technology, music, art, physical education, and a modern foreign language. These would take up 70 per cent of the school day, with the rest of the day left open for options. The children would be tested with nationally approved, standardized tests around the ages of 7, 11, 14, and 16. The tests are intended to be "diagnostic." They are not to be used to fail kids. Those who don't meet nationally set targets in various subjects will be given extra help. But there's a twist. The scores will be used to publicly compare the performance of different schools: In effect, to create competition among schools. Thatcher's reforms were passed as the 1988 Education Reform Bill.

A national debate on education is not complete without a fierce debate over standardized examinations. Supporters say they're the best way to ensure that all students achieve at least a minimum level of skills. Schools decide what it is they want children to know and then test them to see if they have mastered it. Opponents say these tests are destructive. They tend to be culturally biased and work against children from working-class and ethnic minority backgrounds. But both sides agree on one crucial result: The system encourages teachers to "teach to the test."

Only a foolish – or extremely courageous – teacher would not drill students on material that will be tested; poor scores by students reflect badly on the teacher. So standardized tests allow governments to reach behind the closed doors of classrooms and further centralize control.

Discredited in the late 1960s, standardized exams are making a comeback. They have been reintroduced in British Columbia, Alberta, and New Brunswick and are at the centre of heated debates in the other provinces. Their popularity has increased as provincial governments come under pressure to make schools more accountable. Scores from standardized tests can be politically embarrassing. They're an incentive for governments to take more control of schools, especially in an environment where schools are criticized for being out of step with a changing economy. In the end, they greatly reinforce the assembly-line mode of schools.

During the 1980s, the B.C. Social Credit government was a big supporter of corporate agendas. In 1982 the government made a "Consumer Education" program mandatory in the schools, which meant students had to pass the courses to graduate. The program came as a complete surprise to the B.C. Teachers' Federation, which dubbed it "Capitalism 11-12." By making the program compulsory, the province was forcing students to cut down on option courses. Teachers who taught optional courses like music, for instance, were left with fewer classes and so were assigned to teach the new consumer education program. Not being skilled in economics, they reached for ready-made packages from the corporate world to use in their classrooms.

The most popular of these packages is called *Project Business*. It's produced by Junior Achievement, a Canada-wide organization of businesses that includes IBM, Xerox, MacMillan Bloedel, and the major banks. The group defines its purpose this way: "The mission of Junior Achievement is to promote economic literacy, an understanding of, and a positive attitude toward business and private enterprise among Canadian youth." Junior Achievement sold the package to schools in the tried and true corporate way: It wined and dined school administrators and teachers. As part of the deal, a business executive gets control of a class once a week to make sure students hear the virtues of free enterprise straight from the horse's mouth.

Project Business is a glossy 195-page package that is supposed to make teaching easy. It's filled with graphs and charts designed to make capitalism fun. There are, for instance, free enterprise crossword puzzles: "If the money received is more than the money spent, a _____ is made (six letters across)"; "The machinery, factories and physical elements are owned by private individuals and they have the right to make a profit (or take a loss). This is called _____ (ten letters down)".

Another test is called "Ad Match." It presents students with two columns and they are to match advertising slogans with the companies they are associated with. Slogans: "It's a good time for the great taste of _____"; "Ohh what a feeling___"; "Taking it to the limit____"; "Where your value is guaranteed ____." Answers: McDonald's, Toyota, Kawasaki, Eaton's.

Students also learn about the "Seven Ms" of production: material, money, manpower, machines, methods, management, and markets. And to put this industrial philosophy to practice, the package is full of games that turn the classroom into stock markets, businesses, or banks.

It costs Junior Achievement $300,000 a year to produce the curriculum package for teachers. An advertisement soliciting corporate donations for the operation shows a bar graph of how the program went from reaching 1,000 B.C. students in 1981 to 5,000 in 1985. Under the banner *Your Investment in Free Enterprise,* the ad tells businesses, "It costs $65 for each student influenced, $325 for 5 students, $195 for 3."

In an essay on *Project Business,* a girl from Lambrick Park High School in Victoria wrote: *"Project Business* has affected my understanding of the free enterprise system in that it has enabled me to realize all the many opportunities offered toward my future and that of British Columbia. The economic climate in British Columbia is quite conducive to supporting any individual, provided he has the initiative and willingness to work, in fulfilling all the business ambitions he may have. I myself have realized the endless opportunities open to me and to almost anyone in the province of British Columbia due to the free enterprise system here."

The B.C. Teachers' Federation tried to balance the propaganda in *Project Business* by developing a curriculum package on labour. Since the majority of students would eventually end up in union jobs, the federation thought it important to brief them on their role as employees in an economic system where they have little power. One part of the package, for instance, dealt with the collective bargaining process. The Socred education minister at the time assailed the labour studies curriculum as socialist dribble. The attack was so vituperative that it scared most teachers from using the package designed by their own union.

By the end of the decade, Prime Minister Brian Mulroney had gotten into the act. On August 25, 1989, Mulroney stood in front of a national convention of the Progressive Conservative Party in Ottawa and proclaimed: "The future also lies in our system of education. It is education systems that will determine international competitiveness rankings in the future .... Our educational system is shortchanging many Canadians and imposing a severe burden on our national competitiveness." At a first ministers' conference less than three months later, Mulroney tied education to international competition another half-dozen times in a three-minute speech. Mulroney and the premiers agreed to establish a task force that would study the relationship of schools to Canada's competitive position and the international economic challenges of the year 2000. Canada's political elite had finally found Sputnik II.

By the late 1980s, another equally urgent voice for reform could be heard. *Challenges and Changes*, a 1988 report on education commissioned by the Manitoba government, said: "In this era of interdependence – when the global community faces critical environmental concerns, a fragile international economy and the shadow of nuclear war – it is imperative that a high sense of ethics and social responsibility be instilled in those preparing to take their place as adults in society." When government committees start admitting we're toying with Armageddon, it's time to really worry, a sure sign we've been joyriding with our existence a long time before anyone officially told us.

To escape the looming global blackout, the Manitoba report said schools should focus on the "new basics": thinking, learning, and creating. It distinguished itself as exceptional by recommending that students should master the process of learning at a time when "process" had become an unfashionable word in education. The process of learning, or teaching students how to learn, is a tenet of the progressive pedagogy of the 1960s, and it is wrongly blamed by back-to-basics proponents as having caused a decline in standards. In an age where the myth of progress is glorified, the blinding desire for certainty allows answers to take precedence over questions. But the Manitoba report bucked this trend, arguing that spoon-feeding bits of information to students is useless. The report adopted the progressive philosophy of education, and even some business groups have adopted its principles.

"The debate about whether we educate students to reach their greatest potential or to enter the workforce is rapidly becoming irrelevant," the Canadian Federation of Independent Business told a committee of the Ontario Legislature in 1988. "We have to do both." Perhaps without knowing it, the business group was calling on schools to simply practice more democracy and submission. It's a dual and contradictory mandate that schools have historically been expected to satisfy. By the time elementary schools in Canada West became free, universal, and compulsory in 1871 – arguably a great act of democracy – the hidden curriculum of submission was entrenched in the structure and pedagogy of schooling.

A B.C. Royal Commission on Education in 1989 described the contradiction this way: "We have long expected schools to serve as agencies for civic and democratic development and as places where our culture and values can be sustained and transmitted to the young. We have likewise come to expect that schools will provide custodial care for children and socialize them into certain norms of behaviour, as well as prepare and select them for later careers." On the one hand, schools are supposed to produce a more democratic society, and on the other they're supposed to spoon-feed existing cultural norms while sorting and slotting people into good jobs and bad jobs.

No report expressed this contradiction more forcefully in Canada than Ontario's 1988 Radwanski report, which caused debate across the country. Radwanski warned that Ontario was at risk of producing "a generation of under educated ignoramuses" unless it started developing students who could think for themselves. To achieve this, he recommended a common liberal arts program for all high school students, with no options allowed. He then left educators scratching their heads again by calling for a curriculum based on "mastery learning," a method of teaching in which information is presented in sequenced bits, each one forming a hurdle that must be cleared before students move on to the next one.

Radwanski also critiqued the practice of streaming. He argued that by discriminating against ethnic minority students and those from low-income backgrounds, streaming perpetuates a cycle of poverty, and that the practice must be abolished. He then ensured that streaming will never be wiped out, by arguing that schools must be plugged into the economy. He wrote: "Education has long been recognized as an important contributor to economic growth, of course – but now it has become *the* paramount ingredient for competitive success in the world economy." The secret, then, is to figure out what the world economy needs. For that, Radwanski quoted a 1987 policy statement by the Economic Council of Canada: "Education is a cornerstone. Its importance in a high-technology world cannot be ignored because the accelerating pace of change will lead to rapid obsolescence of skills. The education system therefore faces a profound challenge. It must prepare individuals to be mobile, flexible, adaptable and versatile. The ability to learn will be the premium skill of the future." But people who are "mobile, flexible, adaptable and versatile" are not necessarily people who can think for themselves. They may simply be docile company people.

Does the economy really need creative thinkers? It may need some, but how many? What if, rather than consisting of a market full of creative thinkers, the economy is becoming more like the shape of a pear: a few highly skilled managers at the top and lots of unskilled, low-paying, service-sector jobs at the bottom? Does that mean we produce smiling automatons? We can be sure of one thing: the essential structure of the economy has changed little since the industrial revolution. Power continues to be centralized in the hands of a few, and tasks continue to be graded and separated, leaving us with the factory model of schools.

Within this model, some changes are more acceptable than others. Teach-to-pass, for example, fits perfectly. Holistic language, however, is fighting an uphill battle because its very nature contradicts and challenges the factory model. Thus, while the messages may be contradictory, the ones more likely to filter through are those that support the hidden curriculum and develop the company people both Radwanski and Bob Keech envision, albeit in different ways. As a case study, B.C.'s educational reform is an example of the conflicting demands being placed on schools, while Ontario's major reforms illustrate how the hidden curriculum tends to reject what contradicts it.

■

In January 1989, after studying the recommendations of a provincial royal commission on education, B.C.'s education minister Anthony Brummet unveiled sketchy plans for a complete restructuring of the school system by 1995. The reasons for the massive change fell under the general category of "ensuring that schools provide young people with the knowledge, skills, and attitudes that will be needed to meet the challenges of a rapidly changing world." The challenges, as the government saw them, were: a "recent explosion in knowledge"; a restructuring of the economy from one based on resources to one with a growing emphasis on "information processing" and the service sector; and new markets in the Pacific Rim. The minister then unveiled the "mission statement" for B.C. schools – the one sentence expected to drive the whole system. It read: "The purpose of the British Columbia school system is to enable learners to develop their individual potential and to acquire the knowledge, skills, and attitudes needed to contribute to a healthy society and a prosperous and sustainable economy."

I met Larry Kuehn three months after the January announcement. As head of staff development for the teachers' union, he had spent a lot of that time collecting documents that spewed out of the ministry of education like ticker-tape at a parade. Covering his desk were regulations that would fill in the gaps in the plans Anthony Brummet had unveiled, the dos and don'ts of the system.

In both senses of the word, Kuehn is a stout man; strong of character and bulky of body. He pointed to the mission statement: "They've done it," he said. "They're making explicit that the central purpose of the system is preparing people to be workers in that economy. They never did that before. They always surrounded it in a liberal rhetoric without really letting anybody know what was really happening. This is probably the classic case of taking the hidden curriculum and making it visible."

The stress of the mission statement, Kuehn said, is on individualism and economic prosperity, while saying nothing about social responsibility. This would have involved a starkly different vision, one the teachers' union had proposed to the government. Schools, the union said, should enable learners to develop as "self-reliant, socially responsible citizens and to acquire the knowledge, skills and attitudes necessary to participate in a healthy, prosperous and democratic society." In the end, "socially responsible" was replaced by "individual potential" and "democratic society" with "sustainable economy." When NDP members of the B.C. legislature tried to reintroduce the words "democratic society" in an amendment, one Socred cabinet minister accused them of wanting to teach students about "socialist systems." The amendment, not surprisingly, was torpedoed. The NDP later took power, but the mission statement of schools remained the same.

According to the reforms, students will be judged on three fronts: intellectual, social, and career. From the time students walk into school, teachers will assess them in these areas and report the progress to parents. The Socred government described career development this way: "To prepare students for their occupational and career objectives: to assist in the development of effective work habits and the flexibility to deal with change in the workplace." This will be tricky for primary grade teachers.

Larry Kuehn began riffling through his papers.

"Where's the bottle? I'm trying to find the bottle. I know it's here somewhere. Oh, here it is. This is the system. A wine bottle on its side. Here," Kuehn said, pointing to a diagram from the Socred government of what the new school system would look like, and it was exactly as he had described it.

At the base of the bottle were the first four years of schooling, kindergarten to grade 3. The government had taken the radical step of wiping out grade levels, a change also made by the Alberta government in 1989. Progressive elementary teachers have been fighting to get rid of grades for years. They argue that children develop at different rates, in spurts and starts, not according to some artificial grade level. Besides, the origin of grades had little to do with pedagogy. They were first introduced in the early nineteenth century in "monitorial schools." Anywhere from a hundred to a thousand children were herded into the same room to be instructed by teachers' aids who took their orders from a teacher. With so many students in one class, grading made the drilling of children more manageable.

In the middle of the bottle, from grades 4 to 10, students would study a common curriculum of humanities, sciences, practical arts (business, home economics), and fine arts. The neck of the bottle is reserved for those heading to university. At the mouth of the bottle the government had laid out what the system was to produce: "personal enrichment/ self-initiated career activities [read: entrepreneurship]/ post-secondary access/ world of work." Nothing about social responsibility.

The changes are dressed up in the right language. Education minister Brummet said: "The system will focus on the preparation of educated citizens, who have the ability to think clearly and critically, and to adapt to change." The common curriculum, he said, should be taught in an integrated way rather than having each subject treated separately. This paves the way for ridding schools of disciplines that artificially divide the world into 45-minute periods of physics, biology, chemistry, and so on. Instead, schools could integrate social, political, and scientific ideas under broad courses like the environment, which make a lot more sense to students. Both of those goals – critical thinking and integration of knowledge – are quite progressive. But universities, the bastions of artificially divided academic disciplines, began to pressure the more recent NDP government in B.C. to drop the integrated studies approach.

In the senior high school years, the regulations call for sequential learning: a student knows A before moving on to B, knows B before moving on to C, and so on. In other words, information is presented in a linear fashion and students are tested along the way to make sure they grasp the content before moving to the next level. In the senior high school years knowledge is to be both integrated and sequential, a paradox that the hidden curriculum is left to resolve. It's no mystery which one the hidden curriculum prefers: spoon-feeding students sequential bits of information is what it does best. It also follows that sequential learning in the senior grades will pressure teachers in earlier grades to teach in the same way.

B.C.'s royal commission on education said nothing about sequential learning, perhaps because most of what it stressed suggested the complete opposite. But sequential learning is back in vogue. In Canada, George Radwanski, more than anyone else, was responsible for resurrecting it. His report to the Ontario government said, "Learning should be seen as sequential, with the curriculum divided into manageable learning tasks or segments that a child must master before moving on to the next phase." When a child hits an obstacle in this sequential drive, the school would then provide individualized help. "The risk of simply being left behind and accumulating an unmanageable deficit in knowledge and skills is greatly reduced." Radwanski said the system would be a less rigid version of the mastery learning style popularized by Benjamin Bloom in Chicago in the mid-1970s, but he didn't explain how.

To some extent, sequential learning is based on a simple definition of equality that gives all students the same bits of information to master. By the time they graduate everyone has passed the same amount of bits.

Chicago schools adopted this method in the 1970s. Reading was broken into 283 sequential subskills the students had to master. In a 1985 study of the program, researcher Harriet Talmage found that teachers hated it. The method wrongly assumed that all students learn in exactly the same way, and that piling one subskill on top of another would amount to the acquisition of a complete skill. External tests proved the teachers right. The students' reading scores had dropped substantially from the time the program began. By 1981 parents had figured out there was something wrong and a group of them filed suit against the Chicago school board to stop the program. The board did so in 1985.

Linda Darling-Hammond, in her essay "The Over-Regulated Curriculum" in *The Principal's Bulletin*, explained that Chicago's less than stellar experience with sequential learning was not an isolated case. School boards across the United States that adopted the program came up with some incongruous results. Some children had successfully jumped over all the hurdles but were still unable to read. Others were proficient readers but kept failing tests that measured the many hurdles they should have cleared.

Darling-Hammond, a researcher with the Rand Corporation, believes sequential learning is analogous to ordering doctors to follow a check list of procedures for all patients with certain diseases. Everyone would get equal treatment, but no one would get personal care based on a doctor's professional judgement or a patient's unique symptoms.

Larry Kuehn had another problem with sequential learning. Critical thinking skills, a buzz phrase in schools throughout Canada, are not the easiest to test. They're a combination of intuitive and logical thinking; an ability to look at something upside down and to make assumptions when there is no straight path to an answer. These skills are hard to define as an objective, and even harder to test. Trying to do so, Kuehn felt, would result in stressing only those skills that can be tested. "A reductionist view of the world is inherent in a sequential learning approach," he said.

"The model is, in effect, the Ford factory model; that education consists of a sequence of putting things into the student's head and putting things onto the students in terms of behaviours, and one always comes after the other just like in an assembly line. You don't jump ahead."

Still, it's easy to see why sequential learning remains popular. It fits neatly into a society where so much is organized in straight lines. Sequential learning makes the practice of putting people into neat boxes less complicated. If Johnny clears the hurdle he stays on a straight path. If he doesn't he's shuffled into a box stamped "remediation." Sequential learning promotes conformity by assuming that anyone who doesn't respond in a predictable manner is deficient. It sees the classroom not as the dynamic sum of individual relationships, but as an assembly line that promotes competition and alienation. In other words, it shifts into high gear everything schools already do.

The B.C. reforms are a classic mixture of progressive and regressive schooling. Ontario's experience indicates that contradictions and ambiguities in school reform eventually become fodder for the great scavenger – the hidden curriculum.

In 1980, the Conservative government in Ontario began a review of schools that eventually led to a new high school curriculum, entitled Ontario Schools: Intermediate and Secondary (OSIS). The head of the committee developing the new curriculum was Duncan Green, who had been the director of the Toronto Board of Education in the 1970s when a group of progressive trustees began tackling racial and class biases in the system for the first time. Green's committee was made up of representatives from education, labour, and business, including Sonia Bata of Bata Shoes, Greg Murtah of the Ontario Federation of Labour, and Ron Watts of the Council of Ontario Universities. The extent to which schools were not producing students capable of taking on the world economically was blamed largely on the poorly implemented progressive reforms of the late 1960s.

Murtah and Watts both stressed that while the pressure was on to plug schools into the economy, the government was interested in more than simply producing cogs for the industrial machine. In fact, the OSIS curriculum developed by the committee supports this view. Its documents are filled with the "critical thinking" messages of the Hall-Dennis report, *Living and Learning*, an example of how rhetorically entrenched that philosophy has become in education. However, the government's boast that OSIS was a "back-to-basics" curriculum was not an empty one. Queen's University sociologist Alan King said OSIS was a reactionary document. "It was a control document. It was an attempt to get control of the schools and control of the time kids spend in schools."

OSIS was introduced in 1984 and it increased, from 9 to 16, the number of subjects students were forced to take. Then it did something teachers still can't figure out. It lowered the number of credits needed to graduate for students heading to university and increased the number needed for students in non-university programs to get their high school diploma. Not surprisingly, in a report to the Ontario government in 1988, Alan King predicted the drop-out rate would increase among students in non-university courses, where children from low-income families tend to be found.

Duncan Green provided a more startling judgement of OSIS. By the time he testified before a committee of Ontario politicians in October 1988, Green had just finished a four-year stint as the province's assistant deputy minister of education. He told the committee that OSIS was designed to eliminate streaming. It took the seven program streams that had existed since the early 1960s and created basic-, general-, and advanced-level courses. Therefore a student who was bright in math but struggling in English could take an advanced-level math course and a general- or basic-level English. Quality-conscious universities had their academic interests protected. To qualify for university, students had to pass six select courses, called Ontario Academic Credits, offered in grade 13. The plan failed miserably. Instead of floating from one level to another, students were streamed or locked into one of the three levels beginning in grade 9 and forced to take all their courses at that level. In the end, rather than having basic, general, and advanced *courses*, Ontario schools created basic, general, and advanced *students*.

"Levels of difficulty were intended to apply to content," Duncan

Green told politicians on the committee. "They were not intended to apply to students. It worked in reverse."

Green places much of the blame on a society, particularly its business leaders, that insists on labeling human beings as if they were cans of soup. "When kids get out of school, we ask whether they've got a B, a C, or an A on their heads," he said. It's a view many principals perpetuated. As managers, they had another reason for streaming students: it made the school day easier to organize. This is perhaps the most striking example of the power of the hidden curriculum. It took a policy aimed at destreaming schools and turned it into one that streamed more efficiently.

After almost 40 years in education as English teacher, principal, school board director, and high-level government bureaucrat, Duncan Green concluded: "I don't know whether the school system can become the great equalizer it was meant to be. We always want to know who was first and who was twenty-fifth." He was talking about the hidden curriculum.

Tackling the hidden curriculum was the last thing on Ontario Premier David Peterson's mind when he rose to speak at his party's annual "heritage dinner" in March 1987. As supporters supped on $300-a-plate roast beef dinners, Peterson described the province's 40 per cent drop-out rate (later revised to 33 per cent) as one of the highest in the industrial world. He declared: "You have to question the efficiency of a system that is not serving young people" who need "new skills to compete in the modern, changing world." He struck an all-party committee of the legislature to review virtually all aspects of elementary and secondary education. Throughout much of the debate that followed, teachers joined the students in suffering from a numbing blend of skepticism and cynicism, much of which was entirely valid. The Liberals planned to overhaul a school system that had been radically changed by the Conservative government only three years earlier with the implementation of OSIS. And both governments had embarked on changes for the same reasons: to develop students better prepared to wage international competition.

School systems are massive bureaucracies. It can take years before a government policy trickles down to the classroom, and this was the case with the reforms of 1984. The Liberals were intending to change a system that was not yet fully in place. For instance, most of the curriculum guidelines for OSIS had yet to be produced. Those that had been dealt exclusively with the advanced courses for teenagers bound for university. The fact that they were produced first indicates where the political clout in the system lies.

The guidelines for courses at the general and basic levels of study, where 40 per cent of students are enrolled, had yet to emerge from the bureaucracy when David Peterson announced that change was on its way. Many teachers in general and basic programs settled on teaching watered-down versions of the advanced level courses, which made no sense to students who weren't heading to university. Finally, although there were serious problems with OSIS, no one was certain of its total impact since the first group of students to begin their high school studies under the new curriculum had not yet graduated.

Trying to change a system already in the midst of change lent a farcical air to the debate that followed. The all-party committee struck by Peterson started its hearings in the spring of 1988, and Duncan Green was the first witness. Green went through a list of major school reforms since 1950 and said: "Sometimes I wonder how the plant grows when the plant is pulled up so often to see how its roots are doing."

Jack Clemens of the Ontario Chamber of Commerce followed Green before the education committee. He stated: "With rare exceptions reality comes crashing in on all of us at some point and that reality is easier to bear if we have not been excessively shielded from it for prolonged periods of time. With that as a prelude, you will not be surprised to learn that we support both some form of standardized testing and the 'right' to fail."

The business community wanted tests in reading, writing, and mathematics at every grade level. Those who didn't meet the targets would get help. If that didn't work, the big stamp: *failure*. The right to fail. There are fewer limits than we thought to the freedoms we enjoy in a liberal capitalist democracy. The *right* to feel like a loser: It sounds like something we should take pride in.

The Chamber of Commerce is right about one thing: the essence of Western capitalist reality is winning and losing. From this, according to the Chamber, a cold logic should prevail. Since some are going to lose anyway, it's best to get them used to the idea as soon as possible. It's true that most elementary teachers try desperately to shield children from being stamped losers; they have seen how the stigma corrodes human dignity. But they also know that children are not the same and that they develop at different speeds. The thought of destroying a child before he or she blossoms strikes horror in most teachers, but the hidden curriculum ensures that it happens nonetheless. Our economy demands it, and the statement by the Chamber of Commerce illustrates the pressure on schools to maintain their process of judging, sorting, and slotting students into winning and losing streams. In Ontario alone, 17 per cent of children are failed in elementary school, an incredible 80 per cent of those in grades 1 and 2. And many more are taught to be losers in more subtle and complex ways. In their thirst to have schools sort more efficiently, the business leaders didn't recognize that the shielding process furthers their own ends. By softening the blow of being stamped a failure, it makes the label easier to carry in a society that lumps into that category almost anyone who doesn't wear a white collar to work.

Ontario's education soul-searching has led to a worthy but relatively minor reform that has caused a major uproar. Before leaving office in 1990, the Liberal government announced it would push back the streaming of students by one year, until after grade 9. The new NDP government embraced the Liberal policy and set a three-year phase-in period. As the September 1993 deadline to de-stream schools by one year approached, the high school teachers' union in Ontario hit the roof.

The leadership of the Ontario Secondary School Teachers' Federation initially opposed the move. This put the federation in lonely territory. When the NDP government asked for public comments on the de-streaming plan, 75 per cent of the 825 written responses were favourable. Federation president Liz Barkley then charged that the de-streaming plan was poorly researched and put together without teacher consultation. To top it all off, she called for education minister Tony Silipo's resignation.

The federation's complaints about the de-streaming plan were groundless. Consultations leading to the reform began in 1987, spawned some 60 pilot projects across the province, and involved the teachers' union every step of the way. Also, de-streaming for one year is not exactly reinventing the wheel. Elementary teachers have been conducting classes with students of mixed abilities for more than a century, and the research on how to conduct de-streamed high school classes is voluminous. The real problem is the resistance of many high school teachers to change. The small group of grade 9 teachers affected by the change will have to modify their teaching methods and act more like their elementary colleagues. This requires retraining, not a favourite pastime of teachers, especially older ones who tend to be set in their ways. Unfortunately, the government has done little to ease these anxieties, offering little funding to retrain teachers and not producing curriculum documents for the new division of study – grades 7 to 9.

The ministry of education indicated that the new curriculum would have students follow integrated courses of study, rather than the academic disciplines now in place in high schools. Instead of dividing the world into periods of math, physics, chemistry, and so on, students would actually get a chance to understand how those disciplines interrelate. High school teachers protective of their subject areas fought hard against the idea, and by 1993 it seemed the government was ready to back down and keep the artificial disciplines.

No schooling reform would be complete without a built-in contradiction. While the Ontario government postponed streaming for one year, it also began to produce a set of standards that students must meet at various grade levels. Some educators fear that teachers will be forced to spoon-feed content to meet those standards. Once a standard is set, tests are needed to evaluate whether students have reached them. The more you test, the easier it becomes to sort, and the hidden curriculum loves to sort.

Ontario's NDP government struck a Royal Commission on Learning in 1993 to once again take a look at how the system's roots were doing.

If society were immune to change, it would not spend forever searching for an educational panacea. We would set up schools in a way that satisfied our present needs and that would be that. Change, however, is one of the few certainties of existence, and this puts schools in what seems like an impossible predicament. Anthropologist Jules Henry explains that the first concern of human beings when faced with a new idea is to ensure that it doesn't kill us. Our immediate reaction is to retreat towards what we know. "Thus throughout history the cultural pattern has been a device for binding the intellect," Henry states in *Culture Against Man*. "Today, when we think we wish to free the mind so it will soar, we are still, nevertheless, bound by the ancient paradox, for we must hold our culture together through clinging to old ideas lest, in adopting new ones, we literally cease to exist." This unique human tendency to look forward and fall back gives flight to our anxiety and leaves us flirting with disaster.

The profound political and social changes of the 1980s were like a global shakedown after decades of Western consumer abundance spurred by a Cold War economy. Pollution penetrated our cocoon of smug ignorance and demonstrated that the enemy was within. Mother Nature is fighting centuries of industrial pollution by giving in and slowly dying. The Cold War may be over, but nuclear weapons remain. When the world can be blown up hundreds of times over, knowing that things used to be worse is of little comfort. We're left groping in an age starstruck by economic progress, in which technology, competition, and consumerism join in a frenzied display of public masturbation. Our natural tendency to retreat in the face of change is reinforced by a nostalgia for a simpler time and a refusal to look beyond the mythologies that blind us. As our fear of change grows, we pressure schools to preserve a culture that's busy charting its own ruin. The economy becomes the main concern, not only because profits keep business happy and re-elect governments, but also because the economy has for centuries served as the litmus test for our quality of life. And so, in looking forward and falling back, we bombard schools with mixed messages while beefing up the hidden curriculum. In the end, the status quo and its blinding mythology of economic progress are reinforced.

Conclusion

JAMES IN A BOX

There is little that's new in the debate on school reform. The fundamental arguments have been around for over 30 years. Should education be a "child-centred" process of discovery or must every child master a minimum body of knowledge somehow deemed important? Do we teach a common, liberal arts curriculum or do we make schools "relevant" by offering options and job training? Do we stress "equality of outcomes" or are we better served by a survival of the fittest philosophy? Is the flexible organization of open or free schools more effective than the rigid structure of traditional schools? Do we embrace Old Education, New Education, conservative, progressive, neo-progressive, liberal, radical, or holistic? All the arguments have been repeated with monotonous regularity. And with each debate, the complaint that schools are failing persists. "There was never a time when critics did not complain that educational standards had fallen," states Canadian historian C.E. Phillips.

Canadian schools are facing a crisis. Structured and operated according to the industrial model of the nineteenth century, schools are horribly out of tune with an emerging post-industrial society at the doorstep of the twenty-first century. Students are living in a world where information "explodes" and communication is "revolutionized." Spoon-feeding facts on an assembly line is pure silliness when facts change by the hour and brains are hooked to machines in the symbiotic world of "virtual reality." We're witnessing a fundamental shift in our under-standing of the universe, moving from a world that resembles a sequence of building blocks to one where all reality is interconnected and holis-tic. In this new context, creativity and imagination are at a premium, especially when knowledge sheds its illusion of truth to become an end-less process of integrating information. Developing a new ethics be-comes a matter of survival in a world where experiences are increasing-ly mediated by technology, and are, as a result, becoming more artificial.

Cultural critic Ivan Illich argues persuasively that all the pedagogi-cal and structural changes in the world won't stop the hidden curricu-lum from doing its not so invisible work. Illich recommends that we "deschool" society – in effect, get rid of the school as an obligatory ritual for all. This must be the ultimate goal of all school reform.

Illich wants people to assume responsibility for their own learning, an obvious necessity in a post-industrial society. He wants to break a key myth of the hidden curriculum – the belief that most learning is a result of teaching inside the walls of a school. Most learning occurs casually during work or leisure, and the greatest learning achievement of all – the acquisition of language – occurs largely in the home. In any event, with computers becoming as common as telephones, it's naive to assume that schools will keep their monopoly on education. Already, companies are pumping out educational packages of all kinds on computer disks. It doesn't take business smarts to recognize that this type of interactive learning will catch on, especially as children and parents grow more dis-satisfied with schools. By putting people in touch with learning services or with others wanting to pursue the same interests, these educational packages will help create what Illich calls "educational webs." For one thing, Illich recommends that people be given educational credits to buy instruction at skill centres of their choice. But he recognizes that a deschooled society would only work if governments passed laws that prohibit discrimination based on prior schooling. For a society no more ready to give up schooling than to give up television, Illich's vision remains a theoretical ideal.

Still, giving learning back to people and seeing it as an activity that occurs largely outside of school buildings are goals that must guide edu-cational reform. Norman Henchey, an education professor at McGill University, states, "To reduce the education system to the system of elementary and secondary schools is like reducing the health system to intensive care units."

Short of tearing down the walls, there are reforms so obviously demanding of immediate action that it seems only ignorance or stubbornness can explain their absence. There's a chasm between what schools are and what they can be. I do not, however, claim it is within my ability to provide a "blueprint for change." As a journalist, I'm more interested in, and qualified for, describing what I see. There is little I can add to the volumes of specific recommendations for reform that have been suggested by educators, researchers, and those interested in the more abstract pedagogical principles. As a general statement, however, the mandate of schools should be to develop creative and independent thinkers through programs of holistic study, all of this taking place in a more humane environment that respects human dignity.

At the heart of this educational process lies a concern for literacy as I've described it throughout this book: for people to recognize that today's guiding mythologies are theirs to shape and change; and this process of making new myths goes hand in hand with rebellion. Educators seem to have forgotten that the myth of progress, which they faithfully reproduce, was born in a rebellious burst of creativity when science, art, and history converged to shape a radically different view of the universe. That myth has guided our behaviour for some 400 years, but the creative forces and events that merged to shape it have fossilized into unquestioned and not-so-comfortable rituals. Progress is a euphemism for environmental plunder; democracy and justice have been reduced to cocktail party platitudes; human dignity is the plaything of the powerful; relativity means "anything goes"; and morality is left to religious zealots, mediocre politicians, or unread philosophers. For many, the great myth has lost its blinding lustre, but the power of change seems beyond their reach. Resignation triumphs and everywhere life is distinguished from death by only a listless breath. We need to create a new collective story before, out of cynicism and indifference, we self-destruct with the existing one.

The Western myth of progress promised a consumer heaven on earth through scientific achievement. In this sense, it was much the same as the utopian promises of communism. The new myth or story we require promises to leave utopia to the gods. It promises no final chapter or happy ending. It promises only to exist from the moment a child enters nature and a desire becomes a gesture and then a name. It's a story that waits to be told as a book waits to be read. What counts is the tale's construction. Schools should develop builders of tales – people who construct narratives with a passion and lucidity that limit rebellion by respecting a common and inalienable human dignity. The central goal of schools should be to develop storytellers in revolt.

Storytellers in revolt are critical thinkers, people in a constant state of questioning, who take nothing as given until they've turned it upside down, analysed it, and made up their own minds. It's a process driven by lucidity and relativity, where conclusions evolve with experience and absolutes are left to gods. The status quo may have been legitimate yesterday, but the world of today and tomorrow can belong to anyone. And herein lies the dilemma: Is it realistic for a society to demand that its schools challenge its very foundations? Bernard Shapiro has his doubts.

"I think it is true that teachers might pay more attention to social issues," Shapiro says. "It's fair to caution, however, that there may be a terrific price to pay for that by the individual teacher. To come to serious grips with important social issues is to raise in the classroom problems and issues and perspectives that are not going to be popular with the people on whose livelihood the teacher depends. You can't ask individual teachers to bear the burden of being particularly saintly in a bureaucratic environment. And so you need to create the context, at a broader level, in which this kind of conversation and emphasis is acceptable. Because right now, I would say that at least for a lot of boards of education it would not be acceptable, and for a lot of provincial and federal governments it would not be acceptable. You can't pretend that the world out there is somehow more accepting of questions than in fact it is. Radical questioning, which is the best way to develop really responsible citizens, is not something that communities uniformly find acceptable. And one cannot ask individual teachers in those communities to martyr themselves on that particular altar, however valuable it would be if lots of us did it."

It is sad that something as simple as expecting teachers to encourage questioning becomes such a difficult issue in a society obsessed with purifying its own reflection. It gives validity to the argument expressed by Illich that no reform can tame the hidden curriculum of "unending consumption," as he calls it. School reform that stops short of Illich's radical approach is forced to take place in the context of an educational system held hostage by its environment. There is little that schools can do to further an egalitarian society when, all around them, capitalism produces poverty and injustice. The trauma inflicted by some families on children is also beyond the healing power of schools. The family has remained a sacred and secretive institution for too long. In several books, including *But the Truth Will Out,* German psychologist Alice Miller argues that children are victims of "an insane system of child-rearing." She describes the dominant approach to raising children as the beginnings of a process of murdering the soul. Children's unconditional love, trust, naivety, and physical weakness place them at the complete mercy of parents. Too often, the result is psychological or physical abuse. The pressures and vicissitudes of modern society are placing even greater strains on the child's primary means of support. For many professional couples, parenting has been reduced to a competitive drive to create another Mozart. As the first institution of socialization, the emotional battering inflicted on children in abusive families has lasting effects. Schools shouldn't be expected to overcome this family abuse, but neither should they compound it.

Changes on these social fronts, as Shapiro notes, require a concerted effort from all sectors of society and can't be left solely to schools. It's reasonable to expect, however, that schools develop students who recognize that both capitalism and family violence are not products of nature. To build myths, one must first recognize them. Shapiro puts the challenge to teachers this way: "How you balance just accepting the status quo and trying to nudge it along a bit, that's the whole treat. How do you go just far enough so that you sharpen people's edges without jumping out of a twentieth-storey window."

So if helping children raise radical questions threatens teachers with fates usually reserved for martyrs, then the choice is clear – there's no more honourable way to go. Radical questioning is already expected from a small number of students in those schools and programs that pave the way to the high-paying, high-status jobs. And whether we like it or not, youths are themselves questioning the legitimacy of our social system in large numbers. Rebellion seems to come naturally to modern youth. Perhaps only youth culture can ask radical questions, at least in a mass sense. Adult radical voices are often hidden or muffled, cloistered in universities or waiting unread between the covers of books.

As noted in earlier chapters, the hidden curriculum has the unintended effect of making most students aware of the hypocrisies and injustices inherent in both the school game and society at large. The tragedy is that teenage rebellion, vibrant and confused, usually falls prey to co-option or resignation. But building on the vague awareness sparked by rebellion can pave the way to meaningful social change. The challenge is to guide the aimless revolt from one that negates human dignity through resignation to one that affirms it through action.

A crucial first step is to make the hidden curriculum the focus of the official curriculum, to teach students how to "read" what they feel bearing down on them every day; to help them identify the narrative of the great myth, name its components, and trace its history; in short, to humanize what pretends to be divine. Students need to understand that they're spontaneously revolting against the physical manifestations of a collective dream that has hardened into brick walls, straight rows, and assembly-line work. In practice, this kind of teaching would not be much different from the media literacy courses offered in Ontario. By studying rock videos, for example, students are taught how to decipher the underlying sexist or violent messages. The aim is to "demystify" the mass media, to demonstrate that its tales are nothing more than the subjective constructions of individuals. Media literacy should begin in kindergarten, and so too should literacy in the hidden curriculum.

Encouraging storytellers in revolt will require changes to the structure and process of schooling. Schools need, as much as possible, to hand over control to students. If the purpose is to help them understand that myths are theirs to mold and remold, then students will eventually insist on changing their school environment. They need the power to substitute hierarchy with democracy. They need a greater role in determining timetables, the content of courses, evaluation processes, and the rules they intend to uphold. This decentralization of power was attempted by free schools in the 1960s. To develop builders of tales is to give responsibility for education to the learners.

Decentralizing power won't be easy, even though the evidence indicates that there is little to justify the controls of traditional schools. Adult society's fervour for suffocating its young is expressed in the back-to-basics movement's attempt to make schools more rigid than they already are. No small part of the problem seems to be an almost pathological need within the system to maintain clear hierarchies, almost an adult vindictiveness whose purpose is rooted in a dark instinct. "For your own good" is an adult euphemism for misguided resentment. With age, a permanent sense of loss often replaces the vitality and exuberance of youth. The excitement that burned in a rebellious and youthful heart is easily smothered in nostalgia and missed opportunities. Life is for the young and wisdom is poor consolation for old age. Misery, as they say, loves company and what was bad enough for us becomes bad enough for others. And so the pressure from many adults is to keep schools as boring and control-crazed as when they experienced them.

The more things change, the more some adults feel like the earth is moving beneath them. They desperately cling to what they know but the effort, inevitably, is in vain. The factory model of schooling is not only dehumanizing to both students and teachers but also obsolete. Social behaviour and relationships are in a period of profound flux and yet institutions, as is their wont, remain firmly anchored in the past. They blindly continue to practice and preach a tale that has long since gone stale. The electronic age has circumvented the lockstep, sequential, and hierarchical structure of a print-based, industrial society. Information, once the preserve of "experts" or the powerful, is now widely and, with television, indiscriminately disseminated. Children have a front-row seat to adult hypocrisies, and many of them learn to access computer information long before they've read their first novel. The distinction between adults and children is blurred, and authority is undermined. If schools remain inert, cynicism and resentment among students are sure to grow.

If free schools are to be used as working models for reform, it's important to remember that they died largely at the hands of teachers, like so many educational reforms of the past. Teachers are the key to all reform, and without better training they'll continue to act like "clerks of the empire." Faculties of education must be put through the kind of intense scrutiny now reserved for schools. Nothing short of a complete change in curriculum and teaching methods will do. Once in the classroom, teachers should be given more support and control over their jobs.

If they are to empower students, they themselves must feel that they are more than just cogs in a wheel.

The exceptional demands placed on unexceptional teachers became a major criticism of free schools. Many teachers are unexceptional, but only a minority don't care to improve their craft. It doesn't take an exceptional teacher to understand and practice holistic methods and critical pedagogy. It does, however, take a change of attitude. Teachers can no longer pretend to be all knowing. They should have the courage to share with students a sense of bewilderment and a passionate, inspired search for personal meaning amid the confusion of life. A good teacher is one who helps students understand the process involved in the journey, one who lights a path through an endless tunnel. Students must be engaged rather than controlled. Discipline, of course, is important; without it, nothing would ever get done. But the discipline needed to work through a problem is much different than the discipline needed to obey orders. One is propelled by desire, the other by passivity. Teaching methods such as drilling are rituals of submission that should be banished from the classroom, except for those rare moments when memorization is useful. Drilling has the effect of a sledgehammer on a child's natural enthusiasm for learning. Education should be seen not as a process of molding or changing people but as one that gives students the tools to grow to their fullest potential.

Resources for reform are always limited, but there's no question as to where they should be focused. The elementary years are when the passion for learning is either nourished or destroyed. The focus must be on learning without fear. The only failures at this stage are teachers and school administrators. Children shouldn't be judged by preset, arbitrary standards. Those with a "cultural capital" that corresponds to that of the school are more likely to succeed when everyone is being asked to pass through the same filter. Not surprisingly, those from white, middle-class, or more affluent backgrounds tend to make it through. To value and build on the knowledge, culture, and strengths that each child brings to school would make the process more equitable. To do so, schools should broaden what they define as intelligence. At the moment, students capable of manipulating abstract symbols – those who can let x equal y in a vacuum – are showered with marks and dignity. Children who have difficulty separating abstract thought from their emotions are penalized for failing to sever body and mind. Those who filter the problem through their personal experiences, through what they already know, are penalized for seeing things in context.

This preference for what psychologist Margaret Donaldson calls "disembodied thought" explains the respect society bestows on people who work with their minds and the quiet disdain it holds for those who work with their hands. Intelligence and talent come in different forms, and children skilled in the use of their hands, in drama or music, for example, should be no less valued than children proficient in mathematics. It's simply a question of shifting the weight and creating a better balance. Age-grading must stop, and children should be allowed to progress at their own rates. They should be evaluated according to the progress they make and not ranked against everyone else in the class. There are no winners and losers under the stars, just people trying to find their way in the dark.

The segregation of students according to arbitrarily deemed ability – at both the elementary and secondary level – is educationally questionable and morally repugnant, and should be abolished. The wounds inflicted on the dignity of students placed in the lower streams is reason enough to end the practice. If teachers can't conduct classes in which students work in groups, with the faster and more motivated students helping the less so, then they shouldn't be teaching. Group work is perhaps the best way to temper the reckless individualism encouraged by the hidden curriculum with a dose of co-operation and, by extension, social responsibility. Group work inevitably teaches a certain degree of relativity. The opinions exchanged in groups drive home the message that the experiences of someone from Cambodia, for instance, produce a world view that can be radically different from the dominant one in the West. One person's myth is another person's mystery. Group work creates the environment for the refining of old tales and the building of new ones.

Generally, critics of the education system on the left equate the end of streaming with the setting up of a common curriculum in which all students would study the same courses. A common curriculum, they argue, would give everyone access to the same knowledge. This theory is well intentioned but misguided. As society becomes more culturally diverse, the chances of designing a curriculum that satisfies all groups is next to impossible. Usually, a liberal arts curriculum is suggested. This opens the endless debate about whether Shakespeare, for instance, is more useful than knowledge of African folktales. A liberal arts curriculum also shows a complete disregard for the system's clients. Many students are bored to death by the old disciplines, and while they may be convinced that Shakespeare is more valuable than rock videos, they have met few teachers who can make his work as exciting to them. Schools should instead provide as many options as possible. A student with a passion for mechanics has no less potential to think critically than a student engaged by the sciences. Only an uncreative teacher could teach mechanics without engaging students in everything from quantum physics to a study of the assembly line as the stifling metaphor for Western society. None of the courses, however, should be conducted for the purposes of job training, except in the sense that they develop people who can think for themselves, which is what members of the business community claim they want. Apprenticeship programs and specific training for jobs are better left to industry.

With the end of streaming in secondary schools should come the death of another educational dinosaur – the division of the school day according to academic disciplines, what communications professor Joshua Meyrowitz calls a system of "organized ignorance." When students walk out of classrooms, the world does not strike them in packages of 45-minute periods. It strikes them whole, its infinite connections and contradictions blazing. Reflecting the unity of nature may be impossible, but to try and capture it in neat academic boxes seems a rather crude and arrogant attempt at enslaving what scientists can't understand. We live in a more humble time, more aware that the universal balance struck by order and disorder will likely remain beyond the limits of logic. It might make more sense to divide the curriculum into broad subject categories, such as the environment, popular culture, technology, sports, and arts. All the traditional content, and much more, can be taught within such categories. In a course on the environment, for instance, students may finally get a chance to recognize how biology, chemistry, and physics interrelate. A simpler reason for the change is that these broad subject categories make far more sense to students and are bound to make schools more interesting. Teachers puzzled about how to make schools more relevant need only look at their students. What can explain the embarrassing fact that schools ignore so much of popular culture, for example, when their clients are the walking embodiment of it?

The universities are perhaps the biggest stumbling block to ridding schools of academic disciplines. They remain the fortress of bureaucratic expertise in which academics jealously guard their turf – historians keep anthropologists at a distance and psychologists make sure no one mistakes them for sociologists. They pressure high schools to reflect this view of the world and, indeed, universities must shoulder the blame for much of the structural inertia of schools. In Toronto, for instance, high school science teacher Ted Anderson helped design a provincially approved course called Science in Society. Under this broad category, Anderson teaches the traditional disciplines of physics, chemistry, and biology. The course is also designed to help students understand the sometimes deterministic impact of technology and the ethical questions it raises. Universities have made clear they don't like this unorthodox treatment of science, and Anderson fears this hesitation may drive students away from his course. Universities act as an institutional anchor for the myth of progress, insisting, for instance, that schools maintain their apartheid-like practice of streaming and standardized examinations to ensure that academic undesirables – those who have failed to at least mimic, if not ingest, the rituals of the hidden curriculum – be sifted out of the school game.

In the end, it's neither the kinds of courses taught nor their content that's most important, but the process practiced. An education that encourages students to search for personal meaning and care about social change is of the essence. Whether it happens in a class on popular culture or in Latin is of no consequence. Our desire is for builders of tales; people for whom seeing through myths is as easy as reading street signs; people who will revolutionize society through art or science; people who will revolutionize their families or workplaces through actions big or small.

For the architects of social tales, the most powerful tool available is language, both written and spoken. Writing is especially crucial to the process, because words on paper are a permanent representation of our thoughts. We can then stare at them, reflect on them – "is this *really* what I believe?" – revise, refine, elaborate, or abandon them completely.

It's an exercise in making choices and, in this sense, writing empowers the mind. Schools should develop students who manipulate language as easily as clay. It's a skill that shouldn't be the preserve of English classes; rather, it should be taught and stressed in all subjects. Roman Catholic school systems, despite their reputation for indoctrination, have used this model successfully in discussing moral values across the curriculum.

Introducing children to literature and poetry from the very start of schooling is vital to mastering the art of constructing tales. Poetry's ability to capture human truth in rhythmic and crisp symbolic images captivates children. In his enchanting book, *The Songlines*, Bruce Chatwin wrote that poetry's charm is to sing the sense of movement within our very cells and to recall our nomadic beginnings. Is it, as Rousseau believed, that children are closer to the essence of being than adults are?

One school principal remembers a wager that Toronto educator Don Rutledge made with a group of teachers. It was the late 1960s and introducing young children to "adult" poetry or literature was seen by most teachers as a waste of time. Children would never understand it, they said. During the 1950s and 1960s – a time when American textbooks dominated the curriculum – the small amount of exposure to poetry that elementary students did receive was of the cute and sentimental kind that was quickly forgotten. In giving this kind of poetry to students, teachers usually followed the commercial holidays of the year, such as Valentine's Day or Hallowe'en. Rutledge bet that elementary students would comprehend poems used in senior high school grades. He selected *Not Waving But Drowning*, a powerful allegory by the English poet Stevie Smith. The poem is about a woman standing on a shore watching a "poor chap" in the sea. She mistakes his wave for help for a friendly salute. "I was much too far out all my life, and not waving but drowning," says the man. Rutledge read it to students in grade 6. They understood it. No longer dubious, the teachers followed Rutledge to a grade 5 class, and then a grade 4 class. At both stops most students still understood the poem. They would say things like, "It's about a guy who doesn't fit in." Rutledge and the teachers found themselves in a combined grade 2 and 3 class before the students described the poem only as a lesson in water safety.

Children should also become familiar with myths, legends, and fairy tales. They are replete with the narrative forms we use to organize and understand experiences. Plato believed that Greek myths provided the most appropriate education for children to become ideal citizens. He saw myths – and the same can be said for fairy tales and legends – as the stories that reconcile the inner world we feel and the outer world we see.

"The deep inner conflicts originating in our primitive drives and our violent emotions are all denied in much of modern children's literature," states Bruno Bettelheim, "and so the child is not helped in coping with them . . . . The fairy tale, by contrast, takes these existential anxieties and dilemmas very seriously and addresses itself directly to them: the need to be loved and the fear that one is thought worthless; the love of life, and the fear of death. Further, the fairy tale offers solutions in ways that the child can grasp on his level of understanding."

In her essay "Myth, Legend and Fairy Tale: Serious Statements About Our Existence," Johan Lyall Aitken states, "The symbolic language is something that a young child seems to understand almost viscerally; metaphoric speech is the child's own speech." Aitken, a professor of education at the University of Toronto, deals extensively with the sexist and racist elements found in many fairy tales. She notes that for every tale promoting patriarchy and racism there's another that doesn't. Furthermore, "there is infinitely more that is sexist in life than in art" so withholding such tales from young children is not the answer. As with all literature, the duty of teachers is to place works in their historical and social context and help children examine the prejudices they may convey. Once that's done, myths, legends, and fairy tales are powerful tools for the imagination.

A child who takes possession of a tale gains control of what poet Ted Hughes calls a "unit of imagination." If the story is learned well, the child can re-enter it at leisure and give its many meanings more thought – an exercise in imagination, mental control, and contemplation. In effect, as Hughes notes, the story becomes a word; any fragment of it serves as the "word" by which the whole story's meaning can be brought to life. Hughes uses the stories of Christ and Hitler as examples. A single word or scene from the Christ story – the Nativity, the Crucifixion – is enough to bring the whole story alive. Along the way it illuminates much of European and Middle Eastern history, "just as you need to touch a power line with only the tip of your finger to feel its energy," Hughes says in his essay "Myth and Education." In this sense the word acts like a gate to a cultural reservoir, unleashing the ideas and meanings forged throughout history: in short, the things that guide our lives today. Hughes asks us to imagine what would happen if, somewhere in the reciting of a poem, we heard the phrase, "The Crucifixion of Hitler." For those who possess both stories, combining these words would create a psychic explosion. They would trigger an immense inner working. How can Hitler and crucifixion exist together? "All our static and maybe dormant understanding of good and evil and of what opens beyond good and evil is shocked into activity. Many unconscious assumptions and intuitions come up into the light to declare themselves and explain themselves and reassess each other," Hughes states. Similarly, it was the colliding myths of early Greece – which had several Christs and Hitlers to deal with – that illuminated the philosophers and poets.

When the dust of colliding tales settles, we emerge with a clearer understanding of good and evil. Evil has always been around, but it's the details of the Hitler story that most vividly illustrated it for us and changed the consciousness of modern man. Hughes argues that the Christ and Hitler stories show "how stories think for themselves, once we know them. They not only attract and light up everything relevant in our experience; they are also in continual private meditation, as it were, on their own implications. They are little factories of understanding." As people grow and their circumstances change, they extract new meanings from the patterns of stories in their minds. Revelations are not born solely of collision. At some point in our lives, stories begin to converge naturally, like rivers joining the sea. And some day, out of collision and natural convergence, someone will interpret the Christ story in a way so new and overwhelming that the course of history will change. In the meantime, there is much fumbling in the dark. There are stories the ruling elites would rather we did not redefine, and of these the myth of progress is the most sacred. We are expected to embrace the myth while sleepwalking through the ruins of its nihilism. But the rubble tells a tale of lies and deceit that leaves us hollow. We recoil and, without knowing it, begin to question, reinterpret, and slowly rebuild. The primary aim of educaton should be to illuminate this now-buried process, to develop minds that actively search for colliding tales, to develop storytellers in revolt. Sadly, as one final tale from Vancouver's Grace Elementary School indicates, schools too often have little more to offer than a silent surrender of the mind.

"James is in a box." Karen Riley had mentioned this several times and naturally I was having some difficulty understanding exactly what she meant. Shortly after the tape-recorded math drill, Riley delivered in a little sing-song voice the names of those who were ready to go to gym class. "Brian's readee, Bob's readeee, James is readeee." James may have scored points by being ready, but not enough to get him out of trouble. In front of the whole class, Riley reminded him of a rendezvous with the principal. She added that he couldn't watch the video that afternoon because he was "still on report." She looked at him and he sat up straight, his hands clasped on his desk, catching her gaze for a split second before he turned away nervously to scan the floor and ceiling, as if searching for an escape.

James is an aboriginal boy who Riley said more than once "terrorized" the grade ones by attacking them in the schoolyard. With his left arm around their necks and his right hand twisting their arms behind their backs, he would deposit them in a corner. Riley said he learned the game from a television show. For this, Riley put him in a box.

"James comes to school," Riley said, "smelling very strongly of urine so he may or may not be a bedwetter; he's extremely unclean. His mother is sort of there but it's hard to determine whether she's on drugs or alcohol or whatever. And he just has a pathetic situation to go home to. There's nobody there but this depressed woman. And he doesn't relate well to the other children. He's never really learned how to socialize properly and he has a real hard set of circumstances to deal with."

Riley was aware that James was lashing out, yet her response was to place him in detention during recess and lunchtime. He was also prevented from taking part in special events like the baseball game the class had played earlier that week. "That made him really, really mad," Riley said. I asked her if her method of punishment through deprivation ever backfired. "Very rarely. Usually there's a button you can push, something that they really want that you can take away from them for a little while and modify the behaviour that way."

The experiment in behaviour modification – the box – had James sitting alone doing nothing: simple but, according to Riley, maddening. "He's restrained. He can't move. It's just driving him crazy. He wants out but I mean, he worked himself into a box and now he's going to have to work himself out. I'm going to start him with five minutes on the playground and if he doesn't strangle anybody, I'll give him seven minutes the next day. But I mean, you have to be careful or you end up torturing yourself more because I don't want to be babysitting him every recess for the rest of the year."

After lunch the class watched a video, which meant James had to stay in his box. Riley's class was on the second floor of the school's annex. From there I made my way to the main building, up the stairs to the main hallway, and there I saw James. He was sitting in a chair against the wall, directly across from the principal's office. A wide table was inches from his chest and, because of the chair's armrests, made it almost impossible for James to move. Riley had described it accurately. James was in a box.

I asked James what he thought about his punishment.

"It's a bit too hard," he said.

"A bit too hard? Why?"

"Missing everything, missing going outside, can't watch films, can't go outside to play baseball. It's a bit unfair."

James was a handsome boy: tall, high cheek bones, a square jaw, and deep-set eyes. His black hair shot straight out from the top of his forehead like the brim of a baseball cap and he had difficulty looking me in the eyes. His speech was a little slurred and, probably due to my presence, his sentences trailed off into embarrassed chuckles.

"Why do you take it, James? Why don't you run away?" I asked.

"My mother will get informed."

"And then what would happen?"

"I don't know. I'll probably get grounded at home then. Yeah, then I wouldn't even be able to go out for a few weeks, then."

"How does it feel to sit here?"

"Sometimes it's a bit embarrassing. Sometimes a bit fun."

"Why would it be a bit fun?"

"Usually I talk for about 15 or 20 minutes to my friends."

He said he found school better than being bored at home. However, he preferred his previous school and listed the names of several teachers who would vouche for his popularity. His family had to move " 'cause our next door neighbour, with their stereo, they made a lot of noise." He aspired to go to university and felt teachers at Grace were nice "most of the time."

"Why would they do this to you if they cared?" I asked.

He paused for a moment, then looked me right in the eyes and said, "You got me on that one."

By this time James seemed more comfortable. I guess I had become one of his 20-minute distractions. The last thing I asked him was how long he had been sitting there. He pulled himself back against the chair, pushed the table out a little, grabbed a set of keys dangling from his belt, and pointed them to a wooden armrest. There, he had carved four parallel lines with a fifth slashed across them, like a prisoner counting time. On the other armrest he had carved his name. I took it as a clear message for history: here, James spent five days doing time.

Sometimes, the more you find out about something, the more incomprehensible it becomes. I told Grace principal Robert Penner that I thought James' treatment was cruel. He shuffled in his seat, visibly uneasy – "Well, that's kind of containment, okay" – but noted that while he went along with the punishment the idea was the teacher's, not his. Like Riley, he had a clear understanding of James' volatile home life. In fact, Penner offered two more reasons why James acted out in school.

First of all, his mother's alcohol abuse forced James to take on the duties and responsibilities of a parent. "He controls his own life," Penner said. "When he comes to school, people tell him what to do, *they* parent. 'Wait a minute, I call the shots, not you.'" Secondly, James is cursed with intelligence. "He's a very bright boy," said Penner, "and it's with the brighter kids we have the most difficulty because they start to catch on that everyone's life is not like their life and that brings out a terrible anger in them, reasonably enough. Again, you or I would be angry, and he's going through that."

Let's get this straight: James is a nine-year-old aboriginal boy for whom childhood is a luxury. He lives in poverty with an alcoholic single parent and, in case that isn't enough, he has the misfortune of knowing that the shit he's being covered with seems to be aimed especially at people like him. So why do they lock him up? Perhaps we've created so many victims we've grown weary of them, as if to say, "Damn! Not *another* poor, abused, alcoholic Indian story; put it there with the rest of the bunch."

Riley saw physical confinement as a way of modifying behaviour, but Penner said much more was at stake. He described it as a "struggle of wills," and the point was to subdue, if not crush, James' will. The previous year Riley had won a similar battle with a child who would break out into screaming fits.

"She fixed him with a cold eye and said, 'You're not ever going to do that again,' and he didn't," Penner said. "I mean, she actually willed it out of him. It was a struggle of wills; direct confrontation between what the child wanted to do and what she wanted to do, and she won. I'm a little reluctant to stop it because in the final analysis it is that willingness to engage someone closely that has the most hope for change."

As a way of getting a difficult situation under immediate control, their response is effective and may even seem reasonable. However, it makes for an ugly band-aid. It's the kind of educational exorcism that some schools in the past pursued with blind zeal. I'm thinking specifically of residential schools for aboriginal children. Forcing them off reserves, placing them in boarding schools, preventing them from seeing their families, and beating them for using their language; all in the name of trying to mold them into little white people. This kind of brute force has disappeared from urban schools, but the psychological warfare Penner talks about still exists.

Wayne Shaddick was Grace's childcare worker. "James isn't jumping through hoops right now," he said. "James is acting out, in my opinion, a larger depression. You can see it with him: his clothes hang on him, the dark colours. When he speaks it's almost a pained expression on his face. And when you scream at a boy like James, you're ripping at old wounds. And so, you want a simple response to your question and he's thinking, 'I've always been bad, life has always been bad for me,' and there's just a million other things coming to his mind and so he doesn't respond appropriately. But he doesn't respond because he needs more than the average kid needs. And so, you embarrass that boy in front of the class and those are scars he carries for the rest of his life. He may jump through the hoop yet and he may not frustrate the teacher, but I would be surprised."

I asked Shaddick why he allowed James to be kept in a box. He had told the principal he didn't like the idea, but in the school's hierarchy of authority Shaddick is at the bottom. "If I don't tolerate it, I'm outta here, on my ass."

From the moment children walk into school, the hidden curriculum begins shaping them from the inside out. The total control of time and space, the competition, the relentless judgement – all of it imposes a frame on the mind that tries to shackle the human spirit. As far as the children are concerned, the rules have always existed. They acquiesce because approval from the community is conditional on playing the school game and suffering its judgement. They internalize a system of imposed standards by which they measure themselves and, as anthropologist Jules Henry notes, learn to dream of failure even during moments of success. Through no fault of his own, James had been dealt a handful of sand and was still expected to compete in the game of social mobility. He had committed no crime yet was condemned. Gnawed by an internal sense of guilt, he sought the crime, like some Kafkaesque character, in order to make the sentence comprehensible and bearable. With some helpful hints from television James gave vent to his torment and was punished, but at least then it made sense.

Working with James to end his cycle of self-blame rather than perpetuating it would constitute a real education. It would simply be a question of helping him understand what he already felt in his gut, but the rest of society has to be ready to hear it.

I asked Penner what James and other children like him are supposed to do with their anger and confusion once they figure out the whole world isn't an inner city. "Well, some of the traditional things are available," he said. "I mean we have a heavy-duty sports program. There's all the outlets and activities that we have here. We ski, we go snowshoeing, we swim, we skate, stuff like that." He paused, and then added that he'd like students to get more of a chance to play out – and "act out" – their anger and confusion. "Staff aren't too keen about that. It makes their job harder. I mean, if you light the population up, you might not be able to put them out."

Light the match.

Notes on Sources

The most enjoyable time I spent while researching this book was in talking with hundreds of children and teenagers over a three-year period. Much of the research also involved watching classrooms at work and interviewing parents, teachers, school administrators, and educational researchers. The following is a summary of the most important written sources used in each chapter.

INTRODUCTION

From the time of the first school, people have been writing books on how to improve them, so there's no lack of valuable texts on the subject. Among them, the most provocative on the hidden curriculum is Ivan Illich, *Deschooling Society* (New York: Harper & Row, 1970). Illich influenced people who call themselves "critical pedagogists" and a good Canadian introduction to their ideas is David W. Livingstone & Contributors, *Critical Pedagogy and Cultural Power* (Toronto: Garamond Press, 1987).

A standard textbook on the key paradoxes of schooling and the research they've spawned is by Christopher J. Hurn, *The Limits and Possibilities of Schooling: An Introduction to the Sociology of Education*, 2nd ed. (Boston: Allyn and Bacon, 1985).

For truly informed and enjoyable reading on the cultural irony of education see Northrop Frye, *On Education* (Markham, Ont.: Fitzhenry & Whiteside).

An insightful survey of the attitudes of youth is found in a study for the Minister of State for Youth by Donald Posterski and Reginald Bibby, *Canada's Youth: "Ready for Today" A Comprehensive Survey of 15–24 Year Olds* (Ottawa: Canadian Youth Foundation, 1987).

The section on scientific literacy and critical thinking is based on "Notes for Remarks" by Bernard Shapiro, Deputy Minister of Education, to The Science Teachers' Association of Ontario Conference, Toronto, November 1988.

For a feminist perspective on education, see Jane Gaskell, Arlene McLaren, and Myra Novogrodsky, *Claiming an Education: Feminism and Canadian Schools* (Toronto: Our Schools/Our Selves and Garamond Press, 1989).

1. EGERTON RYERSON AND THE HIDDEN CURRICULUM

Many of the examples of early Canadian revolt against the hidden curriculum come from the book by sociologist Bruce Curtis, *Building the Educational State: Canada West, 1836–1871* (London, Ont: The Falmer Press, 1988). Articles by Curtis on the more subtle ways schools try to mold the inner selves of people include "Preconditions of the Canadian State: Educational Reform and the Construction of a Public in Upper Canada, 1837–1846," Structural Analysis Program, Department of Sociology, University of Toronto, July, 1981, and "The Speller Expelled: Disciplining the Common Reader in Canada West," *Canadian Review of Sociology and Anthropology*, Vol. 22, 1985.

For a synopsis of how the structure of schools came to mirror the assembly line see Dale E. Shuttleworth, "Public Education: An Industrial Model in the Post-Industrial Age," *Orbit*, December 1988.

A study of the social pressures that led to a hidden curriculum of social reproduction is Neil McDonald and Alf Chaiton, eds., *Egerton Ryerson and His Times* (Toronto: Macmillan Company of Canada, 1978). Also an invaluable study of the evolution of the Canadian curriculum in the context of social change is G.S. Tomkins, *A Common Countenance: Stability and Change in the Canadian Curriculum* (Toronto: Prentice-Hall, 1986).

A detailed account of educational history is C.E. Phillips, *The Development of Education in Canada* (Toronto: Gage, 1957). A brief history of the invention of childhood can be found in Neil Postman, *The Disappearance of Childhood* (New York: Laurel, 1982). Also, Neil Sutherland, *Children in English-Canadian Society: Framing the Twentieth Century Concensus* (Toronto: University of Toronto Press, 1976).

A seminal work on the mesmerizing effects of the machine is Lewis Mumford, *Technics and Civilization* (New York: Harcourt, Brace & World, 1963).

The second part of the chapter, dealing with post-war changes in education, is partly based on the essay by Jack Quarter and Fred Mathews, "Back to Basics," in David W. Livingstone & Contributors, *Critical Pedagogy and Cultural Power* (Toronto: Garamond Press, 1987).

The catalyst for the progressive movement of the late 1960s, the Hall-Dennis Report, is the Ontario Royal Commission on Education, *Living and Learning: The Report of the Provincial Committee on Aims and Objectives of Education in the Schools of Ontario* (Toronto: Ontario Ministry of Education, 1968).

The seminal work on the "white noise" from the hidden curriculum is Jules Henry, *Culture Against Man* (New York: Vintage Books, 1963).

2. THE THREE RS: RESISTANCE, REBELLION, AND RESIGNATION

A useful survey of youth attitudes is Alan King et al., *Canada Youth & AIDS Study* (Ottawa: Health and Welfare Canada, November 1988).

The book that first introduced me to the dynamic between the hidden curriculum and youth rebellion is David H. Hargreaves, *The Challenge for the Comprehensive School: Culture, Curriculum, and Community* (London: Routledge & Kegan Paul, 1982). A classic on capitalism and "self-damnation" is Paul Willis, *Learning to Labor: How Working Class Kids Get Working Class Jobs* (New York: Columbia University Press, 1977). A good summary of Willis' work can be found in Liz Gordon, "Paul Willis – Education, Cultural Production, and Social Reproduction," *British Journal of Sociology of Education*, Vol. 5, No. 2, 1984. For a feminist critique of Willis see Angela McRobbie, "Settling of Accounts with Subculture," *Screen Education*, Vol. 34, 1980.

A Canadian version of Willis' "lads" can be found in Patrick Solomon, "The Creation of Separatism: The Lived Culture of West Indian Boys in a Toronto High School," a paper presented at the American Education Research Association's annual meeting in New Orleans, April 5–8, 1988.

An understanding of subculture begins with a reading of Phil Cohen, "Subcultural Conflict and Working-Class Community," *Working Papers in Cultural Studies*, Vol. 2, 1972. For a look at how Cohen's thesis is played out on a larger scale see Dick Hebdige, *Subculture: The Meaning of Style* (London: Methuen, 1979).

An analysis of human revolt throughout history is found in Albert Camus, *The Rebel: An Essay on Man in Revolt* (New York: Vintage Books, 1956). This book had a profound impact on my view of student revolt.

A fascinating look at the unwritten classroom contracts between students and teachers is found in Arthur G. Powell, Elinor Farrar, and David K. Cohen, *The Shopping Mall High School: Winners and Losers in the Educational Marketplace* (Boston: Houghton Mifflin Co., 1985).

Finally, the social pressures that bear down on students are discussed by critical pedagogist Michael W. Apple in his book *Education and Power* (London: Routledge & Kegan Paul, 1982).

3. HOME SWEET HOME

The belief among many teachers that the home environment is more important to school achievement than schools themselves is a direct result of James Coleman et al., *Equality of Educational Opportunity* (Washington, D.C.: U.S. Government, 1966). A study that contradicts Coleman and maintains that schools can make a difference is Michael Rutter et al., *Fifteen Thousand Hours* (London: Open Books, 1979).

A detailed account of the difference between good and bad schools is Peter Mortimore, *School Matters: The Elementary Years* (London: Open Books, 1987). For a summary of Mortimore's four-year study see Peter Mortimore and Pam Sammons, "New Evidence on Effective Elementary Schools," *Educational Leadership*, September 1987.

A study that leaves little doubt about the positive effects of parental involvement on children's achievements is Suzanne Ziegler, *The Effects of Parent Involvement on Children's Achievement: The Significance of Home/School Links* (Toronto: Toronto Board of Education, 1987).

4. STREAMING

The report that made streaming a hot topic in Canada is George Radwanski, *Ontario Study of the Relevance of Education and the Issue of Drop-outs* (Ministry of Education, 1987). Statistical information on the profile of drop-outs used in the Radwanski report is found in Ellen Karp, *The Drop-out Phenomenon in Ontario Secondary Schools* (Ontario: Ministry of Education, 1988) and Michael Sullivan, *A Comparative Analysis of Drop-outs and Non Drop-outs in Ontario Secondary Schools* (Toronto: Ontario Ministry of Education, 1988).

The standard text on the disasterous side effects of streaming is Jeannie

Oakes, *Keeping Track: How Schools Structure Inequality* (New Haven: Yale University Press, 1985). For a summary of the thesis, see Jeannie Oakes, "Keeping Track, Part 1: The Policy and Practice of Curriculum Inequality," and "Keeping Track, Part 2: Curriculum Inequality and School Reform," *Phi Delta Kappan*, September and October 1986.

A startling look at how schools in different socio-economic neighbourhoods reproduce the class structure is Jean Anyon, "Social Class and the Hidden Curriculum of Work," *Journal of Education*, No. 162, 1980.

For a synopsis of how schools impart different knowledge to different groups, see Donald Fisher, "The Political Nature of Social Studies Knowledge," *The History and Social Science Teacher*, Vol. 18, No. 4, May 1983.

A seminal and powerful work on how schools mold a child's mind while battering dignity is Richard Sennett and Jonathan Cobb, *Hidden Injuries of Class* (New York: Vintage Books, 1973).

A comprehensive and valuable book dealing with streaming and the contradictions in education is Martin Carnoy and Henry M. Levin, *Schooling and Work in the Democratic State* (Stanford, Cal.: Stanford University Press, 1985). One of the much quoted studies on social class and education is John Porter, Marion Porter, and Bernard R. Blishen, *Stations and Callings: Making It Through the School System* (Toronto: Methuen, 1982).

For a cross-Canada look at the effects of family background on education see Paul Anisef, *Accessibility to Post-Secondary Education* (Ottawa: Secretary of State, 1984). For a strictly Ontario perspective see Paul Anisef, Norman Okihiro, and Carl James, *The Pursuit of Equality: Evaluating and Monitoring Accessibility to Post-Secondary Education in Ontario* (Toronto: Ontario Ministry of Education, 1982).

A study on the poor achievement of students in Vancouver's inner-city neighbourhoods can be found in a report by the Vancouver Elementary School Administrators' Association, *Inner-City Schools: Principal's Position Paper*, January 1988.

A description of the education achievements of children from different social and economic backgrounds in Toronto is Gerry K. Tsuji et al., *The Every Secondary Student Survey, Fall 1987* (Toronto: Toronto Board of Education, June 1989). See also *The Upgrading of Secondary School Students from Basic to General Level Programs* (Toronto: Toronto Board of Education, May 1986). Also Bill Ahama, *Participation of Different Ethnic Groups in Post-Secondary Education* (Ottawa: Secretary of State, April 1987).

One of the first attacks on streaming from parents can be found in "Downtown Kids Aren't Dumb; They Need a Better Program," a brief to the Management Committee of the Toronto Board of Education from the Park School Community Council, November 16, 1971.

A hard-hitting report on the cultural bias of schools that never officially saw the light of day is The Professional Development Advisory Committee of the B.C. Teachers' Federation, "Essential Educational Experiences," Draft 5, Jan. 11, 1977.

The absurd cultural bias of IQ tests is described in Jim Cummins, "Psychological Assessment of Immigrant Children: Logic or Intuition?" *Journal of Multicultural and Multilingual Development*, Vol. 1, No. 2, 1980. Also, Jim Cummins, "'Teachers are not Miracle Workers': Lloyd Dunn's Call for Hispanic Activism," *Hispanic Journal of Behavioral Sciences*, Vol. 10, No. 3, 1988.

The problems faced by black students and some ways to overcome them are described in *Education of Black Students in Toronto Schools* (Toronto: Toronto Board of Education, May 1988).

A teacher's guide to ridding the classroom of cultural bias is *The Role of the Reader in the Curriculum: The Second Report* (North York, Ont.: North York Board of Education, 1986).

For a quick course on critical pedagogy theory, and some fascinating portraits of student life, see Peter McLaren, *Life in Schools: An Introduction to Critical Pedagogy in the Foundations of Education* (New York: Longman, 1989). For a look at teaching in an inner-city school see Peter McLaren, *Cries from the Corridor* (Toronto: Methuen, 1980). Finally, a comprehensive review of research indicating that meritocracy is a myth is found in Christopher Hurn, *The Limits and Possibilities of Schooling: An Introduction to the Sociology of Education*, 2nd Ed. (Boston: Allyn and Bacon, 1985).

Also interesting is the Report of the Royal Commission on Education, *A Legacy for Learners* (Province of British Columbia, 1988).

5. FEAR OF FAILURE
The central theme of this chapter comes from Jules Henry, *Culture Against Man* (New York: Vintage Books, 1963).

All students are haunted by the fear of failure. But those who are not promoted to a higher grade – supposedly for their own good – rarely recover academically. For a comprehensive review of the research on grade retention, and the negative impact the practice has on the academic life of students, see Thomas Holmes and Kenneth Matthews, "The Effects of Nonpromotion on Elementary and Junior High School Pupils," *Review of Educational Research*, Vol. 54, 1984. See also Mary Lee Smith and Lorrie A. Shepard, "What Doesn't Work: Explaining Policies of Retention in the Early Grades," *Phi Delta Kappan*, October 1987. A Canadian perspective on the ill effects of retention can be found in "Promotion or Retention?" a submission by the North York Board of Education to the Select Committee on Education of the Ontario Legislature on Sept. 26, 1988.

The psychological stress placed on preschool children by parents determined to produce "superkids" is vividly described in David Elkind, *Miseducation: Preschoolers at Risk* (New York: Alfred A. Knopf, 1987).

An analysis of the importance of play – rather than academics – for preschoolers is Bruno Bettelheim, *A Good Enough Parent: A Book on Child-Rearing* (New York: Alfred A. Knopf, 1987).

6. PUNCH PRESS EDUCATION

A description of how time can be a battleground in schools can be found in Andy Hargreaves and Rouleen Wignall, *Time for the Teacher: A Study of Collegial Relationships and Preparation Time Use Among Elementary School Teachers* (Toronto: Ontario Institute for Studies in Education Press, 1988). Also Andy Hargreaves, "Teacher Development and Teachers' Work: Issues of Time and Control," a study presented to the International Conference on Teacher Development, Toronto, February 1989, and Hargreaves, "Cultures of Teaching: A Focus For Change," *OPSTF News*, February 1989. For a survey of how women are shut out of the top administrative jobs in education see *Affirmative Action Report* (Toronto: Federation of Women Teachers' Association of Ontario, 1988).

The conflict between human rhythm and the linear tick of school is described in Peter McLaren, *Schooling as a Ritual Performance* (London: Routledge & Kegan Paul, 1986).

An examination of how society is trapped by its linear obsession with time is Edward T. Hall, *The Silent Language* (New York: Doubleday, 1973). Also by Hall, *The Hidden Dimension* (New York: Doubleday, 1969) and *The Dance of Life: The Other Dimension of Time* (New York: Double-day, 1983).

An invaluable study that gives a profile of teachers and their classroom methods, along with an analysis of what makes a good school, is Alan King et al., *The Teaching Experience* (Toronto: Ontario Secondary School Teachers' Federation, 1988).

An account of the poor training student teachers receive is found in Michael Fullan and F. Michael Connelly, *Teacher Education in Ontario: Current Practice and Options for the Future* (Toronto: Ontario Ministry of Education, January 1987).

A good summary of the challenges facing Canadian schools in light of technological change is Norman Henchey, "Education for the 21st Century: Canadian Imperatives," *A Working Paper Prepared for the Canadian Teachers' Federation,* Feb. 23, 1983.

A report on how schools are spoon-feeding facts is *Science for Every Student: Educating Canadians for Tomorrow's World, Report 36* (Ottawa: Science Council of Canada, 1984). See also the important work by Gordon Wells, *The Meaning Makers: Children Learning Language and Using Language to Learn* (Portsmouth, N.H.: Heinemann Educational Books, 1986).

Teachers who are fed up with being "clerks of the empire" may find it valuable to read Henry A. Giroux, *Teachers as Intellectuals: Toward a Critical Pedagogy of Learning* (South Hadley, Mass.: Bergin & Garvey Publishers, 1988).

A study on the impact of technology that goes beyond the usual deterministic and fatalistic musings is Joshua Meyrowitz, *No Sense of Place: The Impact of Electronic Media on Social Behavior* (New York: Oxford University Press, 1985). Also invaluable is Neil Postman, *Amusing Ourselves to Death* (New York: Penguin Books, 1985).

7. LITERACY

An important work that describes how the holistic approach to language reflects the way language is learned at home is Gordon Wells, *The Meaning Makers: Children Learning Language and Using Language to Learn* (Portsmouth, N.H.: Heinemann Educational Books, 1986). I am also grateful for the use of several unpublished essays by Wells, including, "Creating Classroom Communities of Literate Thinkers" (1988), "Developing Literate Minds" (1988), "Talk About Text: Where Literacy is Learned and Taught" (1989), "Language in the Classroom: Literacy and Collaborative Talk" (1987). Also "Apprenticeship in Literacy," *Interchange,* Vol. 18, Nos. 1/2 (Spring/Summer 1987).

Setting up the first holistic language program in Toronto is discussed in *The Dundas Report: Education in the Inner City* (Toronto: Toronto Board of Education, 1980). The Toronto founders of this program were greatly influenced by linguist James Britton. A good collection of his ideas is

Gordon M. Pradl, ed., *Prospect and Retrospect: Selected Essays of James Britton* (London: Heinemann Educational Books, 1982).

An outstanding short series of five books for teachers on the importance of reading, writing, and storytelling across the curriculum is *Growing With Books: Children's Literature in the Formative Years and Beyond, Resource Guide* (Toronto: Ontario Ministry of Education, 1988).

A concise book on the fascinating workings of the young mind is Margaret Donaldson, *Children's Minds* (London: Fontana Paperbacks, 1978). Donaldson and other child psychologists owe much to the pioneering work of Russian Lev Semyonovich Vygotsky. See Vygotsky's *Mind in Society: The Development of Higher Psychological Processes* (Cambridge, Mass.: Harvard University Press, 1978). For a first-hand account of social experiments leading to Vygotsky's theories see A.R. Luria, *The Making of Mind: A Personal Account of Soviet Psychology* (Cambridge, Mass.: Harvard University Press, 1979).

Literacy as a means to social change is discussed in Paulo Freire and Donaldo Macedo, *Literacy: Reading the Word and the World* (South Hadley, Mass.: Bergin & Garvey Publishers, 1987).

A work that influenced the back-to-basics literacy movement is E. D. Hirsh Jr., *Cultural Literacy: What Every American Needs To Know* (New York: Vintage Books, 1988). A synopsis of Hirsh's argument can be found in his article "Restoring Cultural Literacy in the Early Grades," *Educational Leadership,* Vol. 45, No. 4 (December, 1987/ January, 1988). In the same issue, Stephen Tchudi and Gretchen Schwartz describe Hirsh's method as an attempt to spoon-feed useless facts.

8. MECHANICAL MIND

My discussion on the workings of the young mind is largely borrowed from Margaret Donaldson, *Children's Minds* (London: Fontana Paperbacks, 1978), and from L.S. Vygotsky, *Mind in Society: The Development of Higher Psychological Processes* (Cambridge, Mass.: Harvard University Press, 1978).

A discussion of the importance of symbols to the human mind is found in The Bullock Report, *A Language for Life: Report of the Committee of Inquiry Appointed by the Secretary of State for Education and Science* (London: Her Majesty's Stationary Office, 1975).

A captivating look at the signs and codes that inform daily life is Roland Barthes, *Mythologies* (Frogmore, Herts.: Paladin, 1973). See also the essay by Robert Graves, "Mythology," reprinted in *The Norton Reader* (New York: W.W. Norton & Co., 1980).

For a fantastic recreation of the first sign, see Italo Calvino's short story, "A Sign in Space," in his book *Cosmicomics* (New York: Harcourt & Brace Jovanovich, 1968).

A fascinating search for the story that tells all stories is Gregory Bateson, *Mind and Nature: A Necessary Unity* (New York: Bantam Books, 1979). Also Northrop Frye, *Myth and Metaphor: Selected Essays, 1974–1988*, Robert Denham, ed. (Charlottesville: University Press of Virginia, 1990).

Much of the historical analysis in this chapter on the effects of technology comes from Lewis Mumford, *Technics and Civilization* (New York: Harcourt, Brace & World, 1963).

A compelling analysis on the relationship between science and culture is Fritjof Capra, *The Turning Point: Science, Society, and the Rising Culture* (New York: Bantam Books, 1983). Science's attempts to grasp the wonders of the universe are made understandable in Stephen W. Hawking, *A Brief History of Time: From the Big Bang to Black Holes* (New York: Bantam Books, 1988).

A teacher's resource guide on how the impact of television can be dealt with in the classroom is *Media Literacy: Intermediate and Senior Divisions* (Toronto: Ontario Ministry of Education, 1989). Finally, a guide on how parents can help their children "read" television is found in Bruno Bettelheim, *Recollections and Reflections* (London: Thames and Hudson, 1990).

9. LOOKING FORWARD, FALLING BACK

When most school bashers were demanding a "back to basics," the report from Manitoba's High School Review Panel withstood the pressure and recommended some more appropriate reforms in *High School Education: Challenges & Changes* (Winnipeg: Manitoba Ministry of Education, 1988).

From Sputnik to Japanese Hondas, how America's competitive obsessions influenced schools is found in Ira Shor, *Culture Wars: School and Society in the Conservative Restoration 1969–1984* (London: Routledge & Kegan Paul, 1986). A summary of the key educational debates in the United States is found in "How Not To Fix The Schools," *Harper's*, Vol. 272, No. 1629, February 1986. Much-needed reforms in the U.S. are covered by Theodore R. Sizer, "High School Reform: The Need For Engineering," *Phi Delta Kappan*, June 1983.

A critique of sequential learning in the U.S. is found in Linda Darling-Hammond, "The Over-Regulated Curriculum," *The Principals' Bulletin*, Spring 1987.

For a sweeping view of how educators monopolize the writing of curriculums across Canada, see the essay by David Pratt, "Canadian Curricula," *OPSTF News*, December 1987.

Finally, the position of Ontario high school teachers during the province's reform period can be found in five booklets, compiled as *Presentation to the Select Committee on Education of the Ontario Legislature* (Toronto: OSSTF, Sept. 12, 1988.)

CONCLUSION: JAMES IN A BOX

For a synopsis of the different movements in educational reform, see Geoffrey Partington, "The Disorientation of Western Education: When Progress Means Regress," *Encounter,* January 1987.

A love for learning is fostered or smothered in the early years of schooling. A report that outlines the importance of those years is *Report of the Early Primary Education Project* (Toronto: Ontario Ministry of Education, 1985).

A book that gives a concise history of the holistic approach to the world and to education is John P. Miller, *The Holistic Curriculum* (Toronto: OISE Press, 1988).

A strong argument in favour of a "common curriculum" is Ken Osborne, *Educating Citizens: A Democratic Socialist Agenda for Canadian Education* (Toronto: Our Schools/Our Selves Education Publishing, 1988). See also an unpublished essay by Mark Holmes, "The Fortress Monastery: The Future of the Common Core," The Ontario Institute for Studies in Education, December 1986.

For the analysis on how technological change will make the traditional model of schools obsolete, I have borrowed from Norman Henchey, "Education for the 21st Century: Canadian Imperatives," *A Working Paper Prepared for the Canadian Teachers' Federation*, Feb. 23, 1983.

A powerful analysis of the destructive consequences of traditional child-rearing is Alice Miller, *For Your Own Good: Hidden Cruelty in Child-Rearing and the Roots of Violence* (New York: Farrar, Straus, Giroux, 1983).

A look at how the classroom computer can be transformed from spoon-feeder to creative learning tool is Jim Cummins, "From the Inner City to the Global Village: The Microcomputer as a Catalyst for Collaborative Learning and Cultural Interchange," *Language, Culture and Curriculum*, Vol. 1, No. 1, 1988.

A convincing argument for the importance of fairy tales in the primary curriculum is found in Johan Lyall Aitken, "Myth, Legend, and Fairy Tale: Serious Statements About Our Existence," in *Growing With Books: Children's Literature in the Formative Years and Beyond, Resource Guide* (Toronto: Ontario Ministry of Education, 1988).

Finally, the magic of poetry and the power of the word are captured in Ted Hughes, "Myth and Education," in Geoff Fox et al., eds., *Writers, Critics, and Children* (London: Heinemann Educational Books, 1976).

Index